CHURCHILL'S TRIUMPH

The Second World War is ending and the three most powerful men on earth gather to thrash out

the det
Winstoi
Frankli
bloodie
men wi
struggle
places i

Meanw
back ho
now his
everyth
the ruii
him, th
Winstoi
fight fo

Michae
that lie
the he
caught

F DOBBS

LARGE PRINT

Churchill's Triumph

CHURCHILL'S TRIUMPH

Michael Dobbs

WINDSOR
PARAGON

First published 2005
by
Headline Book Publishing
This Large Print edition published 2006
by
BBC Audiobooks Ltd by arrangement with
Headline Book Publishing

Hardcover ISBN 10: 1 4056 1400 5
ISBN 13: 978 1 405 61400 9
Softcover   ISBN 10: 1 4056 1401 3
ISBN 13: 978 1 405 61401 6

British Library Cataloguing in Publication Data available

Printed and bound in Great Britain by
Antony Rowe Ltd., Chippenham, Wiltshire

Dedicated to the memory of
Dr Panagis V. Vandoros (codename Pan),
a survivor of Hitler and Stalin

'History with its flickering lamp stumbles along the trail of its past, trying to reconstruct its scenes, to revive its echoes, and kindle with pale gleams the passions of former days.'

Winston Churchill

June 1963

The Mediterranean

PROLOGUE

It was a moment that, in time, would be seen as marking the beginning of the end. He would soon be gone. Dead. Not tomorrow, not the next day, but one day soon. Those around him knew it, as he knew it, too, which made his son's behaviour all the more shameful and impossible to forgive.

It was to be the last cruise of Winston Churchill's long life, an unhurried voyage on board the yacht *Christina* that would take them through the Strait of Messina and into the Ionian Sea before the insistent heat of summer arrived and left them flinching. The *Christina* was almost as much of a legend as the old man. She had started her working life as a humble Canadian naval frigate but had been transformed without thought of cost into the most luxurious vessel afloat. She had handrails cut from ivory and fireplaces inlaid with lapis-lazuli; she had her own surgery, her own cinema and even a red and white Piaggio seaplane. In truth, she was so crammed with marble and mechanical gadgets that she was top heavy and at times developed a noticeable pitch and yaw. Sailing in the *Christina*, her owner explained, was like clinging to the bosom of an opera star, although he usually expressed it in rather more earthy style.

Aristotle Onassis was an undersized swashbuckler of a Greek who had spent a lifetime roaming the seas, a modern-day pirate who had made and lost several fortunes yet always came back for more, and of all his earthly possessions

3

the *Christina* was the most seductive. He used it to make powerful friends, to woo numerous mistresses and to keep his distance from those ordinary folk who would never be either. There was nothing ordinary about Onassis: he always made an impression—he insisted on it—and didn't care much about who was hurt along the way. He took boyish pleasure in telling his female guests that the bar stools on which they were perched were covered with the skin from a whale's genitalia, and that they were sitting on the biggest prick in the world. He didn't give a damn about their reaction, so long as there was one. In his fifty-seven years he had won and lost the affections of money-lenders, monarchs and movie stars yet, no matter who stormed out of his life, there was always a queue at the harbour side waiting to clamber on board.

But Winston Churchill seemed to be an exception. Since they had met five years earlier the Greek had gone out of his way to take personal care of the elderly statesman's comfort, ensuring there was whisky on his breakfast tray, that his favourite films were lined up by the projector and there was absolutely no whistling anywhere on board. Churchill hated whistling, and although he was growing deaf and in all probability would have heard nothing short of cannon fire, the Greek was taking no chances. He placed one of Churchill's own paintings in the salon, moving aside an El Greco to make space, and read all of Churchill's histories to ensure they would never be lost for conversation. Churchill was small and pink while Onassis was still smaller and dark, like an olive— 'He's the only man I can look up to without breaking my neck,' the Greek once joked. It was an unlikely match, the hairy-assed pirate and the pink-cheeked politician, and it raised many an eyebrow, but it worked, and at the age of eighty-eight that was really all that mattered to Winston.

There was only a handful of other guests on board, all carefully selected: Churchill no longer had the energy for new acquaintance and Onassis ensured that the faces around the old man were friendly and familiar—which was why, with considerable hesitation, he had invited Randolph, Churchill's only son, to join them. It was Randolph who had introduced his father to Onassis in the first place, yet the son was rarely asked on board when Winston was around. Randolph was trouble. He'd inherited his father's affection for alcohol and argument, yet while Winston knew his limits and usually stayed within them, for Randolph there were no limits. He would start an argument with a chair if he were left too long on his own and would rake over the embers of any quarrel in the hope of igniting it once more. He loved his father yet, like all the other parts of his life, it was an emotion he was unable to control.

Earlier that day, as the sun was setting and the evening air had filled with the scent of ship's polish and tangerines, they had sailed past the island of Stromboli near the toe of Italy. It was renowned for its active volcano yet had appeared as nothing more than a mauve smudge in the descending gloom. Churchill, with his painter's eye and inescapable love of the dramatic, had remarked how disappointing it seemed and Onassis, as always anxious to please his friend, had tugged on the yacht's siren and tried to taunt the island into

5

activity. 'Come on, you wop bastar-r-r-d,' he had cried. 'Show us what you're made of, balls or blanks.' The island had seemed to tremble—surely it was nothing but the weakening light?—and then a column of fire had formed, thrusting itself ever higher and spawning fluorescent offspring that ran riot across the sky. The old man had chuckled in delight—and it was so difficult to stir the passion in him nowadays—but Onassis was an old pirate, a slave to the sea and its myths. He fell silent, ashamed at his bravado. It was a bad omen.

Later that evening, as the *Christina* continued its voyage through the inkwell waters of the Mediterranean, Churchill made a flamboyant entrance into the dining room, arriving like an ancient Ottoman caliph, borne aloft in a chair carried by four thick-limbed members of the crew. He had broken his hip the previous year and was no longer very mobile, yet still he instinctively raised two fingers and waved them at the other diners. Old men, old habits.

'We shall find him on the beaches,' Randolph mocked, too loudly, his voice saturated with tobacco and whisky.

'So glad you could join us on boar-r-r-d, Randy,' Onassis growled, in his heavy, rolling English as the crewmen settled the father at his place in the middle of the table. 'Don't know why we don't get together like this more often—God's truth, I don't.'

Randolph winced. Even through the haze of cigarette smoke he had little difficulty in making out the warning he was being given. He lowered his head and studied his tumbler, swirling the whisky around before draining the glass and handing it to one of the hovering servants.

The dinner proceeded in Olympian style. The Greek showered praise on those men present, abused many who were not and, in his open and uninhibited fashion, he made a pass at the women. He came round a second time for Lee Radziwill. She was the third and considerably younger wife of Prince Stanislaw Radziwill and was also the sister of Jackie Kennedy, the wife of the US President. Onassis knew and desired the two sisters and, in time, would sleep with both, in much the same way that he had already seduced his own sister-in-law when his wife had run off with his much-loathed business rival and brother-in-law, Stavros Niarchos. 'We like to keep these things in the family,' he would explain, to bewildered English observers.

There was a routine to these occasions. Churchill was the guest of honour and the other diners would try to engage him in conversation, but as their spirits and their voices rose his deafness reduced it all to a sound like the buzzing of gnats round a stagnant pond, and gave him about as much pleasure, so he would say little and sometimes nothing at all. It was rumoured that he was going gaga, losing his mind, but much of it was the deafness and the stifling boredom that trailed in its wake. He had grown tired with being a god, untouchable. That was why he enjoyed the company of Ari Onassis, a man who supplied enough vigour for both of them and managed to shower everything with the finest champagne.

The evening lengthened, candles cast flickering shadows across the dining-table, and the Greek's energy came to focus increasingly on the princess.

Her husband, who claimed descent from William the Conqueror, appeared entirely indifferent to the suggestive hand on his wife's arm; rumour had it that he had his own distractions, yet somehow through the thicket of their short marriage they had managed to produce two infant children.

'So, the boy,' Onassis exclaimed to her. 'Perhaps he will be like his ancestor, William. A great conqueror.'

'Bastard,' Churchill interjected, without lifting his head from his plate. It was his first comment of the evening.

'What . . . ?'

'Bastard,' the old man repeated, lisping heavily. 'Before he became William the Conqueror he was known simply as William the Bastard.'

A flush spread rapidly from the princess's breasts to her cheeks, although whether the rush of blood was caused by her intake of alcohol, her imminent seduction or the fact that her son had been born only five months after her marriage, even she didn't know. And no one was entirely sure if the old man was trying to make a point about the child or had simply fallen half-cock into the conversation.

As the guests sat in silence, bemused, he raised his eyes. 'They said I was much of a bastard, too. Born before my time, in a cloakroom at Blenheim. My darling mother explained that I was very premature, always too eager to get on with things.' His rheumy eyes roamed the table until they attached themselves to Randolph. He waved his knife at his son. 'You, however, were not born a bastard. Your friends say that only a lifetime of diligent application has made you one. I welcome you to the ranks.'

The others laughed, but Randolph hadn't heard the humour and instead perceived only a slight. His brow clouded. 'I am what you made me, Papa.'

The old man considered for a moment. 'A fine writer,' he said, before returning his attention to his food.

But for Randolph this wasn't enough. He brooded a while. Seated at the table were men of extraordinary renown—a prince, a shipping magnate and, of course, his father, the most famous man on the planet. And Randolph? Well, he was, as his father had said, a writer, a journalist who had taken the tart's ransom at the *News of the World*. He had been born to so much yet, deep inside, he knew he'd achieved so very little; even deeper down, he blamed this on his father. Randolph was fifty-two and had spent his entire life living in a shadow. Stood for Parliament many times; defeated on almost every occasion. An excellent writer, yet with a reputation reduced to insignificance beside his father's tattered histories. The father had acclaim, immense royalties and a Nobel Prize for Literature while the son made his way as . . . a journalist. A hired hack. Oh, yes, he was also his father's biographer, but even that accolade had been granted by the old man only after years of hesitation and with all too obvious reluctance. Randolph was sick to his soul of being punished simply because he was his bloody father's son, and it wasn't as if Winston had been much of a father, either.

'Then perhaps one day you will permit me to correct your histories, Papa.'

The old man slowly laid down his knife and fork

to look across the table, but said nothing. Others, however, leapt to his defence.

'Mistakes, Randolph? Surely not,' said the old man's private secretary, Anthony Montague Browne.

'Riddled with 'em. It's not just that they're self-serving and comically one-sided. As an historian myself I find it difficult to understand the errors. So many, even though they were written by a brigade of researchers. Perhaps that's why they lacked focus.'

'Tell me you're joking,' Onassis growled.

'Perfectly true. Every word. They're like one of his paintings. Wobble all over the bloody place. As fiction they're fine, I suppose, very inventive, probably deserved a Nobel prize. But as history . . .' He shook his head and clasped another cigarette between his lips, delighted at the consternation he had caused.

'That is one of the most ungrateful comments I think I've ever heard,' Montague Browne's wife, Nonie, said, her voice quivering with indignation.

Randolph gazed meanly at her, then allowed his eyes to fall like an open hand upon her undersized breasts. 'What would a woman know about it? Particularly a woman like you.'

Nonie's husband stiffened and was about to launch himself into the argument when she laid her hand firmly on his arm, restraining him. They knew Randolph, understood that he was not a man with the patience for fly-fishing and preferred simply to lob sticks of dynamite into the river. It was one of Montague Browne's duties to try to calm troubled waters, not to throw himself into them. His wife, however, had no such professional

10

inhibitions. 'Even by your standards that's damnably foul, Randolph. After all he's done for you.'

Randolph was after her like a goaded bull. 'After all he's done for me? God! I'd have thought at your age you were old enough to know better.'

'And at *my* age, I do,' Onassis intervened. 'I've read your father's histories, every one of them. Br-r-r-rilliant. There's nothing missing, not of any importance. Tr-r-ust me, Randy.'

It was an instruction, and about as close as the Greek could come to ordering his guest to stop. But Randolph had no brakes. He swallowed another mouthful of alcohol and gathered speed. 'It's full of holes, Ari.'

'And you're full of shit, as well as several bottles of my wine.'

'So let's wring the neck of another and tomorrow we shall all be friends again. But the histories will still leak like a whore's knickers.' He plunged once more into his glass. 'My God, if he'd put half as much effort into kicking hell out of the Russians as he spent crawling up Roosevelt's arse we'd be dancing in the Kremlin right now. But no, they led him by the nose. The Special Relationship, he called it, Britain and America standing at each other's side, faithful to the end. Bloody right. To the end of our empire. The Americans came and raped and plundered their way through us like the Mongol hordes, except they had smiles and silk stockings and barely needed to say please. We just rolled over and let them have their way. Particularly you wretched women,' he spat, turning once again upon Nonie. 'What did they say about you all? What was it now,

11

the words on every woman's lips? One Yank—and they were off.'

'What utter rubbish,' Nonie broke in. 'Do you think we women had no self-respect?'

'Pamela didn't.'

And there it was, the undiminished sin. The beautiful Pamela, his first wife, whom he had married just as the war began and only weeks before he was sent to the Middle East. Randolph, sweating now, his complexion shining like a drying fish, stared across the table at his father. The old man stared silently back.

'Come and embrace everything English, that's what you told them.' Randolph's voice was rising, not just in argument but in wild anger. 'You were so desperate to get the Americans into the shooting war that you overlooked all their insults, encouraged any indiscretion.' He pushed away his empty plate as if to leave a clear field of fire. 'So when Averell came and embraced your own bloody daughter-in-law, what did you do? Absolutely bugger all. Didn't raise your voice or lift a finger. You damn well encouraged it!'

President Roosevelt had sent Averell Harriman to London in early 1941 to take charge of the Lend-Lease lifeline that had kept Britain afloat in those most desperate months of the war. He became the most powerful American in Britain and, within days of arriving, had also become Pamela's lover.

'Christ, how could you? While I was away at the war! You . . . you . . .' Randolph, his red eyes flooding, was trembling on the brink of obscenity.

'I seem to have heard that you spent a good deal of your time doing battle with the brothel-keepers

12

in Cairo,' Nonie snapped.

'Were you there, gabby doll? Wouldn't surprise me, but I don't remember fucking you.'

'Enough, Randy!' Onassis barked, too late.

Randolph was no longer trembling on the brink but had started falling, and no one could save him now. 'Enough? You'd have thought it was more than enough when he found out that his favourite American was diving into my wife. So what would you have done, Ari, as a father? What would any self-respecting Greek have done? Cut off the bastard's balls and sent them back home in the diplomatic bag. But what did my beloved father do?' He was pointing a trembling finger across the table, like a rifle. 'He invited them both to Chequers so they could get on with it under his own roof. Provided them with pillows, sheets, champagne, the lot. You talk of brothel-keepers, Nonie. Well, I can tell you that in the Churchill family, remarks like that come too bloody close to home.'

'Chr-r-rist, Randy, that was more than twenty years ago. You sure know how to screw up a good evening.'

'But don't you see, Ari? It's like the whole stinking war. Americans come over, screw the British, then pack their bags and leave. That's what happened. And that's why his histories are bollocks.'

'What the hell could he have done?'

They were shouting at each other, as if the old man weren't even there.

'Fought back. Cried out in protest. Defended our honour. Wasn't that what he was supposed to do? Raise his voice in righteousness when we had

13

nothing else to fight back with. But no, he rolled over like a twopenny tart and let Roosevelt have his way.'

'President Roosevelt was a truly great man,' the American-born princess burbled, much too primly for the circumstances.

'God, I wondered how long we'd have to wait for the Americans to come to our rescue once more.' Randolph's brow was erupting in little spots of hate. 'Your president was a sanctimonious old shit who dropped promises like crumbs from his afternoon biscuit. All his guff about freedom, about democracy, about decency being delivered on the point of an American bayonet, yet that Old Woman in the White House damned near threw away everything we'd fought for. You ask me, it wasn't only his legs that were crippled.'

'We won!' the princess exclaimed.

'And away fled tyranny and terror!'

'We . . . won,' she repeated, much less firmly.

'Go tell that to the Russians. And the Ukrainians, the Latvians, Estonians, Hungarians, Czechs, Poles, the Chinks and the Chonks and that half of humanity we lost somewhere along the way.' He turned once more upon his father. 'Isn't that right, Papa?'

Throughout it all, the old man had said nothing. Now he sat there with his jaw sagging, the folds of his dinner jacket hanging vaguely round his shoulders, a morsel of food clinging to his lapel, a very old man. A trickle of saliva glistened like silver on his chin. Perhaps he was incapable of responding, or had mercifully failed to hear most of it. Yet, as they stared at him, tears of humiliation tumbled from his eyes and he turned to the servant hovering beside him, raising his finger. Moments later, the four crewmen returned and bore him away.

*   *   *

It was a deceit that only Onassis could have conceived. Randolph had to go, and go immediately, but some pretext had to be found to preserve the decencies. After all, it might be the last time he ever saw his father. He shouldn't leave in anger and he wouldn't leave in remorse, so that night Onassis made calls on the ship's telephones and cast spells that seemed most magical. By morning, a message lay on Randolph's breakfast tray from the King of Greece summoning him for an urgent and exclusive interview. It was a coup: the resulting article would more than justify his time on the yacht and mollify his masters in Fleet Street, so the *Christina* set course for the island of Corfu where Randolph was ferried to the harbour, guarded by almost every man on board. He would not be permitted to change his mind.

The *Christina*'s launch made its way through the ripples of a scented sea, with Randolph standing in the prow, gazing ahead in the manner of some ancient explorer. Montague Browne noticed that he was weeping. As he later recorded in his diary, Randolph turned to him: 'I do so very much love that man,' the son whispered, 'but something always goes wrong between us.'

*   *   *

The day was harsh and brilliantly blue, meant for

baking bricks. The other guests departed, the men to form the firing squad for Randolph while the women escaped from the troubled atmosphere of the yacht to a nearby beach. They left the old man alone. He sat beneath an awning on the deck dressed in a blue blazer with glinting brass buttons, his head protected by a Trinity House yachting cap. He seemed a shrunken figure, lost in the arms of a vast cane chair stuffed with cushions, a small table for drinks by his side and a cold cigar drooping from his short, podgy fingers. He had been asleep for some time.

Sleep was an escape from a world for which he no longer cared. Infirmity and boredom had pursued him too long and he had grown tired of the chase. It had been a remarkable year, marked by many milestones. During its course, he had become the oldest man ever to have been prime minister, outlasting even the garrulous Gladstone. He had also become the oldest serving brother of the Elder Brethren of Trinity House, the group of men who provided the pilots that brought mariners safe home to port. Many of the telegrams celebrating the occasion had talked of the ships he had brought home, laden with food for a starving nation, but now, in old age, his mind would stray to those other ships that had foundered on his watch, taking their crews with them. On some days, when he dwelt on such things, every banging door would sound like a collapsing bulkhead, every seagull's cry like a seam about to burst in an imploding hull or the sobbing of a man with no means of escape. Would he meet these men, when his own time was done? And what would they say . . . ?

Other honours had been poured upon him. He

16

had been made an Honorary Citizen of the United States. It was an historic gesture: the only other man ever to receive that had been Lafayette, the French revolutionary leader who had fought alongside Washington nearly two centuries earlier and done so much to defeat the British, damn his eyes. And in that same crowded year the National Congress of American Indians had declared him a fully fledged heir of the Iroquois tribe in direct descent through his mother, Jennie. Churchill was half American, but eternally English.

Just occasionally during those lonely watches of the night he would wonder whether such things mattered in the afterlife, if there were an afterlife. He had long ago decided that if he found himself at the gateway to Heaven he would knock politely and hope to be greeted by an enormous number of family and friends, those he had loved and long ago lost, those who had gone before. His mother would be there, shining like a distant star, as she had throughout his childhood, and his brother Jack, along with his infant daughter Marigold. Death would answer so many uncertainties, soothe so many pains. Ah, but his father—would he be there, or was he to be found in what might be termed 'another place'? Throughout the extended pain of their relationship the younger Churchill had managed to maintain an almost obsessive devotion for his father; he hoped that one day, perhaps, Randolph would do the same.

There would be his own time of judgement, of course, and the judgement upon him would take longer than most, balancing the many moments of his life, weighing them. When he had been younger—at least until he had been eighty—he

17

had never bothered with self-doubt. Some things he had got right and others outrageously wrong, yet he had always insisted that the worst sin was not to have done what might prove to be wrong but to have done nothing at all. His motto had been simple, forthright. Keep Buggering On! So he had charged forwards. He had always suspected that History would judge him kindly, if only because he had written so much of it, but what about Eternity? What verdict would that pass upon him? 'I am ready to meet my Maker,' he had once declared, 'but whether my Maker is ready for the great ordeal of meeting me is another matter!' Yet now there was no longer any sense of challenge, only tedium, and the biggest ordeal was waking to face another interminable and pointless day.

When he woke once more, he was in a foul mood. He opened his eyes and was at first blinded by the brilliance of the light that cascaded from every polished corner of the deck and the sea beyond. His eyes began to water, his head to ache. He knew his cigar was cold and he found his champagne glass empty. Damn this life. As his eyes adjusted to the light, he saw the outline of a servant, one of the yacht's crew, clad in white coat, hovering near at hand.

'Gimme a drink,' he said gruffly.

The figure didn't move.

Churchill waited. Nothing.

'Gimme a drink,' he repeated, his old voice rising.

Still nothing.

The old man's hand went to his head, touching his brow, trying to dispel the fog of confusion. He wondered whether he was having another stroke. It might be that he was now living only on the inside and had become merely an inert observer at his own death. Terrors such as these prosper in old age. But then again, perhaps the crewman was Greek, or French, spoke no English. He tried another tack.

'*Je suis Churchill!*'

Now the other man stirred. '*Et je suis polonais.*'

I am Polish . . . The words rushed at Churchill like a wind across the water, beginning to sink beneath the encrustations of age, to worm their way deep inside, exciting him, stretching the constricted blood vessels that carried purpose to his brain, flexing them, bringing him back. 'Then, Monsieur Polonais,' he said, 'I would like a glass of champagne. Please.'

'As you wish,' the man replied.

Ah, so the bugger spoke English, if with an accent, yet sufficiently well to understand orders. He disappeared for a few seconds, lurching on some crippled leg, and returned with a glass—no, confound him, two glasses! He placed one beside Churchill and was drinking from the other himself. What type of servant was this?

Something inside Churchill persuaded him not to lose his temper, to ride the insolence, for the moment at least. He still couldn't make out the man's features against the brilliant light reflecting from the sea, but the servant held himself like a man of considerable age perched on but one sound leg.

'So, what happened to your leg?' Churchill enquired.

'Russia,' the servant replied.

'Ah, war wound.' It seemed to help Churchill

19

relax a little. The old days. 'I used to have a valet like you. Bloody rude. Independent. Name of Sawyers. Bugger of a man. No front teeth, no hair, spoke with a bloody-fool Cumbrian accent that tied all his words in knots. But indispensable, in his own way.'

'I remember him well.'

'Damned fool, look what you've done,' Churchill snapped, as in surprise he spilled wine down the front of his blazer. He wiped himself. 'What the devil did you say?'

'You don't recognise me, do you?'

'From where? When?' the old man cried, growing agitated.

'Nearly twenty years ago. In Russia.'

Saturday,
3rd of February, 1945
Saki airstrip, Soviet Crimea

CHAPTER ONE

This must be, Churchill thought, the most God-forsaken place he'd ever seen, at the very edge of the earth. As they flew in for the landing he could see an army of women bent over the runway, sweeping away the snow with twig brooms. The runway itself was little more than a series of uneven concrete slabs cast upon the frozen ground, with a control tower that had been thrown together from rough-planed timber. It had a machine-gun nest on top. The insistent greyness of it all burrowed inside Churchill and froze his doubts so hard he wondered if they would ever leave him.

Sarah Oliver, his daughter, a flight officer in the WAAF, sensed his misgivings and squeezed his hand. 'Still feeling poorly, Papa?'

The previous day he'd had a temperature of 103 degrees, not the best way to begin a hazardous journey, not for a man of seventy. But he shook his head. 'I never wanted to come here, not to the Crimea. Nothing but lice and typhus plague and . . . blessed Russians. My God, I hope the whisky will last, otherwise we might end up dying in this place.'

'So . . . why here?'

'Had no choice. Neither did poor Franklin. A man in a wheelchair has to fly six thousand miles because Stalin refuses to travel more than six hundred. The supreme gathering of the three most powerful men in the world—in a hole like this!' He stabbed his finger at the scene outside. 'If we'd researched the matter for ten years with all diligence, I swear we could have found no more miserable spot. Russia in blasted February!'

The conference of the three Allied war leaders hadn't yet started and already Stalin had won the first round.

'They call you the Holy Trinity, you three,' Sarah said, smiling, trying to reassure him.

'And Stalin says I'm the Holy Ghost,' he replied morosely, 'because I'm the fool who seems to be forever flying about.' He scratched at a blob of grease on his lapel. 'But I think we rather resemble the triumvirate of Ancient Rome—you remember your Shakespeare?'

'You know I prefer more modern pieces.'

'After the fall of Julius Caesar, the three of them—Mark Antony, Octavius, Lepidus— gathered together to carve up the world. Just like us. Then they fell upon each other's throats.'

It was clear his spirits were not to be easily raised. They'd left Malta eight hours earlier, bound for their ultimate destination of Yalta on the coast of the Black Sea, which in February could freeze as hard as Iceland. The nearest operational airfield was Saki, although from five hundred feet up it seemed an utterly reckless place to land. As the four-engined Douglas Skymaster made its approach it gave another sharp lurch through the cold air and Sarah gripped her father more urgently. She wasn't enjoying this, either. 'Why couldn't we have come by ship?' she moaned.

'My sentiments entirely, but the Germans departed the Crimea only a few months ago. They left behind a wasteland drenched in blood and a harbour packed with mines. Regrettably, the bastards failed to leave behind a map for their minefields. So, we endure.'

Then, at last, the tyres were hitting the ground, squealing, once, twice, and the Skymaster was clawing slowly to a halt, bouncing on every rut. When finally the aircraft had stopped, Churchill was pensive, remaining in his seat for a while, staring at the guard of honour lined up at the side of the field, lost in his misgivings.

Sarah waited for him, staring sadly at her father in the light of a winter's afternoon. The sparse hair, the sagging jowls, the eyes that were losing the battle against time. He was an extraordinary man who seemed to possess an almost supernatural capacity for revival and for restarting the motor that had driven him full tilt through a lifetime of hazard, but the gears were now worn, they kept slipping, and each time he set out, the engine was forced to race ever harder to make any headway. Sarah knew why she'd been asked to accompany him to Yalta, for much the same reason as Roosevelt's daughter, Anna, was also coming. For comfort, yes, to make sure their fathers had those little personal things around them that made them feel content, but although no one spoke about it, the daughters were also there *just in case*. To be by their sides, *just in case* anything were to happen. No man can easily contemplate the thought of dying far away from his home, on his own.

Yet there was still plenty of life left in the old dog. Suddenly he launched himself from his seat. 'Let's get on with it,' he muttered grimly.

The American President was waiting for him. Franklin Roosevelt had arrived on a plane some twenty minutes earlier and had been lowered in his wheelchair on a specially constructed lift. Now he was seated in the back of a Lend-Lease jeep, wrapped heavily against the cold as the two leaders set out to inspect the guard of honour together. Roosevelt looked frail, disinterested, and the Prime Minister tried to give the occasion some semblance of dignity by walking beside him. Afterwards they were taken to a tent heated by wood-burning stoves where their Soviet hosts had laid on a feast—sucking pig, caviar, smoked sturgeon, black bread, with endless quantities of vodka and the sweet local champagne. All the while, outside, the guard of honour continued to stand at its post, bayonets like icicles.

When, at last, Churchill climbed into the back of his car alongside Sarah, his mood had not improved. She left him to his thoughts. Of all the Churchill children, she resembled him most closely—the same intense blue eyes, gold-red hair, passionate temper, so stubborn she was known as 'Mule'. It often made words superfluous between them and their silences were never painful. She tucked a rug round his legs and held his hand.

It would take them almost five hours to reach their destination. Yalta was barely more than eighty miles away but the road was slushy, rough, heavily potholed, with signs of hasty repair. At every two hundred paces they saw members of the Soviet militia, many of them women, saluting with their rifles as the convoy passed. And still it snowed.

'I am in agony about Franklin,' he began at last.

'I think we all are,' Sarah replied. 'He looks so desperately ill.'

'He is also desperately misguided. Infirmity and imprudence. The combination could be calamitous. You know, I asked him if we might share the journey to Yalta. He declined. Said he needed to rest. He won't talk to me, Mule. Has pushed me aside.'

'He couldn't do that. You're mistaken.'

'I am most certain of it.'

'Then why?'

'Because he thinks he knows better. Trusts Stalin. Believes we may all live together in harmony once the slaughter is over. He's one of those most dangerous of men, Mule, an idealist. Thinks he can win over Stalin simply by the force of his own personality.'

'Don't you?'

'Only if I've got a bloody grenade in my pocket.'

'But you've said such nice things about Marshal Stalin.'

'And I shall continue to do so. It's called diplomacy, and it is filled with terminological inexactitudes.'

'Which means?'

He sighed, as though already exhausted. 'In a few hours' time I shall embrace the Marshal warmly and he, just as warmly, will embrace me. Doesn't mean we like each other. Nearly thirty years ago I sent an army to Russia with the intention of crushing the Bolshevik infant in its cradle. I failed. Stalin hasn't forgotten that. Neither have I.'

Ahead, they could see the terrain changing, rising into mountains. On both sides of the road were strewn the remnants of broken tanks and rusting military equipment, and as they passed

27

through village after desolated village, not a single house appeared to be intact. They could see no livestock, no signs of preparation for the coming spring, only hungry eyes peering from the darkness of empty windows. This was the Crimea, still gripped in a German winter.

As the hours rolled and bumped past they tried to entertain themselves by reading aloud extracts from Byron and munching dry ham sandwiches, which they washed down with a little brandy. He always brought sandwiches with him to Russia; in this place you never knew what to expect. Then the brandy got the better of the old man's constitution and he leant forward to rattle at the partition window separating him from the driver and armed guard seated in front. 'Stop the car,' Churchill ordered.

The guard shook his head, indicating that they should continue. A shouting match quickly developed that wasn't resolved until Churchill grabbed the handle of the door and started to open it as though to jump out. 'I need a leak, you fool,' he shouted, as the car drew over. 'Just wait till you're my age and they start bouncing your bladder over these bloody roads!'

As he stepped from the car he found himself in yet another graveyard of charred and tumbling walls. It was still snowing and the hamlet appeared deserted except for a couple of nervous dogs that barked from a safe distance. He could taste the air: it was still thick with brick dust, and there was the sense of something sweetly sour and rotted about this place, as though someone had taken the lid off an old dustbin. It was a smell he had carried with him from the trenches of the last war.

It wasn't until Churchill had finished his business out of view of the car and was buttoning himself up that he saw two small children. A brother and sister, he guessed, the elder no more than nine, rake-thin, with harshly cropped hair to ward off infestation and a threadbare horsehair blanket that was their only means of protection. Tears marked the girl's cheeks but she made no sound. Their eyes spoke of horrors and their skin was so filthy it was impossible to know where bruises smudged into old grime. Slowly, from beneath the blanket, the boy stretched out a hand and muttered a few words that Churchill did not understand.

'My poor lambs,' Churchill whispered. He began feverishly searching his pockets—for what he wasn't certain, as he never carried any money— and while he fumbled the blanket fell from the children's shoulders. Their bodies had become a canvas of sores, scars and infection, and where the girl's left arm should have been there was nothing but a desperate, blackened stump. They had no shoes, the girl was clad in a sack and the boy was wearing a grey German field tunic that still bore its dark stain of death. His hand went to his mouth, begging for food, and Churchill cried out in anguish. He stepped forward, but as he did so they were gone, vanished into the grey gloom of snow. From nearby he heard the guard shouting in impatience; Churchill swore softly at him, didn't move, couldn't move, as tears trickled down his cheeks. When at last he had clambered back into the car and they were on their way once more, he said nothing for many miles.

Then they began to climb into the mountains.

They made another stop, this one planned; another feast set out on groaning tables, with Soviet dignitaries—Molotov, the wretched foreign minister, and Vyshinsky, odious prosecutor—dancing attendance and insisting they eat. Churchill cursed the memory of the stale ham sandwiches and whispered urgently to his daughter. While he ate and engaged the attentions of his Soviet hosts, she busied herself on his errand.

By the time they were on their way once again the short winter day was drawing to its end. Sarah sat with two bulging canvas shoulder-bags at her feet. The old man squeezed her hand in gratitude, but said nothing. An hour further on they approached the ruins of another village. Firelight flickered between the cracks: there was life here, of sorts. Once again Churchill demanded that they stop, and this time Sarah joined him as he stepped from the car and disappeared into the shadows. When, a few minutes later, they returned, the guard failed to notice that they were no longer carrying their shoulder-bags, or that the rear compartment no longer smelt so strongly of sucking pig and smoked fish.

'It seems so desperately inadequate, Papa,' Sarah whispered.

'Of course it is.' He sobbed in genuine distress. 'Everything I do nowadays seems so. But at least, Mule, we shall know that we tried, and that some good, no matter how little, has come from this wretched conference in Yalta.'

*   *   *

30

Elsewhere on the road, another car was bumping its way through the mountains.

'He really has degenerated, Anthony. He's become just another silly old man. All over the place.'

'Winston, you mean?'

'It's inexcusable. We travel halfway round the world to sort out the peace, yet Winston won't even read the papers I give him. It really is a terrible shemozzle.'

'Shemozzle, indeed, Alec.'

The two men fell into silence, contemplating the dreariness of the scene outside the car. Anthony Eden, the foreign secretary, and Sir Alexander Cadogan, the permanent under-secretary, were, as so often in their careers, following some way behind Churchill. Neither found it a comfortable position. Eden was the suave and elegant politician, the diminutive and intellectual Cadogan his most senior official; both were quintessential figures of order, and they found it inconvenient and frequently exasperating to work for a prime minister who most evidently was not.

'He's not the only one, of course, Alec. Look at the Americans. Half their delegation is dying on its feet—and Franklin looks like an impressionist picture that's been left out in the rain. We should be holding this conference in the catacombs.'

'We need to stick a few pins in their rumps. Make sure they take a little guidance—'

'Our guidance.'

'Otherwise we'll achieve nothing. These meetings are all the same. Our masters dine and our masters wine, which is all very well, but nobody knows what on earth has been settled—least of all

31

themselves. Winston is the worst.'

'Oh, but he's done so much.'

'Anthony, forgive me, but this is the most decisive point of the war. Everything we've fought for hangs upon this moment and upon this meeting. It's no time for nostalgia.'

The Foreign Secretary sighed. 'At times he does seem like an old ship with the wind torn from her sails. And the truth is, I never know when his heart will rule his head.'

'His heart *always* rules his head, Anthony! He has a couple of drinks and gets a little buffy, then he's away on one of his great sentimental waves. Fine for music hall, less useful with Marshal Stalin, I fear.' The car hit one of the many hurriedly filled potholes that marked the road out of Saki and the civil servant bounced in his seat, shaking both his dignity and his natural reserve. His fingers brushed fretfully across his carefully trimmed moustache. 'Frankly, Anthony, I shall be much happier when you've taken the reins.'

Eden sat quietly for a moment. There was no denying his ambition, or his ability—everyone said so. But it was better in such matters not to seem too keen.

'We've beaten him like a plough horse. I suppose he can't go on for ever.'

A pause.

'You would be so much better, Anthony.'

Another pause.

'Thank you, Alec. I shan't forget your devotion. We must all move on.'

'Well, since you mention it, I suppose you've realised . . .'

'Come, Alec, you can confide in me.'

32

Cadogan stared out of the window. It was many moments before the words came. 'Washington. I'd like Washington.'

'We already have an ambassador. There is no vacancy.'

'Neither is there at Number Ten, Anthony. But time will tell. And the Americans' intellectual grip is about as thin as restaurant coffee. All grand phrases and foggy bottoms. No denying there's a job to be done.'

'And you would be the man to do it.'

'It's my turn to thank you.'

'All in good time, Alec. Everything in good time.'

The car bounced on, and they fell back into silence.

*   *   *

Frank Sawyers was having a difficult day, not that there was anything unusual in this. Every day in the service of Winston Churchill was a challenge. The British war leader was a demanding and often sharp-tongued taskmaster, who worked preposterous hours, indulged in extravagant appetites and expected everything—and everyone—to work to his whim. As his valet, Sawyers was expected not only to put him to bed but also to be there to wake him up in the morning. It was therefore fortunate that Sawyers wasn't married and was never likely to be, and that he had a sense of the ridiculous that enabled him to laugh through his master's excesses when others, including well-salted admirals, battle-hardened generals and gin-sodden cabinet ministers, simply wilted.

He wasn't the best-looking fellow in the world, short, in his forties with a shining pink pate and a dominant lisp, but Sawyers was always meticulously turned out and set himself high standards. He also knew that Churchill couldn't operate without him. Truth be told, he would have trouble getting dressed without him, and although Sawyers had never lifted a rifle in anger, he reckoned he'd done as much as many to win this war simply by keeping the old bugger going. He bore many scars from the Churchillian lash, but others recognised his abilities. At a dinner in the Kremlin the previous year, the Russian leader himself—Marshal Stealin', as Sawyers liked to refer to him in his sibilant Cumberland accent—had toasted him, not once, but twice. Mind you, the Marshal had been more than halfway towards alcoholic oblivion so had probably mistaken him for a cabinet minister or, at very least, the Keeper of the King's Closet. Now, there would be a job . . .

Sawyers was a servant, but in his own way a bit of a snob, so it helped him along his bumpy road to know that Churchill always insisted on the best—vintage champagne, hand-rolled Havanas, silk underwear. The problem was, the master never quite found the means to pay for it all. To finance his lifestyle he would contract to a publisher to write another history but spend the advance long before its time, requiring him to undertake to write yet more histories to pay off his debts. As his literary agent used to say, rarely had so much been owed to so many. The histories would eventually be written, of course, and the advances earned several times-over, but in the meantime, Sawyers had to be an excellent household manager, even something of a forager, and these skills were never in greater demand than during his first few days in the Crimea.

Yalta wouldn't have looked out of place on the French Riviera. It sat in a natural amphitheatre that was crowned with forests of pine, and had grown into a seaside resort of elegant villas and promenades interwoven with rustling olives and small vineyards. But then the Wehrmacht had arrived. The desecration they had inflicted had been almost total, for what they had not ruined during its capture had been raped as they departed. Barely a window survived or a roof remained intact. It had become a land of memories, which made it all the more remarkable as the choice to host the most important gathering of the war, yet Stalin refused to travel outside the Soviet Union and Yalta, in February, was at least warm. As the road from Saki unwound in the lee of the mountains, snow and slush gave way to sweet, scented breezes fresh off the sea.

The three delegations—Russian, American and British—were to be housed in separate facilities. The Russians stayed at the Yusupov Palace in Koreiz while the Americans were placed nearby in the old tsarist summer palace called Livadia. The British, meanwhile, lodged nearly thirty minutes away, at the Vorontsov Palace. The Vorontsov was a strange confection of styles, a confusing mixture of Scottish baronial castle, Moorish villa and Swiss chalet, perched on the heights at the southern tip of the Crimea from where it gazed out over the waters of the Black Sea like a cross-eyed bull. It had survived the carnage that had reduced the surrounding areas to wasteland only because Field Marshal von Manstein had made it his personal headquarters, yet even so, two weeks before Churchill was due to arrive, the Vorontsov had had nothing: no windows, no doors, neither plumbing nor furniture. But when Sawyers and the vanguard of the British party got there they discovered a stylish dining room, antique furniture, rare carpets, wall hangings and many grand portraits. Every item had been shipped by rail from Moscow, four days' journey to the north. The linen was spotless, the flowers stood fresh in the vases, and goldfish swam once more in the stone pool of the orangery. They'd even replanted the gardens. No effort had been spared. The entire staff of the Hotel Metropol in Moscow had been conscripted and brought a thousand miles south to act as bed-makers and broom-wielders, rounded up in the middle of the night by the NKVD secret police and told to pack. Most of them had imagined they were headed for the gulags, not a holiday resort.

Although the Vorontsov was called a palace it was not large, and no amount of endeavour could alter the fact that there were simply not enough rooms to go round. As a result, most of the British delegation was shuffled off to an annexe where air vice marshals shared a bucket for a latrine and lowly colonels were forced to sleep eight to a room. And the fleas declared war on everyone, regardless of rank.

The most insurmountable problem, however, was with the bathrooms. There were only four, and once Winston Churchill and his Foreign Secretary, Anthony Eden, had laid claim to theirs, the rest would have to queue—or use the facility set up in the garden, which came complete with a Russian *babushka* armed with a sponge who would scrub your back like a naughty child. In spite of their public-school backgrounds, not many of the Englishmen found the courage to take up the challenge.

It was inevitable that compromises would have to be made, and this, for Sawyers, came close to disaster, for Winston Churchill was not a man of compromise. The Russians had attempted to make his quarters as comfortable as possible—the plumbing still leaked a little, but he splashed about in his bath so much that he'd never notice—yet the bed would never do. It was a single bed, a narrow bed, and no part of Winston Churchill was narrow. Sawyers tried to indicate as much to the Russians who were moving furniture around the palace like worker ants, but they were harassed and said, *'Da, da,'* although they didn't understand English, which only became clear when nothing happened.

For a moment Sawyers wondered whether to volunteer for a posting to an Arctic convoy, then scolded himself for being so weak. He knew what to do. He had seen his master do it on many occasions. So he stood in the middle of the bedroom and screamed. Roared. Threw a monumental tantrum. Stamped his foot and swore—and would have thrown his cigar into the fireplace, if only he had one. The worker ants milled around in a storm of confusion, dashing in and out of the room and chattering in gibberish. It was some time before a voice of sanity broke through.

'I speak little of your language, sir. Can I be of assistance?'

37

A young man in his late twenties, tall, gangling, fine features but with a broad, Slavic forehead and a thick thatch of dark hair, was being ushered forwards by the other men. His feet seemed heavy, every step taken with reluctance.

'At last.' Sawyers sighed.

The other man drew closer. 'What are your orders?'

'Me? Orders?'

'You are officer, no?'

Sawyers laughed.

'But . . .' The other man, already wary, became confused. 'You are in charge of Mr Churchill's apartments, and you are not officer?'

'Not on your life.'

'In Russia, you would be at least full colonel.'

'Me?' Sawyers shook his head. 'I'm just a bloody butler.'

'But you are making outrage. Everyone is worried that you will complain to NKVD and get us shot.'

'No need for a firin' squad, just a new bed. For Mr Churchill. Man size, not this children's cot.'

The man interpreted to the others who were crowding round the doorway. They began to shake their heads.

'They say there is no such thing left anywhere in Crimea.'

'Way I see it, if my Mr Churchill can spare the time, I'm sure your Marshal Stealin' can spare a bed.'

As the Marshal's name echoed round the room, private concern was replaced by general alarm. Voices fell to a hoarse whisper. The young man wrung his hands—Sawyers noticed that the left had two fingers missing.

'They say it will be done,' the man announced eventually. 'Even if they have to make it themselves.'

'Thank you. Y' may just have saved my life.'

The young man came no closer but craned his neck forward to examine the Englishman with the caution of a physician looking for signs of plague. Sawyers could see sweat broken on his brow.

'Then I will ask you to do same for me,' he whispered.

But at that moment, from somewhere out in the corridor, came the military bark of a guard, and with that the anxious stranger fled, along with all his friends.

*   *   *

The bed arrived only hours before its intended occupant. It was brought by a dozen workmen who puffed and muttered, crying out to each other to ensure that no damage was inflicted upon either the huge mahogany frame or any part of the room. It required taking the sliding door that separated the bedroom from the main living room off its runners, and they were also forced to remove the bedside table. A smaller table was put in its place, the whole operation supervised by a man who spoke no English but who, to Sawyers's educated eye, seemed to be nothing of a workman. His hands were soft, his air arrogant. He did no more than lift the lamp from the old bedside table and replace it carefully upon the new. But the young man had also returned. He spent much of his time glancing nervously in the direction of the supervisor.

'They have brought bed all way from Moscow,' he declared, but Sawyers was determined not to be impressed.

'Sounds fair enough—seein' as Mr Churchill has brought himself all the way from London.'

The young man drew nearer. 'Make another outrage. Pretend you have trouble with plumbing,' he whispered urgently.

'What's to pretend?'

Yet even as he responded with his typical dose of servant's sarcasm, he knew he should take this young man seriously. There was no mistaking the flecks of dread that grazed across his grey eyes. Whatever game was being played out here, it was in earnest. Sawyers wasn't at all certain whether it was compassion or simple curiosity that drove his response, but in any event he cleared his throat and lifted his voice: 'And about time, too, what wi' Mr Churchill arrivin' in a few hours. We've only just got his bed and still there's water floodin' across bathroom floor. Call this a palace? What would Marshal Stealin' say?'

As always, the Marshal's name cast a curious spell across the Russians. The bustle of reorganisation melted into unease, as if a herd of antelope had smelt the musk of lion. Even the supervisor stiffened. Words were exchanged, angry, low words, and soon the young man was hustling Sawyers into the bathroom. Sawyers went to close the door but the other man shook his head, indicating the supervisor outside. He turned on every single tap and flushed the lavatory. 'NKVD,' he whispered, beneath the roar of rushing water. Sawyers was forced to bend close to the bath to hear him. Steam stung his face.

'My name is Marian Nowak,' the other man muttered, 'and I am very pleased to meet you. I am Pole. From Hotel Metropol.'

Sawyers knew the hotel well from previous trips to Moscow with Churchill. It was the place reserved for foreigners and was staffed by those who had some fluency in languages. Sawyers also recalled the British Ambassador's warning that every member of staff in the Metropol was involved with the NKVD security service and was not to be trusted.

'You must help me.'

An unmistakable cloud of suspicion passed across Sawyers's face.

The other man grew more anxious. 'We do not have much time.' He began banging at one of the bath pipes with a wrench.

'What d'you want?'

'Get me out of here. Please. Take me with you when you leave.'

'Why should we do that?'

'Because I can help you.'

'How?'

'I know about Katyn. I was there.'

Sawyers was now certain he was falling into a trap. For almost two years the whispers of Katyn had rushed across the conscience of the world like stormclouds across the moon. It was a crime of extraordinary proportions, a crime against the Poles—all Poles, everyone was agreed on that—but the rest was covered in accusation and smothered in doubt.

Poland. The first sacrificial lamb of the war. Once a proud and independent nation whose

41

empire had stretched from the Baltic to the Black Sea, yet its position and wealth had always been the envy of others. Over preceding centuries the fortunes of Poland had waxed and had waned, but mostly they had waned until, in the autumn of 1939, they had been utterly wasted. That was when Germany had pounced upon her from the west, taking her in its jaws and swallowing much of her whole, while to the east the Soviets, like jackals, had lain in wait to snatch the chunks of the carcass that remained. Within a few weeks, Poland was entirely gone, but still she wasn't to be spared. Two years further on the Wehrmacht had pushed across the blood-drenched fields that had once been Polish soil to fall upon the Soviet Union itself, and twenty million Poles were caught once again in the crossfire. The torture continued.

It was yet another two years before the Germans announced the discovery of a mass grave in the forest of Katyn, north-west of the Russian town of Smolensk. As they dug through the dirt of the forest floor they found the bodies of thousands of Polish officers, each bound, blindfolded and shot with a bullet to the back of the head. A Soviet bullet, it was alleged.

The Soviets denounced the claim as propaganda. And when the exiled Polish government in London called for an investigation of the massacre by the International Red Cross, the Soviets denounced them, too, claimed the exiled Poles were playing into Nazi hands by echoing their black propaganda and doing their dirty work for them. Moscow as good as accused the Poles in London of complicity in the crime of Katyn, and from that moment on the Soviet government refused to talk with them, denying their claims and their status as the legitimate government of Poland.

Which caused all sorts of problems for the British and Americans. They had long recognised the legitimacy of the London Poles, but now they needed the Russians more—much more. Couldn't win the war without them. Couldn't afford to get tangled up with nonsense in some faraway forest. So they sat back in embarrassed silence and did nothing. Katyn would be upon the conscience of them all.

And now it had come to the Crimea, had found its way right into Churchill's bathroom. As the steam formed a thick mist round him, Sawyers started shaking his head. He had a mole's nose for trouble, and this reeked of it. 'No thanks, Mr Nowak,' he said. 'Just fix the leak, if you will.'

'But you must listen!' the other man snapped, grabbing his sleeve.

Very carefully, Sawyers removed the other man's hand. And now the supervisor was calling, sensing that all was not in order.

'I can help you,' Nowak persisted, pleading. 'Look—at bedside lamp. Examine. It has extra flex. For listening device. You must not trust Russians . . .'

But already it was too late. The supervisor was at the door. Moments later, Sawyers was out of it.

*   *   *

The short winter's day had long since come to its close by the time Churchill's car approached the neo-Gothic outlines of the Vorontsov Palace. The

43

meandering drive down from the mountains had physically drained him, while the sense of desolation they encountered on all sides had lowered his spirits, so by the time he walked into the suite of rooms that had been set aside for him his temper was short. He did not take it kindly when he learnt that Sarah's room was nowhere near his own.

'What the hell sort of palace is this, Sawyers, when my own daughter is treated as a second-class citizen and packed off to the maid's quarters?' He flung his cap angrily at his servant; it missed. He slumped into a hideous overstuffed chair and lit a cigar. He sighed, and the sound seemed to drag the last reserves of energy from him. His shoulders sagged, his body wilted. 'What the devil are we doing here?'

'Saving the world. Leastways, that's what you told me at Chequers,' Sawyers responded, scurrying to find an ashtray. When eventually he located one, a fine piece made of heavy crystal, he was intrigued to discover it had the Romanov imperial crest engraved upon it.

'Save the world?' Churchill snapped. 'But we can't. Even if we could, we've no time. No time.' Ash tumbled down his jacket, but he took no notice. 'The President has decreed he will stay here only five days, six at the most. Six days—when we have been fighting for our lives for almost six years.' The words came tinged with bitterness. 'Six miserable days. Why, the Almighty himself required seven.'

'You need a bath, zur,' Sawyers replied.

'I need a bloody drink!'

'No, zur, you need a bath.'

'Damn your impertinence, Sawyers. Since when did you start issuing the orders?'

'It's true. I may be impertinent. But you still need a bath.'

Something in the servant's steady blue eye and stubborn lip made Churchill pause. Sawyers was already turning on the taps, sending a cascade of water into the cast-iron tub, and beckoning to his master. Churchill heaved himself from his chair.

'Funny goin's-on around here, mind,' Sawyers whispered, when at last Churchill came close. 'Seems the room is bugged.'

'What? *What?* Where?'

Sawyers raised a finger to his lips to quieten the other man. 'The bedside lamp, so I'm told. And that's not all. Place has been crawlin' wi' all sorts of workmen ever since I arrived, yet this mornin' they disappeared as quick as kids at a broken window and now we got strange-looking servants dressed up in white coats. One fellow's dusted banisters outside the door three times since lunch. Loiterin' wi' intent, I reckon. He's YMCA, or whatever you call it.'

'NKVD, you bloody fool,' Churchill muttered, drumming his fingers ostentatiously against the side of the bath to create still more extraneous noise. 'So, Comrade Stalin's up to his usual tricks. Never doubted him for a moment.' The colour had come back to his cheeks, 'Where d'you say this bug is?'

'Bedside light.'

Churchill stamped across to the bed. He examined the lamp carefully without touching it. At first he could see nothing, yet soon he had found the extra flex leading to a hole in the

45

skirting-board and, after more diligent searching, he identified what he assumed to be a small microphone hidden in the intricate leaf design of the lamp's base. He drew a deep breath, held the lamp aloft to examine its underside, then burst forth with a few bars of 'Rule Britannia' in a voice so grating and tuneless that it made Sawyers wince. 'Britons never, never, never shall be slaves!' he cried, to anyone who might be listening. Then he let the whole thing fall from his fingers. It fell to the floor and shattered into pieces.

'Bugger. Clumsy of me.' He smiled grimly, turning to the servant. 'Come, Sawyers, tell me. Where the hell did you discover all this?'

'From a Polish plumber. Said he needed our help.'

'Every Pole on the face of the planet needs our help. If only it were possible. What else did he say?'

'Said if I were Russian, I'd be at least a full colonel.'

'If you were Russian, Sawyers, you'd have been shot for endless insubordination. Now, if it's not too much trouble, how about my bloody drink?'

'Know what I was thinkin', zur?' the servant replied, standing his ground.

'What's that?'

'Maybe there's somethin' to be said for joinin' a revolution after all.'

Sunday,
4th of February, 1945
The First Day

CHAPTER TWO

His arrival was like the coming of autumn. The first sign was a growing coldness among the blue-capped NKVD guards who were posted around the Vorontsov, followed by a gentle stirring of rough, whispered instruction. Then came anxiety, which began to blow like freshly fallen leaves into every corner. Expressions froze, shoulders straightened, fingers hovered nervously around triggers. Stalin was coming. Early. Trying to take them by surprise.

Churchill, alerted by the cries of the guards, rushed into the hallway to greet him. They had met only three times before, and on each occasion the Englishman's sense of foreboding had grown. They had got drunk with each other, poured scorn upon each other and forced endless quantities of insult and adulation on each other, yet Churchill found there was something hollow in the man, a space where the spirit should have been. There could be outpourings of every sort of emotion, but they were switched on and off like a light, on command. Perhaps it was because he had no woman in his life, there was no longer any leavening, no Clemmie to dig in the occasional claw and remind him that he was merely mortal. There had once been a wife, much younger, whom Stalin had reputedly loved in his own way, but she had died, some said by her own hand on account of his uncontrollable cruelty. That was when the purges had started. Her anguished soul had been pursued into Hell by countless others. It was the price of a

49

husband's broken heart, or so it was whispered. Churchill didn't care to listen to such rumours, he had no idea what was true, but that was the problem—you rarely knew what was true about Stalin, and when you did, you desperately wanted not to believe it. Churchill both admired and hated him, and he had also grown to fear him. Yes, Winston Churchill was afraid, of this untouchable man and of the world he wanted to create, and now he was on the doorstep.

Churchill had only just set foot in the hallway when the door was wrenched open and light flooded in. At first his eyes could see nothing but a silhouette set against the afternoon light—the cap, the greatcoat, the small frame, not much over five foot even in his built-up boots. Yet as things began to fall into focus Churchill couldn't help but smile to himself, for crowding in behind his visitor came a phalanx of men—generals, ministers, toadies, assorted security men—who bent low and bobbed in their master's wake like a gang of medieval courtiers. Churchill would later describe them to Clemmie as spaniels and sycophants; he heard Sawyers giggle and call them fart-catchers.

Sawyers, the wretched man! There he was, at the door, nodding renewed acquaintance with the Marshal, as though he were meeting some fellow at a football match, and getting the first handshake as he helped the Generalissimo off with his plain military coat. Stalin was an unostentatious man for one with such rapacious appetites. One of the pockets of the greatcoat had been clearly and rather clumsily darned, and beneath it his trousers were tucked into the tops of soft boots. He wore no decorations apart from a small gold star upon the

50

left breast of his tunic that identified him as a Hero of the Soviet Union.

'It's a pleasure to meet you again, Marshal,' Churchill began. Stalin said nothing; he simply smiled and held out his hand. The handshake was surprisingly limp, unimpressive, little more than a passing brush of flesh. The complexion, too, was unimposing, roughened and sallow from the effects of smallpox and too many years spent locked away in the Kremlin. The hair was thinning and, when he did begin to speak, the voice that crept out from beneath the thick moustache was quiet and often difficult to hear, but his eyes made all his meanings clear. They were Oriental, penetrating, sharp, yellow. They carried no flicker of warmth. As cold as the road from Saki.

'You are looking well, Marshal.'

'Let us not start with a lie, Mr Churchill. We are all older.'

'But with age comes experience. And with experience, wisdom. Let us hope that together we can use our long lifetimes to make this a wiser world.'

'Let's first make sure we crush the Fascists, shall we?'

He was not a man for poetry but, by God, he knew what he wanted. And that was one of the many reasons for the admiration and fear that Churchill felt whenever he met the man.

'You happy here? Everything to your satisfaction?'

'I seem to have broken a bedside lamp. But apart from that things seem splendid.'

'Lamps? We can get lamps, as many as you want.'

51

'That I don't doubt.'

'There is an old Russian saying—*chem bogaty tem i rady*—you are welcome to what we have.'

'Then perhaps I may be allowed to offer you something in return, Marshal. It would give me great pleasure to show you my Map Room. We can see how things in the west are proceeding. May I?'

Ah, the offensive in the west. Stalin offered a smile, yet there was no humour in it. He had spent two barren years demanding an offensive to relieve the German pressure on the Russian front, and for two years all he'd been given was excuses—'Like kids caught with their hands up their sisters' skirts,' he had once sneered. And when it had finally arrived it seemed less like a general offensive than a gentle overture: they hadn't yet crossed the Rhine, and a few weeks ago they'd even been going backwards. The German counter-offensive through the Ardennes had caught the Americans and British with their heads stuck in their Christmas hampers. They were forced to regroup and rearm, and to offer up yet more pathetic excuses while they watched the Red Army in the east grind its inexorable way forward. So—Churchill wanted to show him how 'things in the west' were going, did he? Seemed like a good opportunity to get the proceedings off to a suitably humiliating start.

'*Da!*' the Russian declared, and the Prime Minister led the way.

Churchill took his Map Room with him everywhere. In the Vorontsov it was located in a small room beside his bedroom, where it was commanded by the admirable Captain Pim. Maps were pinned upon every wall and marked with the positions of the opposing armies in every quarter of the world. It was all there. The American slog through the Pacific. The lumbering British progress in Italy. The stalled advance upon the Rhine. Only in the east had the land been swept clean of the Wehrmacht. From Russia, of course. And the Ukraine. From Latvia, Lithuania, Estonia, Romania, Bulgaria and, now, almost all of Poland. And while all of this was going on, Churchill couldn't even yet claim the Channel Islands.

As they studied the maps together, the Englishman was overcome with a sudden sense of inadequacy. He felt the need to defend his position. His hand wandered to Paris. '*La belle France,*' he muttered, in his execrable French, '*est encore libre.*'

'And de Gaulle sniffing along behind like a dog on the trail of a free dinner.'

Stalin didn't like de Gaulle. Truth was, it was difficult to find anyone who did. The general had an extraordinary capacity for looking down his long Gallic nose and stirring disquiet. But Stalin's insult wasn't merely gratuitous: as usual, there was a point to it. 'He thinks he is Joan of Arc. But unlike Joan, he has inherited his earth.'

De Gaulle led the provisional government in liberated France, installed by the British and American armies as reward for being so consistently bloody-minded with the Germans— although in truth he was almost as consistently bloody-minded with the British and Americans themselves. He spread his disdain with a remarkable lack of discrimination.

'You object?' Churchill asked.

'It is a matter of no consequence. You can

53

impose de Gaulle or Donald Duck, for all I care. If the French will not liberate themselves, they must take what is given.' He sniffed. 'It is the same for Poland.'

Ah, Poland, of course. Stalin was claiming the same rights over Poland as the Americans and British had exercised in France. Tit for tat.

'Something we might discuss,' muttered Churchill, but already Stalin had moved on.

'Your maps interest me. They show the British empire in red.'

'It is our tradition.'

'With us, too. On our maps the Soviet Union is always in red.' Stalin's hands wiped their way across what seemed like half the globe, from Europe to the furthest stretches of Asia, then swept slowly back to take in many new territories: the Balkans, the Baltic—and Poland. 'Our maps will be bigger when this war is over.' It was a statement of fact, but it was also a challenge—or, at least, Churchill took it so. While the Soviet empire would undoubtedly expand, the British empire would not. Its day was done, its map would shrink: that was the thought behind Stalin's remark. The spoils of war were likely to be spread thinly among those who had been there from the start.

And once more Stalin's fingers were racing across the map, like a composer at his score.

'The Germans throw against us children and old men. They are armed with nothing but pop-guns and home-made mortars. Their only hope'—he stabbed his thick finger at the map—'is to concentrate their defence. Move their best divisions to the great rivers in the east, hold them as long as possible.' His finger was tracing the line of the Danube, the Elbe, the Oder-Neisse, the mighty waterways that lay before the Russian advance. 'We must stop them before they can do that. Destroy their communications centres. Berlin. Leipzig. And here.' The finger stabbed forcefully down once more, coming to rest upon the city of Dresden. 'Their troops will all go through here. This city is their great crossroads.' He turned to Churchill. 'I request that you destroy it. Stop the Wehrmacht. Make sure they cannot reinforce the Russian front.'

Over the years, Stalin had made so many requests, not all of them unreasonable, and the British had done their damnedest to meet them. They'd sent off desperate Arctic convoys, given up tanks they needed themselves, even ripped apart their own operational Hurricanes to make sure Stalin got the spares he demanded, but he always wanted more, more and more. Yet now the Luftwaffe was spent, almost smashed, and the skies belonged to the Allies. They could bomb almost anywhere they wanted, with impunity, so there seemed little reason to deny him. Churchill turned to his air-force chief, Portal, who was standing in the background. The Prime Minister raised an eyebrow, the airman nodded, and it was done.

A few days later the beautiful baroque city of Dresden would be gone, burned to the ground by the overwhelming force of the bombers, and with it would die fifty thousand, perhaps one hundred thousand people, although the devastation was so great that no one would ever know for sure. All on an eyebrow and a nod. Churchill would be troubled by that decision for the rest of his life. It

55

isn't known if Stalin ever gave it a second thought.

But now the decision had been taken and Stalin clapped his hands with impatience. 'Prime Minister, our time is short. We meet again. In an hour. With Mr Roosevelt.' Already he was heading for the door. 'And I shall send you someone to update your map,' he called, over his shoulder. 'You are behind the times. Zhukov is another thirty miles further forward. And Chuikov already has a bridgehead across the Oder.'

He was making a point, a boast about Soviet superiority, and they both knew it.

'May God shower many blessings on your British advance. And may you always fight on level ground.'

Damn his eyes! He could even twist a prayer into a taunt. But still he wasn't finished. He looked back from the doorway. 'You will forgive me rushing. The President has asked to see me before we begin. A personal meeting.'

Only the flutter of the eyelids betrayed Churchill, but Stalin noticed. And he probably knew; Churchill had asked not once but repeatedly for a meeting in private with the President, and as many times as he had asked he had been refused. There had been any number of excuses. Yet the Russian asks to see Roosevelt and suddenly he has all the time in the world.

The conference hadn't yet formally started, and already Stalin was two rounds ahead.

*   *   *

'Splendid view, Alec. But they've painted over the window-frame. Can't get the wretched thing open.'

56

For a moment Eden banged away at it, but it was a futile gesture. 'Life,' he added dispiritedly. 'Always filled with sticky windows.'

He lit a cigarette, trying to fight off his dark mood and concentrate on the panorama. For all its architectural misjudgements, the Vorontsov enjoyed a captivating position. From his first-floor window the view tumbled down across newly manicured gardens to the shore far below, where a dark, smooth sea danced gently round outcrops of stubborn rock.

'Strange to think some Jerry was standing here, on this very spot, less than a year ago.'

Cadogan came to join him at the window. 'I keep discovering pale marks on the wallpaper where paintings used to hang. The Germans must've taken them when they left. I ask myself why? Surely it was clear they were losing the war, that they'd never be able to enjoy their plunder. What was the point?'

'Are you sure it was Jerry? I sense the Russians themselves have been hacking away. Every bit of bathroom furniture is new, even the lavatory cisterns. Now, I can't imagine a German dragging away a lavatory cistern, can you? But a Russian . . .'

'They are the most awful brigands.'

'Strange people.'

'Still stranger allies.'

'Needs must.'

'We're going to have our work cut over the next few days, Anthony, and not just with the Russians.'

'With Winston, you mean?'

'No, not him. You and I can always sweep up after him. Heaven knows, we've had enough practice. It's the Americans I'm dicky about. Harry seems so listless. And Ed so . . .'

'Useless,' Eden muttered, through a cloud of smoke, finishing the thought.

'But I rather like him.'

'*Everyone* likes Ed. He has that charming capacity for bearing the imprint of the last bottom to sit upon him. But when it comes down to the serious stuff of *doing* something, he's quite, quite useless.'

Edward Stettinius had only recently been appointed as Roosevelt's Secretary of State. He was graceful, easy-going and irredeemably naïve. Harry Hopkins was none of those things. This informal but hugely influential adviser to the President was a ferret of a man who worked in the shadows and survived on a diet of nicotine and intrigue. He was gaunt, waxy-skinned, desperately frail. That he was still alive was a surprise to his friends, and that he had been able to make the trip to the Crimea a matter for astonishment. It had been almost too much for him. From the moment he had arrived he had been confined to his bed, and with him he had taken the steel wire that bound the US delegation together.

'Perhaps you're right,' Cadogan conceded. 'Ed is always weathercocking. You know I'd done a deal with him? We'd agreed we wouldn't put any other issue to bed before we'd discussed Poland. Put a bit of pressure on Uncle Joe, force his hand. Then Roosevelt arrives and it's back to square one. Bricks without straw once more.'

Outside, the sun was beginning to settle, drawing the colours from the day. The sea became oily, the breeze brittle, mimicking Eden's mood. Behind his elegant appearance he was a nocturnal pessimist, a man who shone for others in the daylight but who, alone in the dark corners of the night, found too few sticking places for his talents. In his own eyes he'd never truly succeeded at anything. Politics. Marriage. Money. Now he feared, at Yalta, he would find yet more failure.

'We'll muddle along somehow, I suppose. As always.' He sighed.

'You know, Anthony, an uncle of mine once advised me never to go abroad. Said it was a horrible place. I'm beginning to think he was right. Last night I couldn't find even a scraping of lemon peel. Had to take my gin-and-tonic *sans citron*. Bloody, I can tell you.'

'And I fear it will get bloodier still before they let us out of here,' Eden muttered, rattling in vain once more at the stubborn Russian window.

*   *   *

Three delegations, three locations. The British with their sticky windows at the Vorontsov, the Russians some distance away at the palace of Yuspov, which had once been the home of a bisexual aristocrat who had helped murder the monk Rasputin. But the grandest of the settings was the Livadia, the place reserved for Roosevelt and the American delegation.

It was a summer palace built of sandstone and marble earlier in the century by the last Tsar, Nicholas. It contained many bedrooms. The Tsar had been said to use a different room every night for fear of assassination, sometimes changing rooms during the early hours. In the end, it had served no purpose. They had murdered him regardless. Indeed, he might have preferred to be shot in his bed rather than in that dank, dreadful cellar, but in the event the choice had never arisen.

While the arrangements were necessarily somewhat makeshift, the delegations were met with the highest standards of Russian hospitality. These included constant military patrols in the grounds that were doubled at night and armed soldiers every ten feet to guard the water supply. What it did not include, however, was privacy, a concept with which Soviet citizens were unfamiliar. There was no escaping the presence of Russian servants, imported from the Metropol to cook, to clean, to relight fires and to lay dining-tables—and, of course, to remake beds. It seemed to matter little if the guests were still in them.

In a palace where there were often no doorknobs and where more than two hundred Americans had to share just six bathrooms, even the most fussy visitors had to compromise on their privacy. That included the President.

The first plenary had shown how tired Roosevelt was. It had been agreed that all the meetings of the Holy Trinity should take place at the Livadia to spare the chair-bound President the discomfort of travelling, yet he had already come six thousand miles. He was not at his best. He had been repetitious, dull, wayward. Even the incessant supply of cigarettes had failed to stimulate him, and he had a worrying cough. The session had been short, little more than an hour, and nothing of substance had been agreed. Stalin had doodled with a red pen, drawing wolves, Churchill had closed his eyes and contemplated, while Roosevelt simply sagged. Like an old man.

They had taken him quickly to his room for rest, and that was when Old Fenya had barged in with an armful of clean towels. No knocking—in the Soviet Union it wasn't customary: there was supposed to be nothing to hide.

As she entered she saw, lying on the silken counterpane, an emaciated figure clad in nothing but a small towel that lay across his loins. His skin glistened from the oil that his black servant, Prettyman, had rubbed in to soothe the aches and sores of sitting so long, but it served only to emphasise the wasted muscle and wafer white skin. When he coughed she could see the pain trying to break through between the ribs. The pulse in his neck throbbed in protest. From a pad on his arms protruded wires that went to a small machine, over which hovered a man in naval uniform. This was Commander Bruenn, the President's hard-pressed cardiologist. So intent was he that for a moment he didn't notice Fenya—Prettyman saw her, but was uncertain what to do: he wasn't used to giving commands. Roosevelt himself slowly raised his head and stared uncertainly.

Old Fenya didn't need to be a physician to understand what she saw. The body was dead from the waist down, the legs little more than bleached matchsticks, and the decay was eating its way through the rest. Twenty-four years in a wheelchair would do that to a man. The eyes were sunken, purple-dark, empty pathways to the exhaustion within.

Old Fenya was used to suffering. She'd lost one husband to the purges, another to diphtheria and two sons to the war. There had been little enough pleasure in her life and an abundance of pain, but never in one spot as much helplessness as this.

She turned, weeping, and fled.

*   *   *

There were other tears that day, but first there was laughter and excitement.

Sarah had gone with the other girls to the port of Sebastopol. The 'other girls' were Anna Boettiger, Roosevelt's married daughter, and Kathleen, the daughter of Averell Harriman. They were known as the Little Three, and they shared the ill-defined but vital duties of smoothing parental arrangements and, when necessary, their fathers' tempers.

Today they had decided on a little sightseeing, and they had been driven west round the coast in a shiny black Packard, accompanied by a Russian naval officer with a prominent gold tooth who declared himself to be Boris and spoke excellent if stilted English. The day had thrown a blanket of grey across the countryside but the views from the coastal road were impressive and their spirits were lifted by two bottles of the sweet local champagne that, by the time they had arrived at Sebastopol more than two hours later, had been entirely demolished.

'That was for our lunch,' Boris declared, in apparent despair, when he inspected the damage. 'I will try to find more.'

They giggled. They knew he had a case of the stuff in the boot.

Sebastopol nestled at the head of a sweeping bay. As they approached it along a road that fell casually down through gentle pine forests, it seemed a most tranquil setting, yet its distant beauty was deceptive. As they drew nearer they could see the outline of wrecked ships, scattered across the harbour like fallen crows. They were entering a graveyard. They kept stumbling across all sorts of mechanical skeletons—charred tanks, broken artillery pieces, derailed railway carriages, even the remnants of planes. And as they drew into Sebastopol, they were unable to find a single building that remained intact. It was as though an earthquake had erupted beneath the town, yet the ruins did nothing to diminish Boris's pride.

'This,' he declared, 'is a very beautiful church.' Indeed, it might once have been, but nothing had survived except for the gaunt outline of a tower.

On all sides, they found themselves being stared at. Everyone seemed to view them with suspicion, not just the Soviet infantrymen and sailors and blue-capped security guards, but also the civilians, the women in shawls who dragged bundles tied in rags behind them, the old men bent over the shafts of makeshift handcarts, those who stood buying, selling, haggling, arguing over scraps of clothing or meagre trays of food, or old books, worn-out tyres, a radio, an ancient heirloom, patched trousers, vodka. Wherever they walked they met eyes filled with envy and loathing, and accusation, for a glance was enough to show that these girls knew nothing of their suffering. Anna tried to give a child a bar of chocolate, but Boris stepped between them and with a few sharp words hustled the little girl away. 'That is not necessary,' he explained, with a forced smile when he turned to Anna. 'The children of the Soviet Union have everything they require.'

Sebastopol was a city of fallen walls and empty doorways, rusting gates that swung drunkenly on broken hinges and balconies that had lost whatever room they had once adorned. There was a bitter taste to the air that reminded Sarah of oversmoked herring. Whenever the breeze got up, small flakes of ash settled on her clothing.

By the time they stopped in an open space amid the rubble, which Boris tried to persuade them was 'a very beautiful square', they were glad of the third bottle of champagne.

After lunch they clambered back into the car, yet the day of discovery was not yet done. On the outskirts of the town they stopped beside a field. It was smothered in weeds. Nearby a cow was grazing, and in a distant corner they could see a copse of hurriedly nailed wooden crosses. An old woman was digging beside one, a handkerchief tied round her nose and mouth. And in the middle of the weed-strewn field was a rusting tank. Boris waved a hand to summon up its joys. 'This,' he announced with a flourish, 'is our main sports field. It is very beautiful . . . in the summer.'

Even for Boris it was an altar too high. He pulled a penitential face and Kathleen began to giggle. The other girls joined in. Boris was deeply offended, so they tried to make it up to him by feigning interest and asking questions, yet when it got to asking about the breed of the grazing cow they knew they were running out of steam. They decided to inspect the rusting tank.

'It is German,' Boris told them, 'not at all beautiful.'

As they came close they could see the scorchmarks of the shell that had killed it, still smeared dark amid the rust. It had been blown on to its side and the turret was open like a gaping mouth. They scrambled up to it, excited, curious, until inside they found things—foul, putrid things—that they could barely tell had once been human. Sarah pointed in horror. A collection of bones clung to the lip of the turret. One still wore a wedding ring.

Then it was Boris's turn to laugh.

'Why . . . why . . . ?' Sarah began, drawing back. 'Why have they not been buried?'

'What?' Boris exclaimed, flashing his tooth. 'But there are so many of them. It will take us years to get rid of them all.'

For him it was a statement of pride. And when they realised this, they asked to be taken home.

*   *   *

The men dined together at the American residence in Livadia that evening: the three ageing leaders, the unimpressive Stettinius, the overdressed Eden, the inscrutable Molotov. Averell Harriman, Churchill's old family friend who was now the American Ambassador in Moscow, also joined them and, with a couple of other Russians and the interpreters, they made thirteen in all. In hindsight, it seemed an unfortunate number.

Roosevelt played host, and the dinner lacked the abundance that, in their turn, Churchill and Stalin would later serve. The fare was straightforward, caviar, sturgeon, beef, washed down with vodka and several kinds of wine. The President was so impressed with the local Crimean champagne that he joked he would like to go into business with Stalin after the war as an importer. 'We split everything fifty-fifty, eh, Marshal?' he enquired.

Stalin merely chuckled, while Churchill wondered why he'd been left out of this little deal. It was, of course, an over-sensitive reaction on his part, but it had been one of those evenings when he felt as if he'd been rubbed all over with sandpaper. Now, already tender, he was about to get a damned good kicking.

Stalin raised his glass. 'To the German officers we shall liquidate.'

'To the forty-nine thousand,' Roosevelt responded, and drank.

It was a schoolboy cruelty, a taunt, that made Churchill blanch in anger.

Fifteen months earlier, in Tehran, the three leaders had engaged in a monumental row. It had been an evening during which Stalin had drunk his fill and constantly needled Churchill, finishing by declaring that at the end of the war fifty thousand German officers should be put in front of a firing squad and shot. 'That'll be fifty thousand less the next time.'

The suggestion had horrified Churchill, who had also drunk his fill. He shot to his feet. 'We British will never tolerate mass executions,' he had thundered. 'We shall have justice, not butchery!'

Through clouds of cigar and cigarette smoke, Stalin's eyes had twinkled in merriment. 'What do you think, Mr President?' he asked, drawing the other man in.

'Well,' Roosevelt had responded, 'let's compromise, shall we? Perhaps only forty-nine thousand.' And he had laughed. If his remark had been designed to soothe the situation, it was peculiarly ill-crafted. Churchill wouldn't tolerate being patronised and had stormed out of the room. He had returned only after Stalin had run after him to assure him it was nothing but a harmless joke.

Yet now the joke had returned, and Churchill knew he was the butt of it. They were testing him, trying to flush him out, but this time, Churchill refused to fly. Perhaps, at long last, he was beginning to learn the art of patience, or more likely he was simply getting old. In fact, no doubt about it. They were all of them old men— Churchill was seventy, Stalin only four years younger. Roosevelt had passed his sixty-third birthday *en route* to Yalta, which made him the youngest, but he seemed old before his time. And he also seemed in a great hurry.

They knew the world was watching them, that history would judge, but none felt this more than the American. He had so much to pass on as his testament—he'd been elected President of the United States four times, no other man alive or dead could share that, but somehow, with his time running out, it was only the future that seemed of importance to him. The justification of his entire lifetime's work had come down to what might happen over a few days in a desecrated royal palace many thousands of miles from his home.

Churchill pushed away his plate and studied his friend. The chandelier that hung from the high ceiling was filled with lightbulbs of every haphazard shape and size, and they cast long shadows across the American's grey face. He had recovered a little from his afternoon's apathy and was performing once again, yet Churchill realised it was just that, a performance, something that was turned on and off and that he no longer fully controlled. The eyes still danced defiance but the hand trembled—he could see that in the meniscus of the wine—and the mind sometimes wandered, had trouble fixing on any one spot, always roaming the distant horizon in search of something that insisted on remaining elusive. They had all been worn down by the years of endless war, all three of them. The stiffness in Stalin's left arm had grown worse and he now often kept his hand in his pocket, while Churchill himself had suffered heart-attacks and pneumonia, and there had been moments when his doctor had feared for his life, yet poor Franklin had suffered most, withering not only in body but also, perhaps, in judgement.

Suddenly, as Churchill pondered, Roosevelt was staring back at him, defying him. So what if I'm sick, so what if I might die? Perhaps it's because I'm so near my own end that I can see more clearly, know more precisely, what I want. And I, at least, don't glorify war, don't rejoice in the bloodshed. Forty-nine thousand Germans? It was only a goddamned joke, Winston! Raise your eyes, lift your soul, before God lifts it from you. We can do what no men have ever done—build a world freed from the tyranny of all war, where we no longer have to endure the horrors that . . . well, to put no finer point on it, the horrors that you wanton Europeans have thrust upon this world twice in a single generation. Time for the New World to sort out the Old, Winston, whether Europe likes it or not.

And, in this palace of memories, Churchill decided to take up the challenge. To try to bring down the President from his lofty mountain and make him face up to the dangers of getting stuck in the Russian mud.

'So, apart from our concerns with Germany, Marshal Stalin, what of the other nations? The small ones. What shall we do with them?'

'Small nations? Why, they will be what they have always been . . . small nations,' grunted Stalin. 'And in their proper place,' he added.

'And what place is that, pray?'

'Behind us. Beneath us. Or do you imagine that nonsense nations like Albania should be treated as equals, dictating to the Great Powers?'

'Not dictating, certainly, but . . . participating?'

'What? How big would the bloody table be?' Stalin said roughly, spreading his arms wide.

And already the conference was in trouble, for the deeply religious Roosevelt had made the establishment of a United Nations organisation the main focus of his ambitions. Churchill smiled inwardly, delighted in the manner of a child who has jumped into a huge puddle and splashed mud over those around him.

Stalin soon splashed back. 'Don't tell me that the British Empire has suddenly come to believe in equality,' the Russian growled.

Churchill's blue eyes sprang straight back at him. 'It is not a matter of equality but more of dignity. There are only three Great Powers. No one doubts our pre-eminence. We are like eagles, soaring above the world. It is a matter of affording respect to those who cannot fly so high.'

'Since when did natives in Nigeria get a vote?'

Stalin muttered, into the bottom of his glass.

Churchill waved a spoon in rebuke. 'The eagle suffers little birds to sing and is not careful what they mean thereby.'

But Churchill's words lost their poetry and perhaps much of their meaning in translation. One of Stalin's men, Vyshinsky, looked up: 'Hell, the louder they chirp, the more likely they'll end up as buzzard bait.'

Whether or not the offence was intended, it was most certainly taken, particularly by one of the younger Americans, who pushed away his plate in disgust. 'Power isn't an end in itself. It's not an excuse for excess. I think the American people would expect us to exercise restraint in dealing with the rights of others.'

'Then the American people should learn to do as their leaders tell them, or what's the point in leadership?' came back the reply that, even through the sieve of interpretation, lost none of its sting.

'I'd like to see you come to Chicago and tell them that.'

'Book me a ticket.'

Throughout it all, Roosevelt had said nothing, but his face spoke of his mounting distress. When at last his words came, they were intended to smooth the ruffled feathers. 'You would get a warm welcome, sir,' he began in his educated New England drawl to Vyshinsky, 'and so would you, Marshal Stalin. You know, all over America, we call you Uncle Joe.'

'What?'

'We think of you fondly.'

'You call me what?'

'Uncle Joe.'

And without warning, Stalin had jumped to his feet, sending his chair toppling. It took only a moment for all the other Russians to follow suit. There was much banging of cutlery.

'How much longer do I have to stay here?' Stalin stared pointedly at his watch.

'The Marshal is very busy,' one of his aides exclaimed excitedly. 'A war to run.'

'He doesn't like to be called names,' said another.

Stalin was now staring at the ceiling and breathing heavily, as though struggling to control his temper. 'How much longer do I have to stay here?' he repeated.

'Oh, at least half an hour, I'd say,' Churchill replied, in a tone that some thought flippant as he chased a portion of cream cake round his plate. Everyone else seemed to have lost their appetite.

Harriman took up the running. 'It's like we call our own country Uncle Sam,' he explained. 'No offence intended, Marshal, I assure you. And, I hope, none taken. Please allow me to apologise if there has been any misunderstanding.'

'We were not calling you names,' the President declared in anguish. 'It's . . . a compliment. A token of affection.' He glanced in desperation at Stalin's interpreter.

The interpreter was gabbling, trying frantically to get the words out before any further outburst made his job and, possibly, his life redundant. Stalin stiffened as he listened, tugging at the tails of his tunic. Only when the final words of apology were offered did he glance at Roosevelt and, with a curt nod, indicate his acceptance.

A white-coated servant stepped forward. He had been standing behind the Russian leader all evening, yet despite being young and evidently fit he had done nothing to help the other servants beyond whispering occasional instructions in their ear. Now he bent to retrieve Stalin's fallen chair. As he did so, his crisp white coat rode up to reveal the barrel of what Churchill identified as a Mauser. Harriman saw it, too, and shook his head in sorrow.

Suddenly it was Churchill's turn to stand. 'While the Marshal is on his feet,' he began, 'I propose that we join him in a toast.' He raised his glass.

They all followed, glad of the opportunity to relieve the tension.

Churchill held his glass high. 'To the King!'

The faces of the Russians, already glowing in concern, now turned to masks of panic. Stettinius scowled, too. Eyes bored into Churchill. Stalin lowered his glass, his lip curled back in a silent curse.

'And to the proletarian masses,' the Englishman added softly.

Slowly the stiffness left Stalin's hand, and at last he drank.

'And may the masses be patient with me,' Churchill concluded, as he sat down. 'You see, gentlemen, I must remind you that I am the only leader here who can at any time be removed from office by the people.'

'That's nonsense,' Stalin contradicted him, as he took his own seat. In fact, he used a term of some crudity, but none of the interpreters felt inclined to co-operate. 'The proletariat can do for us all. Just like they did for our own king.' More crudity. The

72

interpreters squirmed, Stalin chuckled, revealing dark tobacco-stained teeth, and the other Russians joined in.

'If you will allow me, Marshal Stalin, I think I shall stick to elections, which, for all the terror they inspire, at least have one great advantage over your own methods.'

'What's that?'

'They allow you to come back from the dead. As I have proven several times.'

Stalin thumped his hand upon the table. 'Waste of time! Better stick to our method.' A sly smile escaped from beneath the thick moustache. 'After all, it removes the uncertainty.'

Now they were all laughing, except Churchill.

*   *   *

Stalin stayed the half-hour, and more. It seemed that he was determined to take the most out of the evening, which itself took more out of Roosevelt. Eventually, it was the President himself who, with a tired wave of his hand, indicated that the moment had come for his guests to go. 'I need my beauty sleep, the Marshal has his war to fight and, doubtless, the Prime Minister has another speech to prepare.'

It seemed yet another remark aimed at Churchill that had been cut with an unnecessarily sharp edge, but the Englishman didn't respond. Instead he waited until Stalin had left and his own time had come to bid farewell. He bent low, his lips close to the President's ear, his lisp grown heavier with the hour. 'My dear Franklin, we must stand firm. Together we might deal with this man—see

73

how he backs off when we stand square to him.'
Not that Roosevelt had stood square to him . . .
'You saw how I tested him, time and again. He
makes a pretence at anger, stamps his foot, but he
stays. Yet we have nothing in common with the
Russian. He even had the temerity to turn your
dinner-table into an exhibition of arms. There is
no music in this man, no sense of justice or any
fear of God. And that nonsense about Uncle Joe—
he's known as much for years, yet only now does he
try to find malice in it.' Churchill gripped the other
man's arm, felt the bone beneath the sleeve. 'He's
trying to soften us up, Franklin, make us malleable.
But we must not allow him to divide us. We must
be as constant in pursuing the objects of peace as
we have been in pursuing the ends of war.'

Two aching, red-rimmed eyes looked up at him.
'Oh, Winston, why did you have to go wreck my
dinner party?'

*   *   *

Churchill arrived back at the Vorontsov in a
sombre mood after Roosevelt's rebuke. He found
Sarah waiting with Sawyers to put him to bed. The
room was lit by nothing but the flames of a log fire
and candlelight. There was no sign of any lamp.

'Sorry, zur. Clumsy of me. They replaced the
light, quick as you like, but somehow I went 'n'
dropped it again.'

'Damn' fool.'

The servant poured a measure of whisky into a
tumbler and placed it on the bedside table where
the lamp had once stood.

'Have you had a good day, Papa?' Sarah asked.

74

'Let me see,' he began, sipping, then counting on his fingers. 'I've been insulted, abused, offended, ill-treated, ostracised . . . And yet again I seem to have run out of fingers.'

But already he was beginning to relax, to reclaim his optimism in the company of the imperturbable Sawyers and his beloved Sarah. Oh, she could be wilful, opinionated, passionate, just like him. Even the same blue eyes and flame-red hair—when he had had hair. There was no mistaking the connection. She was in her early thirties, an aspiring actress who, against her father's firmest wishes, had eloped with a music-hall comedian and thrown herself into a marriage that was already over. And if she was a little reckless, they all knew from which side of the family she had inherited it. Father and daughter never stopped fighting each other, never stopped loving.

'Get your own bloody drink,' he growled, as she picked up his whisky, but Sawyers was already a step ahead of him. A fresh glass was thrust into his hand.

He sighed. 'So, Mule, what news? What despatches from your front?'

'I went with the other girls to Sebastopol.' She came and nestled at his feet, as she used to when she was a child in front of the hearth at Chartwell, and told her tale, whispering into her glass. She told of the church with no walls, the square with no sides, the houses with no roofs and no windows, the graves and the faces filled with fear, and what she had found inside the burned-out tank. Her voice faltered. She placed her head on his knee and he stroked her hair gently, trying to brush

75

away her sorrows. 'Are there no limits to the suffering of the peoples of Russia?' he whispered. 'My poor kitten.'

'But there was something very strange, Papa. What I couldn't understand was the fact that so many of the ruined houses, particularly the bigger ones, seemed to have trees and bushes growing from them—from right inside them. Through the walls, even sometimes through the empty windows. How could that be? I asked the guide, but he wouldn't say, simply shrugged.'

'And let his silence damn him.'

'Papa?'

'The town wasn't ruined just by this war, Mule. Much of that damage you saw was inflicted by the Russians themselves, during their revolutions, civil wars and bloody, bloody purges. So much violence has visited this place in the last thirty years. It was settled by Tartars—it was they who might have built the church you saw, set out the square. This was their land, until Comrade Stalin decreed otherwise. He had the Tartars moved, torn from their homes. Hundreds of thousands of them, a whole human tribe, condemned to exile and extermination. And now only weeds grow in their hearths.'

Sawyers threw another log on the fire; the flames glinted in Sarah's hair. 'Will you be all right, kitten?' Churchill asked. She nodded.

'That's what he said, the Pole,' Sawyers joined in. 'Can't go trustin' Russians.'

'And he was right,' Churchill growled. 'What else did he say, this Pole of yours?'

'What, apart from—' Sawyers jerked his head towards the bedside table where the lamp should

76

have been '—and the fact that I should be an officer?'

'Get on with it.'

'Well, he said we had to save his life. He was afraid. Said he could help us if we helped him.'

'We could do with a little help.'

'And he said somethin' about Katyn.'

'What?'

'That was it. Katyn. Was there, so he says.'

It might have been a cause for outrage, that a foolish servant could have forgotten such a matter, but Sawyers was far from foolish and he wasn't the one to blame. After all, hadn't the British and American governments themselves done their best to forget about the whole matter? Churchill had wriggled in discomfort at its mention, while Roosevelt, without discomfort of any kind, had dismissed it as Nazi propaganda. At that time the goodwill of their Russian allies had seemed so much more important, but time has a way of playing tricks and turning on a man.

Churchill gazed deep into his glass, swirling the whisky, agitating his mind.

'There was a point when I wanted nothing more than the friendship of Marshal Stalin,' he muttered. 'I hoped that matters might change, as he got to know us, but his pattern has always been consistent, and cruel. Whenever we meet, at Tehran, in Moscow, now Yalta, it's always the same. He starts by feigning anger, threatening to walk out, bullying, so that tomorrow or the next day when he makes some small accommodation, we feel he is being most reasonable and give him what he wants. We have been so eager to make him part of our game, but instead we have been drawn into his. And we go on repeating the folly.'

'Can't you stand up to him, Papa?'

Slowly, sadly, Churchill shook his head. 'This conference at Yalta is not a meeting of equals, Mule. Oh, I know, Britain has the highest moral claim, for we alone entered the war as a matter of principle, not bludgeoned into the fight like the Americans and Russians. Yet what does principle matter among the endless piles of corpses? Some reckon more than fifty million dead, the largest slice of them Russian, while the Americans and British between us have lost fewer than a million.' His voice suddenly dried. 'What have we become,' he whispered, 'when we talk of a million souls as a mere trifle . . . ?'

As she looked at her father's face in the flickering firelight, Sarah expected to see tears, but something seemed to have frozen inside him and locked them away. It was almost as if he didn't deserve to cry.

'We have endured so much. Yet set against our own suffering the Russians can place perhaps twenty million. Soldiers, civilians, women, so many innocent children. All slaughtered. But how many by the Marshal's own hand?' He drained his glass. 'May the ghosts of Katyn come back to haunt him.'

As Sawyers came with more whisky, Churchill waved him away. 'Your Pole, he said he was in danger?'

'That's what he said.'

'We are already in his debt,' Churchill continued. 'And if he was at Katyn, we owe him all the more. I would like to meet this Polish friend of yours, Sawyers.'

'But . . . how?'

Churchill's jaw jutted forward. 'You said he was a plumber.'

'Yes, zur.'

'So!' He rose, handed his glass to his servant and picked up a log from the bucket beside the fire. Then he strode into the bathroom. Three well-aimed whacks at the lead pipework beneath the sink left a satisfying puddle of water dripping on to the floor.

'Sawyers, fetch a bucket. And summon the Pole!'

Monday,
5th of February, 1945
The Second Day

CHAPTER THREE

'Terrible party last night, I thought, Alec.' Eden gazed forlornly at the breakfast-table that had been set up in his room. It was piled high with meat, fish, cheese, even a bowl of caviar, and a huge plate of mince pies—for breakfast? Try as he might he'd been unable to make any of the Russian servants understand the concept of a soft-boiled egg. 'I hate to think what's going on in the President's mind—even he didn't seem to know. And Winston as always being Winston, making his speeches, lighting sticks of dynamite and rejoicing as they explode all around him. Really, he can be so irresponsible.'

Eden was in a flap, but Cadogan had always known he was something of a flapper. An elegant flapper, to be sure. His shoulders were narrow and square, ideally suited to his carefully tailored jackets but, in truth, not broad enough for the responsibilities they were supposed to bear. So things slipped, and he flapped. He was *nouveau,* of course, a half-formed aristocrat who also tried to be a man of the people. It was an untidy compromise, which was where Cadogan came in. He was a full-blown aristocrat, nothing half-cock or semi-common about him: he was the son of an earl and a damned safe pair of hands in the slips, no matter how badly the pitch was playing. A man to clear up the mess that others left behind.

Well, not every sort of mess. Not the mess that Anthony had made of his private life. All those women creeping in and out, and that over-plucked hen of a wife! Little wonder he flapped.

Cadogan returned to the moment. 'Speaking frankly, neither Winston nor Franklin is good material for these occasions, in my view,' he said, searching for a piece of bread soft enough to give his teeth a chance. 'Winston's too emotional, gets wrapped up in himself, throws all his toys out of the pram, while the President . . .' He paused to consider both his words and the goo that passed for jam. 'Sometimes I think he's jealous. Wants to keep all his toys to himself, doesn't want to share. We'll have to sort things out with his staff, as usual.'

'You want me to have a word with Stettinius?'

'Oh, I think not. You know Ed, he's constitutionally incapable of taking the initiative, simply waits for instruction from above yet . . .' a subdued sigh ' . . . instruction comes there none. No, I suggest we go through Averell—he's the best of the bunch. We can do business with him. Lot of common sense.'

'He had the damned fine sense to get himself posted from London to Moscow as soon as Randolph returned.'

'The diplomatic solution.'

'Couldn't you have seen it, though, Alec? The presidential envoy and the prime ministerial son, drawing pistols at dawn.'

'Randolph would never make it from his bed in time.'

'Even so, Averell's safer in Moscow with only Uncle Joe to worry about.'

'Now, there's a leader,' Cadogan began with enthusiasm, raising his glass. 'Knows what he wants and how to get it. In my view, he's by far the most impressive of the Trinity. If only—'

Suddenly he began to splutter, then to choke most violently. His complexion turned the colour of a plum and the glass he was holding banged down so hard upon the table that much of its contents spilled across the starched white cloth. It was some time before he rediscovered the gift of speech. 'God's teeth!' he gasped, staring at the offending glass with eyes that might have been borrowed from a rag doll. 'Thought it was fruit juice. But it's neat bloody brandy!'

Eden struggled to contain his mirth. He squeezed the smile, tried to tuck it back beneath his moustache, but it was no good. Eventually, it broke forth in spectacular fashion, and he laughed like a man possessed. And, as he regained the ability to breathe, Cadogan did so, too.

'Never again,' the civil servant vowed, still spluttering. 'From now on I'm sticking to my gin and tonic.'

'Even without the lemon? You complained bitterly about it yesterday.'

'Anthony, this is Russia. We can't expect everything.'

And that was where, for the moment, Cadogan left it. He was still mocking himself mildly as he left Eden's room. He tripped lightly down the staircase, humming distractedly, when he was greeted by a sight that rendered him breathless for the second time that morning. Standing in the hallway, encased in a large ceramic pot, stood a lemon tree. Its branches were heavy with fruit. He was certain there were no fruiting lemon trees in the Crimea, not at that time of year. They must have flown it in overnight. For his gin and tonic.

'Well, I'll be jiggered,' whispered the Englishman, lost in admiration for the Russians' hospitality and efficiency. Would they stop at nothing?

It was much later that day when Cadogan paused to reflect. The only place were he had mentioned his craving for a slice of lemon was the night before, in the privacy of the Foreign Secretary's room. Suddenly his enthusiasm waned. Once more, and in a less chivalrous frame of mind, he was left wondering whether the Russians would stop at nothing.

*   *   *

The Pole arrived midway through the morning. Churchill was still in bed, wearing reading glasses and dressed in brilliant pink pyjamas made of silk. Papers lay scattered about him. He was smoking a cigar and tobacco ash crawled across his belly like an army of ants. A breakfast tray of substantial proportions lay beside him. It included, as usual, a glass of something red. The young Pole, dressed in the shabbiest workman's garb, stood at the foot of the bed.

'You are?' the old man growled.

Immediately, the Pole set down his bag of tools and stiffened to attention, offering the closed two-fingered salute of the Polish armed forces. 'Corporal Marian Nowak, sir!'

'Then if half of what I've heard of you is true, Corporal, I am very pleased to meet you.'

'It is honour to be with you, Mr Winston Churchill.' He spoke slowly, taking care over his words. Unlike most Poles, he didn't murder the *w* sound.

'Come—sit,' Churchill insisted, beckoning Sawyers to bring up a chair. 'Tell me a little about yourself, and how you managed to make the extraordinary journey from—wherever it is you come from.'

'If I do, Mr Churchill, I trust you with my life.'

'You doubt my goodwill?'

'Of course. I am Pole.'

And already there was tension. Churchill's eyes narrowed, not leaving the young man for a moment. 'If you were any man other than a Pole I'd have you flung from this room for that.' He produced a great cloud of blue smoke. 'But I dare say you and your countrymen have good reasons for mistrust. I can only assure you that I bear you the very best of intentions.'

'Then it is matter of honour.'

'If you care to put it that way.'

'And if you please, I will stand.' The young Pole seemed to be setting terms, and his stubborn resilience wore away at Churchill's mood. He waved a paw for the other man to continue, but the Pole was staring cautiously at the spot beside the bed where the lamp should have been.

'It's gone,' Churchill said. 'Everything is in order.' But he couldn't help lowering his voice to what was little more than a whisper.

'Then first thing I must tell you, sir, is that I am not Marian Nowak. I am—or I was—Count Tadeusz Raczynski, lieutenant in Fourteenth Uhlans.'

'The Uhlans?'

'Uhlans are cavalry regiment. Finest in Poland.'

'But . . . you're a plumber.'

87

The Pole shook his head and smiled ruefully. 'As you already know, Mr Churchill, not good one. Not even with all my fingers. My father is—*was*'—the Pole hesitated as he wrestled with his tenses—'he was aristocrat, but third son of third son. So, no money. That happens in English families, too, yes?'

'It seems to have happened in my own family with compelling regularity.'

'My father was professor, taught at Conservatoire. In Warsaw.' And he told his story. Of the growing tension throughout the months of '39, of being called up as a reservist, of the fighting before the capital and the struggle to hold the bridges, of the relentless attacks of the Stukas and other bombers and of the futile attempts to throw back the panzers with cavalry lances—yes, in one instance, with cavalry lances—and rifles. Of the discovery of a terrible new form of warfare called *blitzkrieg*. And of the weeks spent fighting for every yard, every house and street, and in the end for every cellar and sewer, holding on, in hope.

'We were waiting for you, Mr Churchill, for your soldiers and your airmen, and army from France. As you promised.'

The old man said nothing.

Then the Pole spoke of the despair, the snatched encounters, the hurried partings, and the flight of the army to the east, only to fall into the hands of the advancing Russians, intent on sharing in the plunder that was Poland.

'That winter they forced us into camps. Mine was Kozielsk. Only officers. Nothing there for us, no shelter, no medicines, nothing but guards and barbed wire and beatings. But in spring, just as snows melt and world comes back to life, they took us, sixty, eighty, sometimes two hundred at a time. We asked where we go. They said we go home and pushed us into trucks. And every day, more trucks. Then it was my turn. I don't believe they take us home, I think perhaps a labour camp. But they took us to forest.'

'Katyn.'

The Pole nodded slowly. 'As we climb down from trucks, guards surround us. All NKVD. They shout, start to tie our hands behind backs. And we hear noises from forest, time after time, like axe falling on woodcutter's block. Those who arrived in earlier truck are being taken away into forest. And other trucks are already leaving, but they are empty. "You said you take us home!" one of us shouts. Guard hits him, laughs. "This is your home," he says, "for rest of eternity." So then we know.'

Churchill struggled for words. Then: 'It is said there were thousands of them. Of *you*.'

'Many thousands. All officers, leaders.' He made a slicing gesture with his hand. 'Cut off head of Poland, no need to bother with rest of body.' His voice was calm, precise, but his breathing had grown more laboured, his chest pumping. 'We see—*saw*—what was happening. Some of us jumped from back of truck, before our hands were tied, and we ran. Blindly. Better to die in escape than on our knees waiting for bullet. And leaves had come to forest, it was spring, it gave us cover. They shoot, we scattered. And . . . I survived. God was running with me that day.'

'He favours the brave.'

'I walked for week—more. Always at night.

89

Steal little food, throw away my officer's uniform. I grow very weak. Then I stumbled across labour camp filled with Polish soldiers. I know there is only one way for Pole to survive in Russia, and that is as part of their slave machine. Alone, you die. So next day I smuggled myself on to work detail and into camp. They not look for that, not someone trying to get *into* camp. And I became Marian Nowak.'

'Why that name?'

'Nowak was soldier in my command. First man to be killed. At border, even before war starts. He argued with SS officer, was shot, like dog. He was brave man, loyal man. Simple man. Good man, if you want to become invisible in labour camp.'

'And he was—a plumber.'

'I do not know. When they ask, it was first thing in my head. There was so much confusion in camp, they have little idea who is there, so many without papers. And when they ask what I can do, I think it safer to be plumber than some sort of prince. So I trained myself to be plumber. Russian plumbing not very complicated, Mr Churchill. And I have small gift with languages, so lifetime later I end up at Hotel Metropol.'

'And no one ever asked? No one made enquiries?'

'Of course. This is Russia. But it is also war. Chaos. And yet war will soon be over. We will have normal service once more. And Marian Nowak comes from Piorun, in western Poland. Soon, very soon, Russian army is there. Then they discover that Marian Nowak is dead six years ago. And his adventure will finally be over. The gentlemen of NKVD will insist.'

Churchill retreated within a cloud of tobacco haze. He was unsure of this man. The story stretched not only the emotions but also the imagination—yet so many did. The Soviet world was an edifice of impossibilities in which there were no such things as straight lines or common sense. When eventually Churchill emerged, his tone was guarded. 'Sawyers says you want our help.'

'Yes. I want your help to live.'

'How?'

'If I stay in Russia I am dead. In months certainly, perhaps in weeks. I want you to take me with you when you leave.'

'I am afraid that would not be possible.'

'Why not?'

'Because we are a diplomatic mission, not a baggage train. There are rules and conventions which must be observed.'

'Like spying on your guests?'

Churchill's temporary lapse into silence indicated that the young Pole had scored a point.

'There are rules about many things, Mr Churchill. Stalin listens to none of them. He pretends to be liberator, but he sends in Cossacks. You know Cossacks, Mr Churchill? They are very special people, special habits. When Germans raise hands to offer surrender, Cossacks prefer to slice them off with sabres. And last week they liberated German extermination camp in Poland. Its name is Auschwitz. Every female prisoner in camp who was still woman was raped, dragged from huts, even the Russian women, and—'

Churchill waved him down. 'How d'you know all this? You're a plumber, for God's sake.'

'Exactly. And I live with other servants. Drivers, waiters, cleaners. We are invisible. Yet we know everything.'

Churchill shot an uncomfortable glance in the direction of Sawyers, who was, as always, lurking nearby.

'That is why I can be useful to you, Mr Churchill, if we agree to help each other.'

This time, Churchill didn't immediately dismiss the offer.

'I know you do not trust me—cannot trust me,' the Pole continued, 'but I pray with you not to trust Stalin. You, of all people, must not trust him.'

'Why, in particular, me?'

'Because he dislikes you.'

'He has no reason for that!'

'He will never forget what you are and what you tried to do to him after last war. You are not only class enemy but his country's enemy, too—a double danger. I think he is afraid of you a little, Mr Churchill. But Mr Roosevelt is different. Stalin likes him. He pities him, respects his courage because of his legs. And is nice to him because he thinks President is open to persuasion. You are not.'

'Is that meant to be an insult?' Churchill said, angry now. A knot of tension was binding them all.

'It depends from which side you measure it.'

'And all this you know from gossiping with servants?' Churchill bawled, but the Pole stood his ground.

'Stalin says you are man who smiles before trying to slip copeck from his pocket. Roosevelt, he says, is different. The President is interested only in bigger coins. But Stalin believes you will dip for copeck simply for pleasure.'

That had to be the end of it. Churchill would strike back: it was the only way he knew. The young Pole would be swept away in the onslaught that would inevitably follow such a brazen insult. But, instead, something turned inside the old man. The face that had been crossed with concern lightened and, little by little, a chuckle emerged, one that grew in strength until the old man was wiping his eyes with the corner of his bed sheet. 'I don't know who you are, or what you are,' he chortled, 'but one thing's for certain, you're a bloody terrible plumber!'

'So, in this matter of honour, you will help me, Mr Churchill?'

Churchill reached once more for his cigar, a sure sign he needed more time for the struggle with his thoughts. 'I'm not sure. I can't see how anything can be done, but . . .' He waved towards the bathroom. 'Better fix the leak. Then we'll see.'

The Pole stood firm, reluctant to leave without an answer.

'I will think about it, and if I think it appropriate I will summon you,' Churchill said dismissively. 'So you'd better not make too good a job of the pipework.'

'That is not problem.'

'Anyway, what shall we call you? Nowak? Ratsinski?'

'It is pronounced Raczynski. But I do not think there will be much need for Polish aristocrats after this war, so . . . let it be Nowak. A brave man died with that name. I am proud to live with it.' He picked up his bag, yet hesitated once more. 'Mr Churchill, you must understand, I do not worry for myself. I am not so important. But last time I leave my home in Warsaw I have—I *had*—wife and baby girl. I need to know. What happened. So I must respectfully insist you take me with you, not for my sake, but for my little girl.'

'I understand, Mr Nowak.'

'Thank you, sir.'

Then he was gone, and soon the sound of dropped tools and clattering pipes floated out of the bathroom.

Twenty minutes later, the job was done and the Pole was at the door, preparing to leave. Churchill was still in bed, trying to ignore him.

'One thing I forgot to tell you,' the Pole said, almost as an afterthought. 'The meeting between Mr Roosevelt and Stalin yesterday. It was very private—only two leaders and interpreters. Apart from when they ask waiter to bring coffee. That was when they discuss British Empire.'

'What?' Churchill exploded, sending an avalanche of papers tumbling to the floor.

'Perhaps there are other things I have forgotten to tell you,' the Pole said. 'We shall see.' He offered a smart salute as he left.

*   *   *

The incident occurred shortly after Churchill had left for the Livadia. Sawyers related it to Sarah that evening.

'I were in his bedroom mindin' me own and ironin' me trousers, not dressed for visitors, when door opens. No knockin' or nowt, mind. And in comes this young lass. How can I put it to you, Miss Sarah? Even in her uniform you could tell she

94

had what you might call . . .' he stretched for the word '. . . an athletic disposition.'

He wriggled his eyebrows and Sarah giggled. Sawyers was a gifted mimic with an elastic pink face that seemed to store any number of dramatic expressions; a generation earlier he might have been in music hall.

'So she's standin' there, smilin', carryin' this tray of cakes. And me standin' at ironin' board all knobble knees and shirt-tails. So she's beckonin' to me, sort of suggestin' like we might have tea together, as gals do. And the more I'm shakin' me head at her, the more she's wavin' at me. I had to stand on me principles very firm, I did, very firm, Miss Sarah.'

'A man of iron, you are, Sawyers.'

'And blow me down if ten minutes later an electrician doesn't burst in. No knockin'. No hello, no how's-your-father—nowt. Miserable face he had, all saggy, like an 'and-me-down sweater. But big shoulders, b-i-i-ig.' Sawyers spread his hands extravagantly to indicate the girth, and his eyes bulged with amazement. 'And he had a screwdriver the size of a bayonet stickin' from his bag, God's truth, he did. So he ignores me and starts fiddlin' wi' plug. You know, the one we broke wi' bedside lamp? Has his back to me so's I can see nowt of what he's doin'. So I shouts at him, but he don't flinch, let alone turn. So I shouts some more, and he just gets on wi' job even faster. It were clear he weren't going to move. Brazen he were, Miss Sarah, bra-a-azen. And I guessed he must be one of those YMCA characters.'

'NKVD.'

'Probably one of them buggers, too. So I'm

95

standin' there practically in me altogether wonderin' what on earth I can do. I can't let him go fixin' what Mr Churchill took such care to smash. So I takes me courage in me hands, so to speak, and I cross to the door. And I'm closing it, like. Very quiet. *Very* quiet. And that were the first time he takes any notice of me. So then I cross the room and I'm kneelin' down right besides him.'

'What—in your . . . ?'

'Me altogether, that's right, miss. And all of a sudden he's got eyes like an owl, he has. Strugglin' to take everythin' in. Should've seen him, Miss Sarah. Eyes rollin' all over the place. He looked at me, shirt buttons strainin', me legs all uncovered and pink, then he looks over to closed door. That's when I give him one of me smiles.'

'One of those Brighton-seafront smiles, eh?'

'Oh, miss!'

'And what did he say?'

'Dunno. He were runnin' away too fast for me to hear.'

She burst into laughter, hugging herself with pleasure. She wanted to hug him, too, but he was a servant and that would be going too far. Yet he was the most devoted of creatures, almost superhuman in his loyalty to her father, and in her view that allowed him the little mysteries of his private life. Suddenly, however, her expression changed. Little creases of concern gathered round her eyes. 'But what would you have done, Sawyers, if . . . if he had . . .' She trailed off, unwilling to complete the thought.

It was the turn of Sawyers to give himself a hug of English pleasure.

Nowak. From Piorun. It was a small community nestling in the fold of a broad, winding river, and set back from the major routes on which the armies of invasion had marched throughout many centuries. It had often been overlooked, much to its good fortune. Everything in Piorun was on a small scale: modest houses, narrow doors, straw roofs, gardens separated by low fences over which the women would lean and gossip, keeping an eye on the children. Few owned more than a single horse or cow, and most of those who did had had them confiscated. There was little industry: the people found a living largely in the patchwork of surrounding fields and scattered forests, yet they shared a keen sense of community that was focused around the main packed-earth square, which was both meeting point and market-place. It held the only two buildings of any significance in the town: the church, and the two-storey wooden building on the opposite side, that served as either mayor's office or school, depending on which entrance you used. A row of young alders stood along one side, giving shade to the mayor's office, and a garland of leaves and flowers hung above the church door, but by February it had been reduced to a handful of withered brown stalks. The square stood at the end of what was mockingly called Boulevard 3rd May, although in truth this was little more than a rutted ribbon of rocks and mud. The boulevard was one of the few pretensions of the plain, simple people of Piorun.

It was also fortunate in some measure that Piorun lay only twenty miles from the German border and not much more than a hundred from Berlin. On the first day of the war, the panzers had passed it quickly by. There wasn't any opportunity for the sort of resistance that was to bring disaster tumbling down upon so many other Polish towns. And there were no Jews, never had been. But the war didn't completely neglect Piorun: many young men went off to the army and, when the battle had been lost, threw in their lot with the underground. Most of the other men of working age who remained, and also many of the women, were taken away by the Germans for forced labour as part of what was called the pacification campaign, which only encouraged an even greater number to take to a life among the forests of elm, oak and beech. Some *Volksdeutsche* moved in, as they did all over the Greater German Reich, grabbing the best of the land, forcing the owners out of their homes to live in mud-floored hovels, but in Piorun the *Volksdeutsche* were relatively few in number and huddled together on the outskirts in a community that became known as the Settlement. The inhabitants that remained in Piorun during the Occupation, the old, the young, the wounded and infirm, were left to lead a life of obscurity and, for wartime Poland, relative lack of hardship. No one actually starved—at least, not until the last, most terrible winter of the war.

The local German garrison was the 1147th Fusilier Battalion of the 563rd Volksgrenadier Division—there were so many designations and divisions nowadays, so many gaps that had to be filled, like mushrooms spawning in a dark cellar. Yet the men of the 1147th enjoyed the obscurity of Piorun. There was no glory in it, but many had already encountered the glories of the Russian front and had developed an affection for dullness. They didn't press the inhabitants any harder than necessary, they tried to turn a blind eye to the widespread pilfering and black-market activities, and they worked hard to avoid offering reasons for a visit from anyone higher up the Nazi food chain. Yet as the frontiers of the Greater Reich drew in, everything became a little more brutal. The garrison commander was sent off to find fame at the front—not for any misdemeanour, but simply because he was a whole man—and many of his men were ordered after him. They were replaced by the old and the very young, drafted from the Volkssturm and the Hitler Youth, and those who had experienced the worst of the war, who knew it was being lost, and who neither knew nor cared for the people of this place.

It was a coincidence for this story that the *burmistrz,* or mayor, of Piorun was Stanislaw Nowak, the father of Marian. It would have made no difference to events if he had been a Kula, an Andrzeyevski, a Smolarski or a Gawlik, or a member of any of the other families who had lived in Piorun for generations, for Piorun was very much a family affair. Yet the coincidence added to the sorrow. So when it became clear that Piorun and all the other parts of Poland would not remain much longer in German hands, the abuses began in earnest. A thirteen-year-old boy found out after curfew was beaten to death, leaving terrible marks in the snow. Another who had thrown stones at a passing truck was dragged from his mother's kitchen and disappeared. Rape of any young woman became commonplace. Yet the incident that most stirred the hearts of those left in Piorun was the abuse of a fifty-six-year-old grandmother who was set upon in her own home by three drunken soldiers of the Wehrmacht. They subjected her to unimaginable indignities, and only let her live so that she could tell the tale. Piorun was catching up rapidly with the rest of the country.

And then the rumour spread that the retreating Nazis, as a last act of hatred for the Poles, were executing all elected officials in the communities they were being forced to abandon. The local doctor heard it first, and he whispered it to the inn-keeper. It spread quickly and soon the whole town knew. Stanislaw Nowak was the only elected official in Piorun: he was not only widely respected for his common decency but also related by blood or marriage to many others in the town. So at mass on Sunday—the only community gathering allowed by the German authorities—he was instructed by his fellow townsfolk to leave. The priest—also a Nowak, the mayor's brother—even took for his sermon Exodus 14, the flight of the Jews from Israel. Partly because of the common decencies for which he was renowned, Nowak was at first reluctant to quit his post, but he had already lost both sons to this war and he was told, with inflexible firmness, that it was his duty to draw a line under his family's suffering and to go.

The priest blessed him, every member of the congregation hugged him, and by nightfall he was with the underground of the Home Army in the forest. He was fortunate that, after the worst and most vicious winter of the war, the thaw was setting in: it erased his footsteps and left no trail.

The same thaw was also slowing the Russian advance through Poland, turning frozen tracks to mudslides, but everyone knew that was only temporary. The tide might slow, but it wouldn't turn.

It was mid-morning on Monday when the German Kommandant, Kluge, discovered that the mayor had fled. Within an hour he had arrested Nowak's wife. By the time the light was fading he had announced that, unless the mayor returned, she was going to hang in his place.

*   *   *

Churchill studied his friend the President from across the table in the ballroom at the Livadia. There seemed to be empty spaces in the American's suit, as though he'd shrunk, or perhaps he'd always overestimated his size and, in truth, had never quite measured up. They'd been discussing the unconditional surrender of Germany and were getting nowhere, partly because Roosevelt, the presiding officer at this conference, didn't know where he wanted to go. Kept changing his mind, shifting his position. It hadn't always been like that with Roosevelt—in fact, at times, quite the opposite. Too damned keen to rush in and grab the initiative, or was it just about grabbing the headline?

Churchill remembered the first time the subject of unconditional surrender had come up. Early 1943. North Africa, near Casablanca, where Roosevelt and he had met to decide Allied priorities and to knock together the heads of the feuding French generals. They'd held a press conference and Churchill had listened as the President had suddenly announced a new war objective, without consultation and, perhaps, without consideration, and all built upon some rickety piece of American history.

'Some of you Britishers know the old story,' Roosevelt had begun. 'We had a general called U. S. Grant. His name was Ulysses Simpson Grant, but in his day he was known as Unconditional Surrender Grant. That's our policy too.'

And that was it. A policy born. Fallen out of the desert sky. It was the first Churchill had ever heard of it. Roosevelt had been in the war barely twelve months and already he was trying to take it over. The policy of unconditional surrender was crass, discourteous, simplistic, outrageous, misconceived and, above all, wrong: it would probably prolong the war, make the Germans fight ever harder, to the bitter end. But there it was, dangling in front of the press corps. So what could Churchill do? Declare that the President was talking through his socks? Openly rip holes in the alliance? Show them both up? Instead he said nothing, had sulked in silence about a war distorted, a war extended, a war made absolute, no matter what the circumstances, all for the sake of a cheap headline.

Like so much of Roosevelt's politics, it was a half-formed idea dressed in high-minded phrases. A few months previously the American President had endorsed the Morgenthau Plan that amounted to the destruction of the German state and its reduction to an agricultural outback, yet now he seemed uncertain whether there should be one, two or five German states, whether reparations should be paid, to whom, or how much. Roosevelt

102

wriggled in discomfort. He had a hacking cough and the skin of his face behind his *pince-nez* was sticky. Stalin was trying to engage him, asking his opinion, seeking his advice, using a tone of humility that was quite unknown to his Russian colleagues, yet Roosevelt was not to be won over. He was distracted, wouldn't decide. The man who had plucked the policy of unconditional surrender out of the desert air as if it were a gnat now declined to come to a conclusion about anything. And he leant on such weak reeds—Stettinius and the ailing Hopkins, seated behind, who had his head bent as though in prayer, but probably in sleep.

Ah, but Stalin. The Russian seemed to know precisely what he wanted. Revenge. Reparations. Retribution. By the truckful and trainload. 'We will have half of everything,' he growled, in his soft Georgian accent.

Darkness was falling outside the ballroom. Roosevelt's head sagged as he gave his eyes yet another massage; he seemed unwilling to contradict. He left it to Churchill.

'Marshal, I fear that the Russian economists have forgotten the lesson of the last war,' the Englishman said, careful to lay his criticism at the door of Stalin's advisers rather than the man himself. 'A load of terrifying weight was placed upon the German back. It crippled them. They were so overwhelmed by paying reparations and loans that soon a single loaf cost a billion Reichsmarks and the nation starved.'

'You talk to me, a Russian, of suffering?' It was noticeable how Stalin, so considerate of Roosevelt's opinions, was so willing to cut across

Churchill's.

'I am not against reparations—how could I be? No victorious nation will emerge from this war more destitute than my own. I am happy to accept reparations. But I would be happier still to accept a peace with Germany that will endure.'

'That's why they must be crushed.'

'That was what we tried the last time. It was a policy that played into the hands of the extremists rather than the peacemakers.'

'Germany will have peacemakers when Poland has a pope!'

The insult was intended to finish the topic and Birse, the British translator who was sitting beside the Prime Minister, flushed with irritation as he spelt it out, but Churchill was not to be so easily distracted. He grabbed for a metaphor. 'If you want the German horse to pull a great wagon, Marshal, you must first of all keep it fed.'

'You feed him, then! But I'll be damned if I'm going to let him get close enough or grow strong enough to kick me in the bollocks again.'

The flush on Birse's cheek rose several hues. His pencil flooded across the notepaper and sweat broke on his brow as he translated.

The rising heat also galvanised Roosevelt into action. 'Gentlemen,' he said, pinching the bridge of his nose, 'I sense this matter requires a little further study. It's not one for this table or this evening. I suggest we refer the matter to our ministers and officials—perhaps a reparations commission. We could set it up in Moscow.'

'Excellent suggestion, Mr President,' Stalin exclaimed immediately, and Roosevelt nodded in gratitude.

Churchill sat in silence. He could only nod his reluctant acquiescence as the other two played their game. Another decision delayed. Another settlement postponed, and all the while the Russian armies tramped further west.

'After all,' Roosevelt continued, 'when this war is over the conditions will be entirely different from the last. America will be generous to a fault, as we always have been, but in all candour I cannot see how I could ever get the approval of Congress to finance Germany again. We will not repeat the mistakes made last time. We have learnt our lesson. Europe's problems require a European solution, and when the fighting's over I reckon the American people will decide that we've just about done our bit. Time to head home.'

Suddenly, Churchill found Stalin staring at him, catching his eye, knowing that they both shared the same thought. Was this merely a passing presidential homily? Or was there a point to it?

Stalin picked up his empty pipe, with its characteristic white spot on the stem, a Dunhill English briar, and sucked thoughtfully. 'How long will American troops stay in Europe after the war is over, Mr President?' he asked softly.

'They'll stay while we're working out the peace but . . . it's my view that I couldn't get Congress or the people to keep an army in Europe for long. Two years would be the limit.'

'Your country has already been more than generous—and patient—with us Europeans,' the Russian declared respectfully. Then Stalin turned towards Churchill. There were no words. All he had to say was contained in his yellow eyes, and in the small smile he was unable to resist.

Two years. *Two years!* Inside, Churchill was screaming like a condemned man who had just seen the executioner sharpening his axe. Poland obliterated. Germany in ashes. France prostrate. Britain destitute. And America gone. Nothing would stand between the Kremlin and the Atlantic coast—nothing, that was, but honour, and humanity, and any agreement they might reach together at this conference.

And what Stalin knew of honour or humanity could be crammed into the bowl of his pipe.

*   *   *

He was wallowing in the bath, an enormous cast-iron tub the size of an inland sea that could have met the ambitions of any three of his admirals—but the admirals, like the rest of the British party, were condemned to wait in line in the annexe with towels hanging from their arms or submitting to the *babushka* and her sponge in the garden. For a period of time that seemed to threaten imminent drowning, Churchill disappeared beneath the steaming waters, only to emerge like a pink-skinned Poseidon to glare once more at the hapless Sawyers.

Sawyers was having one of his turns. He wouldn't listen to reason. He'd had the temerity to ask, as Churchill was stepping into the bath, if there was any news about 'our Pole'. It was most unlike Sawyers to raise that sort of business with the Old Man, but the horny-handed, missing-fingered plumber had clearly impressed the butler. Sawyers wanted action.

Yet, for all his love of secrecy and the dark arts,

Churchill wasn't convinced. He had no firm idea about this Pole, the truth of his story or the nature of his purpose. He couldn't even be certain that he was a Pole. But Sawyers had no such doubts, and Churchill couldn't get rid of him, not even in his bath: some of the smaller matters in the refurbishment of the Vorontsov had been overlooked, which condemned Sawyers to standing by the bath with his hand outstretched, acting as a soap-dish.

'Even if it were wise, Sawyers, how could we do anything for him? How could we hide him, smuggle him away?'

'We got more than three hundred people here, and the Yanks about the same. What difference would one more make?'

He had a point. Churchill cast his mind back to his first wartime meeting with Roosevelt, even before America had joined the fray. On that occasion he had sailed across the Atlantic to Newfoundland with a party that numbered barely fifty, but the business of diplomacy, like the business of war, had grown out of control. So many hangers-on, so many desk-sailors eager to escape the greyness of wartime London, to indulge in free hospitality and wash away their cares in new and exotic places. Still, he muttered to himself, maybe the bloody Crimea in February wasn't such a bad idea after all. Teach the buggers a lesson.

'We could slip him in the back of one of the cars,' Sawyers continued.

'No, that would be wrong. Against all the rules. We dare not. Think of the consequences if we were discovered trying to smuggle him out. This conference is already hanging by a thread. Such a thing could bring the whole edifice crashing down on our heads.'

Sawyers sulked. 'You were once on the run. In South Africa, during Boo-er War. They helped you.'

Churchill cursed his bloody impertinence. Such comparisons were grossly unfair. And now the wretched man appeared to be holding the soap hostage. 'We cannot save every benighted Pole.'

'Then how's about savin' the one? Just for a start? Don't he deserve it?'

'Enough of all this common-man solidarity, Sawyers. I'm not bloody Solomon.'

'You're not bloody Marshal Stealin', either.'

Tuesday,
6th of February, 1945
The Third Day

CHAPTER FOUR

'Penny for them, Papa?'

'Oh, nothing, Mule. Just enjoying the sun.'

He had taken a few moments to sit outside and allow himself to be embraced by the warm winds as they trickled off the sea, carrying with them the scent of the zinnias and geraniums that the Russians had imported and planted in pots to give the impression of perpetual summer. Nonsense, of course, even fraudulent, like so much of this place, yet sitting out here was better than staying inside and listening to the intellectual agonies of Anthony and Alec, or being left alone with his foreboding.

Beyond the carefully manicured terraces, the dark, oily sea spread out to the horizon, sprinkled with a frosting of sunlight, while from nearby came the gentle, almost musical sounds of water dripping from the Fountain of Tears.

'It's a copy of a famous Tartar fountain at the Bakhchisarai Palace,' Sarah told him.

'Little too ornate for Chartwell.'

'And far too sad.'

'Sad? How can a bloody fountain be sad?'

'You're such an unromantic beast, Papa,' she said, nudging his elbow. 'It's a tale of endless love.'

He groaned in mock boredom.

'It's about one of the last Tartar Khans,' she continued. 'He broke all the rules and fell in love with a girl who was part of his harem, but he had a reputation for such cruelty that she refused to love him in return. Then she died, and he was inconsolable. So he had the Fountain of Tears

111

built. It would weep for ever, he said, just as he would. Don't you think that wonderful?'

'I think it highly improbable.'

'Oh, Papa, you're such a lost cause!'

'So they tell me.'

'Weren't you distracted with love when you first met Mama?'

'We sat and watched bugs crawling across the stones of the Greek temple at Blenheim. Is that the same thing?'

She squeezed his arm playfully.

'Anyway, who was the magical woman who could cure such cruelty and tame the harshest passions in the breast of man? We could use her wiles right now.'

'She was supposed to be the greatest beauty and came to him as booty from one of his wars.'

'Where?'

'In Poland.'

He groaned once more, this time in earnest. 'Then the Khan was right to build a Fountain of Tears, for her and all her kin.'

Beneath them, they could see a family of dolphins agitating the water. They had discovered a school of sardines and were encircling the fish, forcing them closer together to make them easy plunder. The sea began to froth and sparkle in the sun as the dolphins pirouetted and leapt in what quickly became a dance of death. As Churchill stared, transfixed, seagulls joined in the attack.

Then Cadogan was calling. The car was ready.

'I must go for lunch with the President,' Churchill sighed, 'to see whether we have all become sardines.'

The Germans began their preparations for destroying Piorun early that morning. There was so little of real substance to destroy. Most of the town was built of wood, but they mined the two stone bridges that crossed the meandering river, then they mined the church, and soon it was done. For the rest, incendiary grenades and flame-throwers would be enough.

A loudspeaker truck toured the scanty streets blaring out its message.

The people were told that the execution would take place at four that afternoon in the square. Attendance was compulsory. They were informed that any inhabitant of Piorun found to be missing would be shot, along with the rest of their family.

Yet already the town seemed to have died. No one walked the snow-swept cobbles, no trader set out his stall, no children played, no baby cried, no lessons were taught. Doors were bolted. Two elderly women shuffled with bowed heads towards the church, but found a German soldier on guard outside and quickly retraced their path. Even the scavenging dogs seemed to sense the tension and retreated. From behind shuttered windows, from the corners of dark alleyways and through the cracks in ill-fitting doors, all eyes were fixed on the clock above the town hall as it inched its way towards the hour set for dying.

*   *   *

'I don't understand it, Alec. It disturbs me. It offends me!' Churchill turned on the taps to create a satisfying echo that would outwit any listening device.

'And what is that, Prime Minister?' Cadogan replied primly, still smarting from the indignity that had been inflicted upon him the moment they'd arrived at the Livadia. No sooner had they been told that the President and his other guests were waiting for them than Churchill had frogmarched Cadogan into the lavatories as though he were a naughty schoolboy. It brought back unpleasant memories of his first year at Eton.

'I'd hoped for the chance to have a quiet word with Franklin. On his own. One to one. Now it seems there's a bloody posse waiting for us.'

'Is that a problem?'

'It is when I find it easier to arrange a private conversation with Stalin than with the President of the United States.'

'Perhaps he feels he needs the support of others. He's looking so tired.'

'Might there be another reason?'

Cadogan cocked his over-large head and examined his tie in the mirror. 'We have to consider the possibility that the interests of the United States and Great Britain are no longer as close as they used to be.'

Churchill grunted and bent over the wash-basin like a boxer in his corner.

'We also have to consider the possibility that it's a little of both,' Cadogan continued, adjusting his Windsor knot. 'He intends to go behind our backs'—the knot was once again perfect—'and he doesn't want to be bullied by you about it.'

'I don't bully,' Churchill growled impatiently, jerking the plug from the basin. 'I merely argue with considerable force.'

And at considerable length, but Cadogan daren't suggest that. It was common knowledge that Stalin doodled and Roosevelt cat-napped whenever Churchill launched into one of his sweeping panoramas; the instinct that guided the Prime Minister so well in front of microphones and massed audiences sometimes deserted him in more intimate settings. If only Winston would read his briefing papers and stick to the points the Foreign Office had given him, but that was a little like hoping for salmon to swim around ready-smoked.

'Since it's the President's lunch, perhaps we should listen to him before responding,' Cadogan said.

Churchill snorted. He was sure that an insult lay buried in there somewhere but Cadogan didn't elaborate, concentrating instead on wiping his hands with meticulous care on a harsh white cotton towel, which he dropped into a basket. Churchill, from afar, simply hurled his. The towel didn't make it, flapping to the floor like a swan that had been shot through the heart.

The President's room was poorly lit and had the aura of perpetual dusk—a little like the frail Hopkins, who was also there, along with Harriman and others. As Churchill and Cadogan entered, Roosevelt waved from his chair. He was already seated at the lunch-table; it was his habit to ensure that he had been lifted from his wheelchair and into his place before any visitors arrived.

'Franklin, I see you have us outnumbered.' Churchill strode across the room to shake Roosevelt's hand.

'Winston, I know that's the way you like it. You

enjoy playing Custer, while I get no choice but to be Sitting Bull.'

'It was Sitting Bull's victory.'

'Was it? I've never been sure on that one. Trouble is, Custer never knew when he was beaten.'

It was another of the gentle jibes they'd been using since their first wartime conference in Newfoundland nearly four years earlier, yet Churchill detected an undercurrent to this exchange. Perhaps it was nothing more than his over-active imagination, some of the bruises coming out, but nevertheless he decided on caution. He adopted Cadogan's advice and during lunch he did little but listen. He intervened only for the purpose of discovering more about the President's intentions and, reluctantly and contrary to all his instincts, he didn't delay matters with argument.

The President talked of his plans for the new world organisation—his United Nations. And as he did so, the embers glowed once more and his eyes burned bright with hope. 'Not just an end to this war, Winston, but an end to all wars.'

He talked of it as his legacy, in his educated accent that stretched and softened his vowels and sounded elegant. It also sounded final. As Roosevelt talked and smoked, interrupted only by his own coughing, Churchill pondered how much the President had grown to look like his predecessor, Woodrow Wilson, with his *pince-nez* and his cheeks gouged hollow with fatigue. To sound like him, too. Wilson had led the United States throughout the last war and emerged waving his banner for his own world organisation, the

League of Nations, a government of governments that would bring an end to the old world of shifting alliances. Churchill even thought he remembered Wilson introducing it with similar words about an end to all war. Fine words, the most noble of aspirations. And yet . . . Before its collapse, the League of Nations had spawned weakness, procrastination and appeasement. And, of course, Hitler. It wasn't perhaps the League's fault, not directly, but the rise of Hitler was the fault of those naïve men who hid behind it. Evil fills a vacuum in men's souls and they had as good as invited the Devil in by believing only in good intentions and ignoring any signs of sin. Was Roosevelt another Wilson, another faded idealist whose head was held so high they couldn't see when their boots were being stolen?

'We must learn to live as men, Winston,' the President continued, 'not as ostriches or as dogs in the manger.'

Churchill almost choked. He hadn't ever been an ostrich or any sort of dog. 'And what of Bolshevist Russia, Franklin? Can we persuade them of this purpose?'

'That is our task here, at Yalta. To show them that there's a better way—for us all.'

'You think Comrade Stalin is the persuadable type?'

'I cannot believe he would want to repeat the present slaughter,' Roosevelt said, ignoring his food and slipping yet another cigarette into his holder. 'Stalin is one of the most powerful men the world has ever seen. We cannot avoid him, and neither should we try. On a personal level, Winston, I like to think I can do business with the man—and, I might say, perhaps do it better than anyone. Better than all these officials we have around us.' Roosevelt waved in light-hearted manner at the rest of the table, but there was no lightness in his meaning. 'And if you'll allow me to encroach upon our friendship, Winston . . . better even than you. The Marshal will never forget what you are and what you stand for. Monarchism. Imperialism. Everything the Soviet system is not.'

Churchill recalled the sight in his Map Room of Stalin's paw waving across the Soviet Union and wiping up so many neighbouring countries. And Roosevelt thought the Russian wasn't an imperialist . . . Reluctantly, and savagely, the Englishman bit his lip.

'We all change, Winston. We Americans may have been a little slow, a little reluctant at first to face up to our changing world, but we have come to learn that our own well-being is dependent upon the well-being of countries far away . . .' And so the President continued, wrapped up in what Churchill would later term his 'swaddle of idealism'.

'You know, in all my dealings with Mr Stalin, I've never forgotten that Russia is one of the most profoundly religious societies on the planet. It happens to be governed—for the moment—by a creed of absolute atheism. I don't think it's in God's plan for that to carry on too long, and I don't think it's in Russia's, either. We'll draw closer together, I'm sure of it, not out of ideology but out of plain old Russian self-interest. I think we've already seen that happen during this war. That's why I say we can do business with that man.'

'Business such as Katyn?'

'That old chestnut? Why, Averell's daughter

118

Kathy went there herself. Didn't she, Averell?'

The ambassador nodded. 'Not the most pleasant thing to ask a daughter to do, but we thought it was important to see for ourselves.'

'Tell 'em what she found,' the President instructed.

With almost too much care, Harriman put aside his fork and wiped his mouth on the corner of his napkin. He seemed to have lost his appetite. 'Something happened there, for sure. There were bodies everywhere. Buried all across the forest. And almost everybody she saw had a single bullet to the back of the neck.' He held two fingers to the base of his own skull. 'Apparently, it's a typical German technique.'

Since when? Churchill demanded silently. Since they ran out of gas chambers? What did Franklin require in order to prove Russian involvement? An ice pick in every skull, as had been arranged for Trotsky? The lip was being chewed almost to tatters.

'And they inspected the corpses,' Harriman continued. 'Searched through their pockets. They found letters, newspaper cuttings—all from 1941. That's after the Russians had been pushed out of Katyn, and after the Germans arrived.'

'How . . .' Churchill, unable to resist a response, had been going to say 'convenient', but he changed tack just in time. 'How compelling.'

'Who knows precisely what took place there, let alone who was responsible?' Roosevelt concluded wearily. 'I refuse to listen to rumour and dark whispers . . .'

A pity, Churchill thought. It might have saved you from Pearl Harbor. And an even greater pity to sweep aside the brutalities of Katyn like—what?—ostriches? Or dogs in the manger?

Roosevelt was visibly tired. He had eaten little and was drawing heavily on his cigarette for comfort. Harriman sensed it was time to spare him and move on. 'I can't believe you intend to raise Katyn, not with the Marshal. It will achieve nothing, Winston.'

'It's not Katyn that I hope to resolve, it's . . .'

They had barely begun their business in Yalta yet already so much had happened to disturb him. The sense he had gained in the Map Room of Stalin's territorial ambition. The abruptness with which Roosevelt had washed his hands of Europe. The idealism the American expressed that sounded all too much like romance rather than reality. There was nothing wrong with dreams but . . .

Churchill's own dreams had been different. That morning he had woken in a sweat, tormented by a vision of the map of Europe being turned to stepping-stones. They were dripping in blood, with Stalin's boots marching inexorably forward, stepping upon them, one by one. If he were to be stopped, then better he be stopped as far east, as far away from England, as possible.

'Poland,' he said softly. 'I am concerned about Poland. It is, after all, the reason why all of us are here. Poland led us into this war, and Poland seems destined to determine how we shall finish it.'

'That's not quite accurate,' Harriman interjected. 'Poland led Europe into war, not us. Not America.'

'Averell, my friend, it is the reason why *I* am here. If we cannot rescue Poland from the ashes of this conflict then Britain will have gone to war for nothing.'

'Winston, there are nearly eight million Polish-American voters in America,' declared the newly re-elected President. 'You can rely on us to ensure that Poland won't be forgotten.'

'Poland independent. Free. Democratic. Not a vassal—'

But Roosevelt cut across him: 'Emerson once said that the only way to have a friend is to be one. Be a friend, Winston. The Soviets are our allies—and we shall still need them once the war in Europe is won. After all, they will be the ones to liberate Poland.'

'And are you aware, Franklin, of events in liberated Bulgaria?'

But Roosevelt's mind was already elsewhere. He was looking at his watch. 'Is it so late? They'll be piping Uncle Joe aboard before we know it. Time to clear the decks!' The other Americans stood. 'You will forgive me, Winston.'

So Churchill never discovered whether his friend knew of or cared about the happenings in Bulgaria. Four days earlier, those men who had held power under the old system, and who were set to become the challengers to Russian influence in the new, had been slaughtered. Three former regents, two former prime ministers and twenty other leading politicians, every one of them wiped out. An entire level of non-Communist leadership in the country gunned down, with the print of Moscow left all too clearly on the trigger. Such was the price of liberation. Moscow had explained away the tactics as 'an effective purge of Fascist elements'. To Churchill's mind, it had seemed all too bloody effective.

* * *

It was a silly, sad affair that followed immediately upon the lunch and left behind it so many regrets.

By the time Churchill rose from the President's lunch-table, little more than an hour remained before the time when Stalin would sweep through the door and the day's plenary session would start. Roosevelt, as always a solicitous host, knew that Churchill wouldn't have enough time to return to the Vorontsov and claim his afternoon nap so he beckoned to Hopkins, for no better reason than that Hopkins happened to be closest.

'Harry,' Roosevelt said, 'find somewhere for Winston to lay his old head. I don't want him out of shape and all crotchety for later—it'll only lead to more of his speeches.'

Hopkins needed his bed more than anyone—he was rarely to leave it during the conference—but he did as he was asked. Yet he was tired, ill, short of both stamina and patience. Without knocking, he opened the first bedroom door he came to. Inside he discovered another close presidential aide, General 'Pa' Watson, who was in his underwear and about to take a nap. The General was as physically frail as Hopkins, suffering from advanced heart disease, while Hopkins had any number of ailments that on their own could kill him. Neither man should have made the arduous journey to Yalta, but they did so for the sake of their shared friendship with a president whom they had long served and admired, and who liked to surround himself with familiar, trusted faces.

Neither Hopkins nor Watson wanted to let their man down. So they had come. And they quarrelled. Horribly.

'Get out,' Hopkins instructed.

'Get out yourself. I'm using this room.'

'Winston needs it.'

'To Hell with Winston. I'm sick, he's not. Go find him another room.'

'I said, get out.'

'Then to Hell with you, too,'

What followed was crude, intemperate, deeply hurtful, the sort of thing that is best forgotten between two good colleagues. It left Pa Watson clutching at an insistent pain in his chest and Hopkins trembling. It should never have happened, but it did. It finished only when Churchill, who knew nothing of the row, got his bed.

It was the last time those two old friends, Watson and Hopkins, were ever to speak to each other.

Old men, worn down by war, who couldn't properly finish what they had begun. It summed up the story of Yalta.

*   *   *

Before the opening of the new play comes the final act of the old. It was to be played out in the square of Piorun.

As the clock dragged its hand towards the appointed hour, the square filled with townsfolk. They came in small groups, old men in black caps leaning on their daughters, mothers clutching their children, small gaggles of widows, with their heads low, dragging their feet behind them. The thaw that had delayed the advance of the Russians was a miserable, half-hearted affair: old snow was still piled at every corner and icy winds snatched at the hems of skirts and cheekbones, and dragged tears from the corners of rebellious eyes. Even in Poland, where death had become so plentiful, the townspeople of Piorun refused to allow it to come cheap.

The hand of the clock trembled once more. Five minutes to four. Then the coughing of cold engines. Trucks filled with Germans. A *Kubelwagen* in which sat Kluge and, beside him, the mayor's wife. It drew up beneath the lamppost in the square. It was the only lamppost in the whole of Piorun, an overly ornate cast-iron affair. It hadn't been lit since the first day of September, 1939.

A rope was quickly thrown over the lamppost, a noose knotted at its end. The mayor's wife was made to stand in the back of Kluge's vehicle while the scarf was snatched from her head and the noose placed round her neck. She was a woman in the last years of her life. Her many winters had left their scars across her face, the summers had bleached her hair to a steel grey, and the pain of a life filled with many harvests had bent her back and made claws of her hands, but her head was held high so they could see her eyes. They were dry, defiant.

At one minute to four, a young lieutenant began to read from a sheet of paper, his breath forming little clouds, but the wind carried away his worthless words. The driver gunned the engine, anxious that it shouldn't stall when the moment came. Kluge checked his wristwatch against the town-hall clock. Old bones creaked. Children sobbed. The lieutenant read on.

Then a ripple of agitation passed through the square. Voices were raised. The lieutenant paused in confusion. The crowd began to part. And through it, muddied and exhausted by his race from the forest, stumbled the figure of Mayor Nowak. He was totally breathless. '*Stuj! Stuj!* Stop! Please stop!' he cried, and sank to his knees.

Kluge could not hide his delight. He clapped his leather-gloved hands and stamped his boot several times. Then he ordered that a second rope be thrown over the lamppost. 'We shall have a double celebration!' he declared.

Yet his greed was his undoing, for they had brought only one rope with them. While the German soldiers scurried around in search of another, the Kommandant continued to stamp his boot, but this time in impatience. Then the doctor stepped forward. 'Herr Kommandant Kluge, is there nothing we can do to save our friends?'

'You want to die in their place?'

'No one wants to die, Herr Kommandant.'

'Then what do you have in mind?'

'It appears, Herr Kommandant, that you may soon be leaving our town.'

Even though they had no newspapers other than German and they listened to radio only under pain of death, they all knew what was going on. Many of the *Volksdeutsche* had already left the Settlement, abandoning the white-painted farms they had stolen. They had gone to join the long, straggling columns of refugees that for weeks had been clogging the main routes near Piorun, their horses floundering on the ice, belly-deep in the thick snow, pulling sleighs, carts, even upturned tables loaded with whatever these people could save or steal. But wherever they came from, and however they travelled, the refugees were all heading west. They quickly became targets. By day the SS patrols would drag off any male of fighting age, while by night Polish bandits and German deserters would come for the women. The very old and the very young were left to freeze slowly to death. Babies died quickest of all as the milk turned to ice in their mothers' breasts. Yes, the Germans were leaving Poland, and they would soon be leaving Piorun, everyone knew that. It was only a matter of time.

'War is a terrible thing,' the doctor continued, 'and none of us is sure what we shall meet in the days ahead. But we implore you, Herr Kommandant, not to leave Piorun with innocent blood on your hands. How much better to go with your heads held high with honour—and your pockets filled with our thanks.'

'What?'

'Allow us to purchase the lives of our friends.'

'Ridiculous! There's no more than a thousand Reichsmarks left in the entire town.'

'True enough. Money burns so easily. But gold, silver, jewellery—all these things can be so much more useful is times like these.'

'You've been hoarding? I'll do for the lot of you!'

'Perhaps, Herr Kommandant, as you say, you could do for every single one of us—if you had the time. But I fear . . .'

Kluge's jaw was working hard, chewing over the

126

doctor's words. The war was lost, every German knew it, but whatever else lay ahead was buried beneath uncertainty. And, like all Germans of his age, he remembered the times when you could fill a wheelbarrow with money and still not have enough to buy breakfast for your babies. But a good watch, a gold bracelet, a brooch—even during the darkest days, they sang for themselves.

'An hour, then! Everything you have here within an hour. Or more will die.'

But the insolent dog of a doctor was shaking his head. 'In an hour, Herr Kommandant, it will be dark. These things cannot be gathered in the dark. Give us until the morning. Please.'

The Kommandant hesitated, but only for a second. His garrison was desperately weak, depleted by the demands of glory on the Russian front. And these *scheisskerl* Poles scuttled around like cockroaches. He had neither sufficient men nor enough time to do for the lot of them, no matter how much he blustered. So he took what he thought was the easy way out.

'Everything the town has by ten tomorrow morning,' he snapped at the doctor. 'And if it's not enough, not only will the mayor and his wife die, holding each other's hands, but you and your own wife will be given the honour of showing them how.'

*   *   *

This was a time of trial for Winston Churchill, perhaps the greatest trial of his life. He wasn't a stranger to challenge, of course, he was a man who thrived on being kicked, yet somehow the

127

circumstances in which he found himself now were different, more difficult, and not simply because he had grown old. Even at the start of '39 they'd said he was too old. Too old, too unreliable, too unprincipled, too drunk: that was what they'd whispered about him. But, by God, he'd shown the buggers! Whatever they said about him now—and much of it was still robust and unforgiving—they'd never again wrap up his name in a whisper. They would never be able to forget Winston Churchill, no matter how much they might try.

His entire life had been a trial. He wasn't much of a Christian and he didn't pray, yet every night before he went to bed he would spend a few moments in reflection, placing himself in the dock. After Sawyers had left him and before he turned out the light, he would retrace the events of the day, trying to decide how much he had achieved and whether history would judge it to be enough. He never went to sleep without shaking hands with history. He put others to the test, too. Today he had tested Roosevelt and Stalin at the afternoon plenary. And they had both failed. Miserably.

Afterwards he had returned to the Vorontsov in a black mood. He had stamped. He had cursed. He had thrown things. He had been impossible. So Sawyers had sent for Sarah, and she did what all the Churchill daughters did in such circumstances. She listened.

'Franklin is such a . . . ridiculous romantic!' He waved his glass of wine. It wasn't the first. It circled round the dinner-table like a radar beam searching for its target. 'He comes to Yalta hoping to change the world, like Moses descending from his mountain and bringing his tablets of stone on which are carved but three words. *The United bloody Nations.*' He spat them out in frustration. 'It is the only thing he truly cares about. Peace on earth and unity among all the tribes, he proclaims! Then he spends his day sucking up to the Bolshevist brotherhood in the hope that those heathens will swallow it.' He threw back the last of his wine. Sawyers hovered, waiting to repair the damage.

'And you know what, Mule?'

'Papa?'

'Stalin hadn't even read the papers. The President sent him a draft proposal on the United Nations last December and the bloody man says he hasn't had a chance to read it. Too busy with the war.'

'He must have been embarrassed.'

'Embarrassed? He's no nearer embarrassment than Sawyers is to a double first in theology. Instead he demanded to know what the Benighted Nations would do if Egypt said it wanted the Suez Canal back. I told him it was simple. The Empire would say no. So then he asks what would happen if China wanted Hong Kong back—would the Empire keep on saying no, and if it did, what was the point of the United Nations? It was a wretched set-up, Mule, with Franklin and Stalin like footpads out to waylay the empire—just as the Pole said they would. But even that wasn't the worst of it . . .' His voice trailed away as he remembered.

For a while that afternoon, sunlight had swamped their meeting-place in the old ballroom at Livadia. A great fire of birch logs burned in the hearth and Corinthian columns of white marble

129

stood guard along its walls. They sat at the circular table: Churchill in the uniform of the Colonel-in-Chief of his old regiment, the Oxfordshire Yeomanry, Stalin in the simple khaki tunic of a Soviet marshal. Roosevelt was dressed in a civilian suit, pale grey, like his face. Roosevelt, as always, was chairman, since he was the only one of the three who was head of state. It was only minutes after he had opened the session that the nature of the game became apparent. Stalin, who had arrived with only the most cursory of greetings, had quickly turned intransigent. He became blunt and boorish—largely at Churchill's expense. He had cut across the Englishman, interrupted, ignored, mocked, sneered at him and his empire. Accused him of mounting a crusade against Russia. And the rougher the Russian grew, the more emollient Roosevelt had become. It seemed he would do anything to save his beloved United Nations.

'We should've stood up to him together,' Churchill was to growl later to Sarah. But Roosevelt had chosen a different course. He had let things slide, put off decisions, grew visibly upset with the discord, even waved away the fact that Stalin hadn't bothered reading his proposal. Nothing was too much trouble, so long as Stalin remained on board.

Churchill had stayed in the game, didn't have much choice. He had swallowed his pride, and his anger, and waited for the moment that was most important to him: the moment they were to discuss the fate of Poland.

But yet again the President had let him down. 'I see the problem from a greater distance than either of you two,' Roosevelt began, as soon as they got round to it, 'and I guess that makes me a little more dispassionate—but not unmindful. I have eight million Poles in the United States.'

'And not eight hundred thousand voted for you,' Stalin interrupted. 'I know. I've been told!'

Roosevelt looked discomforted, as Stalin had intended, but he didn't argue the point. 'I know the Poles,' he continued hesitantly. 'They are like the Chinese. They attach great importance to saving face.'

Those around the table were stunned by the inanity of the remark. Blood was being shed across Poland in apocalyptic quantities, and he was talking about the importance of 'saving face'? Yet, for a brief moment, Stalin smiled, one of his wicked expressions of mirth that peered like a ferret from beneath his moustache. He'd already worked things out: the President wasn't concerned about saving Polish face as much as saving his own face before Congress.

'I think we have generally agreed between the three of us that the borders of Poland will have to change,' the American leader continued. 'The settlement that was made after the last war is simply not sustainable. There are large swathes of territory in the east, beyond the Curzon Line, that should rightfully be transferred back to the Soviet Union. Meanwhile, Poland gets compensation in the west, from Germany. I believe we've all considered this and find it a fair compromise.'

After the last war the victors had set up an inquiry under the British Foreign Secretary, Lord Curzon, to establish an eastern frontier for Poland. He had come up with a suggestion for a line that, as best it could, represented a fair demarcation between Russian and Polish populations. But Russia had been weak, in the throes of her wretched revolution, and the Poles had sensed a unique opportunity to press home the advantage over their eternal adversary. So their armies had marched, pushed ever further east until they'd swallowed not only the Curzon Line but merchant cities and oilfields and much, much more that lay beyond. Now the Russians wanted it all back.

'Except, perhaps, for the area around Lvov,' Roosevelt added, scrabbling at his papers, searching for his cue. 'That might remain with the Poles, I suggest. A small concession by Russia but one that—I put this to you, Marshal Stalin—would be seen as an act of considerable magnanimity.'

Stalin's mood had changed: the ferret smile had gone, replaced by a face of stone.

'However,' Roosevelt continued, emphasising the word as though he was already preparing his retreat, 'the question of borders is not nearly so important as dealing with the issue of the governance of Poland.'

'I agree,' Churchill joined in, anxious at last to establish some common ground with his American friend. 'That is the most important question we must decide. For Poland to be strong, her frontiers must be constructed on something more sustainable than ancient enmity and intransigence. The present borders cannot be right. Indeed, I've argued the case before the British Parliament and with the Poles themselves.' He omitted to mention that neither had been impressed. He'd ended up in a brutal shouting match with the Polish government in exile in London, who had had no intention of giving an inch on their borders. 'We went to war for Poland, not to defend any specific set of borders but to guarantee her independence,' Churchill continued. 'That was why we fought Germany. And everyone around this table knows that it almost cost us our life. So the question is the governance of Poland. It is a matter of honour for my country.'

Stalin had been doodling idly with a red pencil while Churchill spoke, but suddenly it was jammed down upon the tablecloth and the broken point shot away like a missile. His lip curled in a snarl. 'Poland already has a government.'

Which was half of the truth. As the Red Army had advanced westward, the Soviets had set up their own Polish government in the newly freed city of Lublin, from where it had poured endless buckets of scorn on those bourgeois Poles who had spent the war in London claiming to be the legitimate government in exile. So there were not only two sets of maps, but also two governments, one sitting idly in distant London while the other was already active in most of Poland. And, in Stalin's view, possession was power.

Roosevelt tried to intervene: 'With respect, Marshal—'

Stalin was having none of it. 'I'm not going to sit here and listen to this shit.' He stood up from the table.

Roosevelt's jaw sagged in alarm. Was the Russian walking out for good? Could this be the end of it? 'The Marshal has indicated his desire for a short recess,' the President blurted, improvising for the record, his voice straining as Stalin turned for the door. The Russian stamped his boots across

133

the parquet floor as Molotov and the others bobbed in his wake. Roosevelt called forlornly after them: 'Gentlemen, I suggest we reconvene in ten minutes. Thank you . . .'

And the bear was gone.

Roosevelt leant towards Churchill, accusation in his eyes. 'Winston! For pity's sake, we need him. We can't do a deal on our own. No more speeches—please!'

'It is for pity's sake that some things need to be said,' the Englishman replied, struggling to contain his hurt. 'And for the sake of honour,' he added, then headed for the washroom.

The recess had been set for ten minutes. It was twenty before the Russian reappeared. More upstaging.

Roosevelt greeted him and, anxious to avoid any further difficulties, suggested they adjourn the meeting until the next day, but Stalin ignored him. The performance wasn't yet over.

He didn't sit down, but walked up and down behind his chair like a caged beast, beating out his frustration with his right hand upon the pocket of his tunic. When at last he spoke, the words came more quickly than usual: the interpreters struggled to keep pace, their task made more difficult not only by the characteristic softness of his voice but also the Georgian accent, which grew more pronounced when he was angry.

'The Prime Minister has said that for Great Britain the future of Poland is a question of honour,' he began, breathing heavily. 'For Russia it is also a question of honour. And of life. And death.' He stopped pacing and gripped the back of his chair. His knuckles were white as his eyes

134

darted back and forth between Churchill and the American. 'Twice in the last thirty years German armies have marched through Poland in their attempts to annihilate us. It has become a corridor for our enemies . . .'

Churchill refrained from interrupting to remind Stalin that Russia had been just as adept at using Poland as a corridor for her own armies. He found himself fascinated by the performance he was witnessing. This was the same old Stalin, like the master butcher he was, beating the steak so that it became more tender.

'It is a corridor that is going to be shut, one way or another,' Stalin continued. 'You, Mr Roosevelt, say that we must be magnanimous about the frontier, bend the line a little—but I remind you it was not the Russians who came up with this line but the imperialist Lord Curzon, with the full approval of you Americans. After the last war you said it was the fair line, the right line—yet now you expect me to crawl back to Moscow and confess to my countrymen that I have won for them even less than foreigners were willing to give them after the last war. And you talk about saving face!' He snorted in contempt.

It was an extraordinary scene. Stalin the tyrant was invoking the power of Russian public opinion! It took Roosevelt completely by surprise. He spread his hands in search of a riposte, but found nothing. Meanwhile, Churchill sat back and sipped his glass of tea, silently admiring the audacity of the man and waiting for the next attack. He knew his turn would come. It was the Russian's script: make Roosevelt feel uncomfortable, and Churchill seem intolerable. It took the Russian only a moment to pick up his cue.

'We are given lectures about creating a strong Polish government. But no one—no one!—wants that more than Russia. Ever since the days when Napoleon and his Grand Army marched on Moscow, the enemies of Russia have taken advantage of Polish weakness.' He levered himself up on the back of his chair, trying to increase his diminutive physical stature, turning to confront the Englishman. 'You surely didn't mean what you said, Mr Churchill. "We must decide . . ." Who do we think we are, to sit here in Yalta dickering about the future government of Poland without the participation of the Poles themselves? The arrogance of it!' He stabbed his finger into his chest, glaring across the table. 'It's said I am a dictator. But I tell you, Mr Churchill, that I am enough of a democrat to say that what you propose is profoundly wrong. My task is to liberate Poland, to free it from beneath the Hitlerite heel, to give it new life, not to sit back and watch it become a plaything for old men.'

If Churchill hadn't been on duty he would have applauded: it was a magnificent performance. Yet suddenly Stalin stopped. For a moment he stood stock still, his brow creased in thought. Then he turned to Roosevelt. 'But perhaps there is a way, Mr President. Will you allow a suggestion from an old dictator? Wouldn't it be better to settle this matter directly with the Poles themselves? Why, let's invite them here—to Yalta!'

Churchill started in alarm. 'Which Poles?' he demanded, knowing Stalin meant only those in the puppet government of Lublin. The Russian was offering Roosevelt a means of retreat, a way to save face, and Churchill knew he must shoot this bird before it had a chance to fly—but already Roosevelt was cutting across him and blocking his line of fire.

'There can surely be no harm in a little more discussion,' he began, looking drained. 'I'm sure we could all agree on that—but clearly that could not be a matter for today.' He was tidying his papers, drawing the plenary to a close, anxious that the other two should have no further opportunity to fall out.

'I shall summon them,' Stalin declared.

'Excellent,' Roosevelt responded.

Perhaps the Russian had meant to suggest he would send for them rather than summon them, but old habits are not easily shaken. Roosevelt hadn't seemed to notice.

And Churchill was undone. More delay, more failure to decide, which meant that the Red Army marched ever further west.

There was nothing left of the day. The Russian was going round the table, assiduously shaking hands in farewell. He enclosed Roosevelt's hand in both of his, a token of genuine personal warmth.

'We must have a meeting of minds on Poland,' the American was saying, almost distractedly, as though he were thinking aloud.

'In God's good time.'

'I am determined, my dear Marshal, that there shall be no breach between us . . . If we cannot agree on this, how can we get an understanding on more vital things?'

From the other side of the table, Churchill's attention was suddenly hooked. More vital things? What was more vital than Poland?

'You know, Marshal,' Roosevelt continued, 'that we cannot recognise the Lublin government as now composed . . .'

No to Lublin—fine. That was what they'd always agreed, Churchill and Roosevelt. But what was this new stone the American was throwing into the river? *As now composed?* Did it mean that if the Lublin government was tinkered with a little, a change here, a new face there, that Roosevelt might consent to it after all? Close at hand, Molotov was scribbling furiously, taking down every one of the President's words in a little notebook.

'You mentioned the possibility of bringing some members of the Lublin government here,' the President continued. 'I'd like to develop your proposal a little. We could perhaps invite some others. I know our State Department has a high opinion of . . . well, you'll forgive me, Marshal, if I can't immediately recall their names.' Roosevelt chuckled. 'Polish names are not things that slip easily from the tongue. But I seem to remember there's an archbishop in Kraków and a couple of professors. If we could pull some of them on board, I feel sure . . .'

Sure? Of what was he sure? The President had noticed Molotov's frenzied scribbling, and now he formed his words more slowly, as though composing a diplomatic submission.

'. . . I feel sure we would be prepared to examine with you the possibility of disassociating ourselves from the exiled government in London and transferring recognition to a new provisional government.'

Churchill was stunned, left gasping for breath.

138

The wretched old fool was giving the entire game away. Didn't he realise . . . ?

But still Roosevelt wasn't finished. He gazed up into the Russian's eyes. 'I can assure you, my dear Marshal, that the United States will *never* lend its support, in *any* way, to *any* provisional government in Poland that would be inimical to your interests.'

'That is most understanding of you.'

'I give you my word on that.'

And only then did Stalin release his grip on the American's hand.

When he moved round the table and came to Churchill, their eyes met, and left nothing unspoken.

'Remember, Marshal, for Britain this is a fight for our honour.'

The old dictator brushed his nicotined moustache with his finger and smiled, a cold, bleak expression that chilled Churchill. 'Of course. It's like the bread riots in Petrograd during the revolution,' he whispered. 'Everyone fights for what they don't have.'

*   *   *

Later that evening, as Churchill tried to drown his pain over dinner, only Sarah was allowed to see, and Sawyers to attend.

'My God, Mule, it was like being lashed to a chair and made to sit through a school performance of *Macbeth* and *King Lear* rolled into one.'

'You always said you liked my school plays.'

'Did I ever come?'

'Once. To Broadstairs. I played Alice—

139

remember?'

'Of course. You were scintillating,' he lisped as he lied. 'Stalin is like something straight out of Wonderland, you know. Whenever he speaks, the world turns upside-down and I begin to feel myself falling . . . I'm not sure what to do any more, Mule. He's an actor. A ferocious bully. And he knows precisely what he wants.'

'You know what you want, Papa.'

'But I have no means of obtaining it, not without Franklin. And that Russian peasant plays him like a trout. Tickles him, torments him, until finally . . .'

Sawyers began removing some of the debris of their dinner, but Churchill waved him away. Sawyers didn't retreat far; he never did.

Churchill started rearranging the table. He pushed around the plates, dragged the fruit bowl in front of him. 'You see, Mule, my darling, here is Russia,' he indicated the plate to his right on which lay the torn remnants of a sucking pig, 'and this is Britain'—the fruit bowl on the left. 'In between us lie France, Germany and Poland.' To represent these he laid out three large boiled potatoes in a line. Poland kept wobbling away from its spot, but Churchill insistently shoved it back.

'Germany will be dismembered, torn to pieces. France lies prostrate and filled with left-wing putrefaction, while Poland . . .' He shook his head in despair. 'At times in its long and glorious history, the state of Poland has been vast, yet at other times it has ceased to exist at all. It has expanded east, west, south—the one thing it has never been is settled. So now we are trying to resolve the matter, once and for all. Move it west. Hack a large slice out of Germany. But the bloody Poles don't want to be moved while the Huns . . .' His head was up and he stared at her with red eyes. 'For the moment, they matter not a damn. But there will come a time—there always comes a time—when the *Herrenvolk* wake up from their enforced slumber with an unquenchable thirst for revenge.' His hand thumped down on the table. Poland wobbled once more.

'You make it sound so hopeless.'

'It's Franklin who is being hopeless.' He stuck his tongue in his cheek, exploring his gums. 'What the hell have you done with my bloody toothpicks, Sawyers?'

'Behind your potatoes. Back of France. Just where you left 'em.'

Churchill glared at his servant. 'Are you sure you've not joined the Bolshevists, Sawyers?'

'Roman church, me, always have been. Every Sunday.'

Churchill took a thin sliver of wood and burrowed with ferocious energy inside his jaw.

'But . . .' Sarah seemed perplexed.

'What is it, Mule?'

'This idea of moving Poland. When you first met the President at the beginning of the war, didn't you agree a charter about these things? About borders not being changed except by agreement, never by force?'

'Ah, the Atlantic Charter. Another of Franklin's dreams, one he conjured up at the start of the conflict when its purpose seemed so clear. We drew it up over breakfast.' He slurped at another glass of wine. 'The Charter, Mule, is not a set of rules but a star, something at which we gaze. From afar.' The old man tossed the toothpick into the fire, and with it seemed to go much of his spirit. He sighed bitterly. 'In the meantime we get on with things as best we can. Which isn't very well at all.'

'But if it was Franklin's charter, why can't he help?'

'Franklin? Franklin? Why, the old fool can't even help himself!' But Churchill immediately pulled a face of remorse. It was an outburst too far. 'Forgive me, Mule. I love that man, with all my heart. Without him we could never have survived those dreadful months when all seemed lost. I shall always smother his name in glory. But . . . but— but—and bloody but.' As he repeated himself, the bitterness returned to his voice. 'We all grow old, Mule, we decay. In different ways. Franklin has become ever more stuffed with emotion and idealism. Far-away things. He sees nothing but his Promised Land, not the desert he must cross before he gets there.'

'Like Poland.'

'How can I make him realise?' Churchill cried out in anguish. 'Stalin's army is already there, marching ever further westward, yet Franklin declares that he intends to take his armies home. What am I supposed to do? Look at the map. Why can't he see? Once the American troops are gone, what will stand in the way of Russia?'

And his fist crashed down, first on Poland, then Germany, and finally upon France. The map of Europe was reduced to a morass.

For several moments he sat in despair, tears flooding from his eyes as he gazed into the future. 'I want to stop this thing before it starts. In Poland. Trouble is . . .' he forced a defiant smile ' . . . I'm

142

not in much of a position to tell Stalin to bugger off, am I? Not on my own. But don't worry, my darling. Something will turn up. Always does. You see, there are three of us around that table, the bear, the buffalo and the donkey. Yet only the dear old donkey knows his way home.'

She squeezed his hand. Tears stood in her eyes and he knew he had gone too far. Time to distract.

'And what the bloody hell are you doing, standing there, Sawyers, with all this mess on the table?'

The servant advanced with a napkin and a knife. 'Always thought about goin' to France for me holidays,' he moaned, scraping away at the mashed potato and inspecting the result. 'Don't seem much point any more.'

'You sure you haven't become a Bolshevist, Sawyers? You're always arguing—bad as the bloody Poles, you are. Worse than Randolph.'

'You had a Pole offerin' to help you. But you turned him out.'

'You *are* a Bolshevist! All this damned workers-of-the-world nonsense. You and a plumber.'

'A Polish plumber. Who asked for help and who offered to give us somethin' in return.'

'I explained why—'

'You said it were against the rules of your conference. What rules would they be, then?'

'Damn your—' Churchill began, but didn't finish. The wine had loosened not only his tongue but also his mind, bending his thoughts, opening up new pathways. And the Pole intrigued him. In Churchill's experience most Poles were congenitally bloodyminded, an ill-assortment of Fascists, Communists, nationalists and fanatical

143

priest-followers who spent their time brawling with each other in preparation for setting upon their neighbours. Yet here was an exception, a Pole who knew what he wanted—and who had offered to help. Stalin and Roosevelt were talking about inviting their own tame Poles to the conference, so wouldn't it be useful to have at least one Pole on his own side—if, of course, Ratsinski, or Nowak or whatever his name was, truly was a Pole? And as Sawyers had implied, damn the bloody man's eyes, the way things were going, what the hell had he got to lose?

'But what could he do for us?' Churchill wondered aloud.

'My old dad said you never know nowt wi'out askin'.'

'Maybe,' Churchill mused. 'Just maybe you're right.'

'I'll get puddin' then, shall I?' Then Sawyers bent to pick up a log from the fireplace, brandishing it with a toothless smile as he moved towards the bathroom. 'And I'll call the plumber.'

Wednesday,
7th of February, 1945
The Fourth Day

CHAPTER FIVE

It had been a night of moving shadows, of rustlings and whispers and sporadic sleet, but the Germans in Piorun took no notice. They were depleted in number and demoralised in spirit; some were children, members of the Hitler Youth and only weeks out of school. The guard for the entire town amounted to no more than a handful of sentries in the square and on the two bridges and, like every German in Piorun, their minds were on other things. As the hours passed, their fears grew. Every door that banged, every restless dog that barked, might herald the arrival of the Russians. No one doubted they would be here by the weekend, perhaps earlier. These Germans wanted nothing more than to leave, to return home across the border, and if they could accomplish that with a little Polish loot in their pockets, all the better. So let the Poles scuttle around like rats in the dark, gathering what they may. In the scale of things to come, they were not the problem.

Many of the men who comprised the German garrison spent the evening at the inn. The bravado of earlier days had vanished, replaced by raw anxiety and a determination to get drunk. They raised many toasts to themselves, each growing more mournful, but the beer was thin and they remained stubbornly in touch with their senses, and with their fears. They grew abusive and accused the inn-keeper of serving piss, and they pissed into a glass, instructing him to drink, but he refused. And when they grew angry with his defiance, he simply asked them what they intended to do with him—hang him now, or in the morning? So they cursed him and demanded that he bring out the vodka they knew he was hiding in the back. He brought out a quart bottle of neat spirit flavoured with fruit juice, and they drank till they retched and could scarcely see.

If they had been able to see, they would perhaps have noticed men and even a few women in uniform, infiltrating the town from across the potato fields. Their clothing was unorthodox, usually an old Polish Army tunic or a Wehrmacht jacket with the insignia and emblems ripped off, or occasionally a bit of an old British battledress. They struggled through the clinging mud in peasant boots, laden with ammunition pouches and many different forms of weaponry, much of it German, and some wore grey fur hats like Cossacks, yet no matter what form of headgear they wore, each had a Polish eagle and crown embroidered on the front. This was the Home Army, the underground, the resistance, the remnants from the defence of 1939 and the Uprising of 1944, those who had taken to the freezing forests and lived for years off potatoes and the most meagre pickings, waiting for a day such as this.

But the Germans saw none of it. They watched distractedly over the square and the two bridges and over their drunken colleagues; no one watched over the fields.

The dawn arrived like a trickle of sour milk that spread along the eastern horizon and brought the long hours of darkness to an end. It crept slowly upon Piorun, accompanied by the sound of complaining geese, and cows growing restless for milking. Stirrup pumps squeaked as thin, tired horses tried to stamp warmth back into their hoofs and dark cotton buds of smoke began to appear above the rough thatched roofs, but as the town stirred, German eyes kept flickering eastward, ears straining for the sound of tanks, or artillery, or aircraft. The tidal wave of death was drawing closer and many people in this benighted land would die before the next nightfall; if that were to include a few Poles in Piorun, it wasn't going to burn a hole in anyone's conscience.

Shortly before ten, beneath a flat sky, two Wehrmacht trucks filled with troops whined their way into the square, which glistened in the meltwater. As the soldiers in their greatcoats clambered out and took up their positions, the church bell started to toll, its note sounding dull in the stiff February air, and at its signal the townsfolk of Piorun emerged from all sides. Many brought bags and bundles.

By the time Kluge appeared, the square was crowded and his *Kubelwagen* had to force its way through the throng. Only when he had reached the front of the church did the bell cease its tolling. Another vehicle followed, in the back of which sat the mayor and his wife and the doctor. The doctor bore obvious signs of a beating; the Kommandant hadn't taken kindly to the discovery that he was unmarried and had no wife to hang beside.

The Germans had remembered to bring extra rope with them today. Three lengths. Nooses already tied. From the school across the square, three stools were brought and placed beneath the lamppost. Then the prisoners were dragged

149

forward and made to stand on the stools, the nooses placed round their necks and stretched so that the mayor, his wife and the doctor were forced to stand almost on their toes. The legs of the stools rocked on the uneven ground, slowly pulling the nooses tighter. Several women in the crowd started to weep. The doctor was making gurgling sounds and his lips had turned blue.

'So, where is it? How will you pay for these lives?' Kluge demanded of the crowd. Yesterday he had rather enjoyed taunting these people, but a day was a wretchedly long time when you were waiting for the Russians and his humour had worn thin. He was anxious to get on with it.

It seemed many moments before the elderly priest, the mayor's brother, stepped forward. His habit was as worn as any peasant's smock, his hair crudely cut, his hands dark and gnarled from the hours that he spent labouring alongside others in the fields. Around his fleshless waist was tied an old leather belt that seemed altogether too large for him, and from his neck hung a simple carved wooden cross. 'Please spare them, Herr Kommandant. We have gathered what we could.' He was older than his brother and his voice was frail, cut down by years of undernourishment and humiliation.

'Then where is it?'

'We have placed everything in the church.'

Slowly and with an uncertain hand, the priest held his crucifix aloft, blessing the prisoners, and as the Poles in the crowd saw his gesture, they fell to their knees, those nearby at first, then others, in waves, like the ripples reaching out on a pond. Finally, the priest joined them on his knees, repeatedly making the sign of the cross on his chest, and the only people left standing were the troops.

The Kommandant stared out across the square at so many Poles bent in submission. It was how he wanted them. The priest had done his job for him.

'Well, we shall see!' Kluge shouted. He turned, his boots splashing through puddles as he walked to the door of the church. For a mere fragment of time before he stepped inside, he remarked to himself how it was almost as if the Poles, by kneeling, were trying to remove themselves from the line of fire. Was this, he wondered, how they intended to greet the Russians? On their knees? He smiled grimly. From what he'd heard, it wouldn't do them much good. The Russians felt much the same about these people as the Germans did, and their prayers wouldn't save them. Yet, for a moment, Kluge envied the Poles their superstitions and certainties. He'd spent weeks wondering how he and his men should greet the Russians, but no matter how many sleepless nights he had devoted to the problem, he still hadn't come up with any convincing answer.

Yet, he told himself, war was full of surprises. He might survive, might even live to be a rich man. Time to see.

The church door creaked wearily on its hinges. Inside, Kluge blinked for a few moments as his eyes adjusted to the darkness. His nostrils flared. The heavy stench of old wood and incense hung in the air, but something else was mingling with it, something familiar, out of place. It was several seconds before he recognised the musky smell of stale bodies, and by that time he was also growing

151

dimly aware that a number of gun muzzles were pointing at him.

'*Gott in Himmel . . .*'

'We very much hope he is, Herr Kommandant. But you are not. You are a prisoner of the Home Army. I regret that we will be much less forgiving,' a voice said, from the gloom. A man stepped forward. He was elderly, his back slightly stooped, but his head was held high and the weathered skin stretched tightly over his skull. He hadn't shaved for several days. Kluge thought there was something familiar about him, but it was probably only the Slavic scowl. Beneath a sleeveless sheepskin tunic he wore a patchwork uniform that even in the gloom seemed comical, although Kluge saw no humour in it, for the Pole spoke with a quiet authority that was backed by an American semi-automatic carbine. The German raised a silent prayer of relief that he was a regular soldier and not SS; the Home Army occasionally gave their Wehrmacht prisoners a chance, but the SS never. Then a rough hand stretched out to relieve him of his Luger, while another took his silver cigarette case. He was unarmed, but even so he was far from being completely helpless.

'Don't be a fool. Every single citizen of Piorun is out there on their knees beneath the guns of my soldiers.'

'And every one of your soldiers has now got a rifle aimed at his chest.'

'We will kill you all!'

'Perhaps. But I promise you will be the first to die, Herr Kommandant.' The Pole's voice had an unnatural rasp to it. Kluge thought he could see the furrow of a scar running across his throat.

'So . . .' Kluge tried to force an air of confidence into his words. 'I accept you have a . . . temporary advantage. That will not last, of course, but I suspect we are both in something of a hurry. So let us deal. If you withdraw from Piorun, I'll agree to let the mayor and the others go. They really don't matter to me. It was never truly my intention—'

'Yes, you'll spare their lives, sure enough—and the lives of everyone else in Piorun. But it's your troops who'll withdraw. The only deal you're getting is this. All your men go from Piorun. And they leave their weapons behind.'

'I think not. Even if I did, we would only be ordered back.'

A dry laugh. 'Oh, Herr Kommandant, you couldn't persuade your men to come back to Piorun, not to drink with the Russians.' A dull metallic click announced that the Pole had slipped the safety catch on his carbine.

Kluge's heart was rising in his chest. He felt anger, of course, and disbelief that he was being confronted by some unwashed Pole, but there was also an undeniable twist of fear. 'Kill me and my troops will open fire. Many innocent lives will be lost.'

'That may be so. But you'll never know. Not with your toes turned up. Eh, boys?' he shouted to the others.

The German looked around him. He could see only eight of them in the church, and most were less well armed than their commander. But there might be others around the square. They would have surprise on their side—yes, and that clear field of fire. They would be fighting for their homes and families, that made a huge difference in the balance of things. And suddenly, Gerhard Kluge realised how very much he wanted to see his own home and family again. It seemed so long since he'd been in his suburb of Dresden, rocking his daughter's swing beneath the boughs of the chestnut tree while repelling the assault of a six-year-old boy dressed as a pirate. Before the war his life as an architect had been so simple. He'd never wanted to be a soldier; and deep down he knew he wasn't a very good one. He had his orders, of course, to defend this place—*to the last breath! To the last inch! Fight and die where you stand!* Orders that came direct from the Führer, a Führer who was already back home in the Reichschancellery, in Berlin, no longer in his eastern redoubt. Kluge could face up to the prospect of dying for his country, if he had to, but he didn't want to die here, not in a stinking foreign sewer. Least of all did he want to give some unwashed Pole the satisfaction of killing him.

There came a cry from the crowd outside; the mayor's wife had nearly lost her footing. There were only moments left for Kluge to decide.

*   *   *

When the plumber arrived, his first impression was that there had been some terrible mistake. He found Churchill standing in the middle of his bedroom, short, overweight, his sparse hair awry, clad in nothing but pink silk underwear.

Churchill was utterly unfazed. He had once greeted the President of the United States stark naked and had no intention of standing on ceremony for a Polish plumber. 'Will they begin to

154

suspect you, coming here so often?' he demanded, reaching for a cigar.

Inside his shapeless worker's smock, Nowak shrugged. 'This is Russia. They suspect if I come. They suspect if I don't come. You can rely on suspicion. But you cannot rely on plumbing.'

Yet Churchill was still not sure. 'So what precisely did you do in Poland before the war?'

'So you also suspect me, Mr Churchill.'

The Englishman lit his cigar before replying, taking his time. 'Let us simply agree that these are suspicious times.'

'As you know, my home town is—*was*—Warsaw.'

'Why do you use the past tense?'

'Because Warsaw no longer exists. Before the war it was one of most beautiful capital cities in Europe. Now there is nothing.'

'What do you mean?'

'How can you not know?'

'We know damn' all about what happens in these parts. I'm afraid that Marshal Stalin doesn't very much welcome visitors roaming around behind his front line.'

The Pole nodded and smiled. 'So Polish plumber knows more than British Prime Minister.'

'Don't gloat.'

'We Poles have forgotten how to gloat.'

'You were talking of Warsaw.' Churchill walked to the window, staring out like a headmaster waiting for the report of some wayward schoolboy.

'In 1939, the Germans came. Bombed everything. So much was destroyed. Then later they destroyed ghetto. And last summer there was Uprising. More fighting. And after it was over, Hitler ordered everything that was left in Warsaw

155

must be destroyed. As punishment.'

Suddenly it was Churchill who had the need to explain. He turned from the window. 'I tried to help the Uprising. Truly I did, but . . .' Then his voice trailed away. What was the use of offering excuses?

Warsaw sits on the Vistula river. By July of the previous year the Red Army had fought their way to a point only a few miles distant, where their guns could be heard clearly in the centre of the city. Warsaw filled with anticipation. Then a radio broadcast from Moscow had declared that 'the hour of action has arrived' and exhorted the people of Warsaw to rise up against their German occupiers. They did, on the first day of August. They rose and confronted some of the finest German divisions, even though they had little but obsolete rifles and weapons that had been manufactured in cellars. In their desperation they made mortars from drainpipes and grenade fuses from strips of old celluloid film. Every street became a front line, every house a headquarters. The women of Warsaw served as nurses, armourers and undertakers, their children as messengers and scavengers for food. They fought, and slowly, inevitably, they were crushed. The carnage was terrible, and didn't cease for sixty-three days.

And while all this took place, a few miles away on the eastern bank of the Vistula, the Russians sat and watched as their two ancient enemies slaughtered each other.

Churchill had tried to help, truly he had. Time and again, and then again, he and Roosevelt had proposed that their air forces should drop supplies to the beleaguered Poles, but to do that their aircraft needed to land behind Russian lines for refuelling. And Stalin said no. He said the Poles were lying about what was going on in the city, and that the battle in Warsaw was merely a sideshow. Churchill didn't believe him, was determined to call his bluff, to send the planes anyway, but then it was Roosevelt's turn to say no. He said it wasn't the right time to confront the Russian leader. Somehow, for Roosevelt, it was never the right time to confront him.

After those sixty-three days of carnage, almost one in four of the city's men, women and children, their sons, their sisters, their parents, their neighbours, their friends, had died or were wounded, and nearly half of the Home Army's forces who fought there had been killed. What remained of the city was razed on the personal instruction of the German Führer. The beautiful city of Warsaw was left in ashes.

It was said by some that the Uprising achieved nothing, but that wasn't entirely correct. It depended on your perspective. From the Russian perspective it had achieved a very great deal. Above all, it had enabled the Red Army to walk into the ruins of the Polish capital confronted by nothing more threatening than the stench of unburied bodies.

'I tried, I did try,' Churchill repeated.

'The Polish people grow fat on British assistance.'

'But at least I tried,' Churchill shouted, angry now.

The Pole didn't bother to respond, and his silence stung Churchill more deeply than any words of rebuke.

'We didn't know what was going on in Poland—we still don't,' Churchill argued, seeking mitigation. 'We have only the word of the Russians.'

'Words mean nothing to Russians!'

'Then that is where you must help me. Tell me all you know of what's happening in Poland. Stalin says that the Red Army is being greeted everywhere like liberators.'

'Cossacks? Mongols? Who liberate food from starving peasants and women from the arms of their husbands? Have you grown so old that you cannot see? Russian liberation is like their plumbing. Worthless!' His eyes were burning with contempt, and not just for the Russians.

Churchill decided he didn't much like this awkward Pole. He poked at the end of his cigar with a match. 'Well, perhaps there's another view on these matters,' he grumbled distractedly. 'And we shall shortly hear it. Marshal Stalin has sent for the Lublin Poles.'

'Then you may be waiting a very long time, Mr Churchill.'

'What do you mean?'

'They are not coming.'

The Englishman looked bewildered.

'It is game, Mr Churchill. And already you lose.'

'I don't understand.'

'At dinner last night at the Yusupov, in Stalin's villa, they all got drunk. They always get drunk, that is how Stalin likes it. When men drink, they talk. And Stalin listens.'

'You were there?'

'Of course not. But many others were. They listen, too.'

'Servants.'

Nowak nodded. 'It is always same way. Stalin, Molotov and others play drinking games. They bet. Stupid things, like guessing what temperature is outside or number of girls Beria screws last month. Every time they get wrong answer, they must drink. That is how Russia is ruled, Mr Churchill, with fear and pepper vodka. So they get drunk—Molotov and Beria always are very drunk—and they talk about Lublin. Stalin says they are most wonderful people, these Poles of Lublin, and Beria asks how any Pole who still breathes can be wonderful. Stalin says it is because Lublin Poles always agree with him. For instance, he asks Lublin Poles what they think of fresh air. They say it is good thing. But if Stalin then says no, it is not good thing, they hold meeting of central committee to denounce fresh airism and declare fresh air is counter-revolutionary. So when Beria hears this, he says to Stalin that next time he must tell them not to—I am sorry, I do not know correct English word. For using lavatory. Emptying themselves. Order them not to use lavatory, Beria says. Then in one week, Polish problem will be completely solved.'

To Churchill, the tale had the depressing ring of truth. 'But they are still coming, the Lublin Poles. After all, it was Stalin who suggested it.'

'Last night, Stalin makes toast to Lublin Poles. Says they are like dirty laundry. They will only be found on day after guests have gone.'

'But why?' Churchill demanded, exasperated by the riddle, yet even as he raised the question he knew its answer. Delay. Indecision. Matters put off. Every passing hour played into Stalin's hands, gave him a firmer grip. They had already been

159

here four days, and still nothing was decided. 'Are you trying to tell me that I am being played for a fool?' he muttered.

'You come here to make a deal with Stalin. That is enough.'

'What am I supposed to do?' Churchill's voice rose in frustration. 'I come here to help, yet every Pole I meet has a different story and a cross-purpose. How is it possible to help those who refuse to help themselves?'

'Every foreigner in Christendom comes to help Poles sort out their problems. But throughout our history it is foreigners who *are* the problem. Foreigners like you, Mr Churchill.'

'Rot and nonsense! You accuse me? Damnit, give any two Poles more than five minutes and they'll be on the verge of another civil war. What you've said is not only wretchedly ungrateful but more than a little bloody arrogant.'

'Which is overwhelmed by your own arrogance to believe you can come here without making matters worse!'

'How dare you?'

'You come saying you will save Poland. With words. And you will sign paper saying it is saved. But Poland will not be saved and soon whole world will know your words are lies!'

The two men were squaring up to each other, their fists clenched, drawn along by the heat of their argument, when suddenly the Pole's face melted and he started to laugh. Churchill shook with irritation. He couldn't seem to get the measure of this insolent young man. 'What's so damnably funny?'

'You are, Mr Churchill. Look at you, in pink

160

underwear, shaking all over. Is this how you will save us all?'

As the Pole continued to laugh, Churchill made a grab for his dressing-gown, a vivid green silk affair, decorated with gold dragons. He wasn't used to being treated like this. The bloody man was mocking him, exasperating him almost beyond sufferance. Trouble was, that didn't necessarily make him wrong.

'Well, Mr Nowak, you have at least proved one thing to my satisfaction,' he said, trying to calm himself as he lassoed the silk belt round his middle.

'What is that?'

'You couldn't always have been merely a plumber. Not with an attitude like yours.'

Slowly the Pole stopped laughing, like water disappearing down a plughole. He gazed at his mangled hand, and his words came wrapped in sorrow. 'Before war, before cavalry, I was concert pianist. Very fine one. It was my life, that—and my family.'

'Oh, my dear fellow.'

'What are two fingers when we lose our entire country?'

'Then you will help me while I'm here in Yalta? I will do my best for your country.'

'You cannot help my country. But I will help you—if you take me with you.'

'I give you my word.'

'More worthless words?'

'The word of Winston Churchill!'

The Pole stared ferociously for several moments before, with more than a hint of reluctance, he took the old man's proffered hand. Then he was

161

gone.

Churchill sat on his bed, his head bowed. He felt exhausted and he no longer had the strength for anger. He was in a palace, but it was also a prison and he had grown to hate this place. He had come to Yalta in the guise of one of the most mighty men on the planet, yet the young Pole had made him realise that it was little more than a sham. In truth he was being left behind. There was no longer any place for a donkey alongside the buffalo and the bear.

Churchill sobbed as, little by little, he lost the battle with himself. He'd known the truth for some time, of course, but had done everything in his power to deny it. It was like growing old. A few years earlier, when the Wehrmacht stood within hours of total victory, through stubbornness so profound it had bordered on dementia, he had saved the world, yet now it seemed that nothing he might do or say would make the smallest difference. The game was as good as over, decided by the boot of the Red Army. So Roosevelt ignored him, Stalin insulted him and even a young Pole kicked him around. This old donkey was fit for nothing but the knacker's yard.

And yet . . . in a world descended into confusion, there was surely some purpose in an old donkey knowing the way home, even if he had to limp his way along. And although young Nowak had spoken about the futility of words, he was wrong. Words could be meaningless, but they could also be most powerful tools, with edges of iron. It just depended on how you used them. As he sat on his bed of cares, surrounded by so many despairs, the thought grew and breathed upon the embers of his ambition. Maybe the game wasn't completely lost. Perhaps there might still be a way through the jungle, a way home.

He sat a long while, pondering, arguing with himself, until at last he arrived back at the point from which he had started all those years ago when he'd met his first teacher and realised what a worthless fool the man was.

Let the world rant and rage against him. But he, Winston Churchill, was right.

Suddenly he shook himself and jumped to his feet. 'Sawyers! Where are you, man? And where in God's name is my lunch?'

*   *   *

The barrel of the carbine dug into the Kommandant's ribs. Behind it, the partisan smiled sourly, one of the German's cigarettes hanging from his lips. 'Your choice, Herr Kommandant. But get on with it.'

'Who are you?' Kluge demanded, playing for time.

'Me?' A pause. It was dangerous to let a German know who you were, yet there comes a point when such things don't matter any more. 'I'm Nowak. Jan Nowak.'

'Nowak?'

'The mayor's brother.'

'I thought you looked familiar. But why didn't I know about you?'

The partisan's smile grew wider, exposing a missing front tooth. 'Our father was a sensible man. Three sons. One for the Church, one for town, and one for trade. That's me, the trader.'

'And you speak very good German.'

'That's prison. Got caught smuggling, so you put me up in your hostel of happiness at Moabit for a couple of years. An excellent education.'

'And a remarkable family story.'

'Yeah. We Nowaks are survivors, we are. Even with a rope round our necks. And you know what, Herr Kommandant? We can also read minds. Your mind. Like I know you're pissing yourself with fear, and wondering just how many more reasons I could possibly have to hate you. So, let's get on with it, shall we?'

The muzzle of the carbine nudged the German towards the church door.

'Now here's the deal. When we get out there, you are going to order your troops to lay down their arms.'

'They will not obey.'

'A German refusing to obey orders?' The Pole blew smoke into the German's face. 'Or are you suggesting, Herr Kommandant, that you're not here doing your duty but simply trying to hang my brother for fun?'

Kluge had no answer.

'Don't worry, Herr Kommandant, my troops won't open fire unless you give them cause to. And you should look on the bright side. Do as you're told and you might all make it back home.'

Kluge was trying to figure out his response, but inspiration eluded him, his mind was whirling as though in a dream, and suddenly he was standing on the steps of the church, blinking in the daylight and looking once more upon the scene in the grey square. He saw a scaffold. A sagging body. Troops. Townsfolk. A mass of faces, eyes intent, staring at

164

him. Waiting.

'First, you let the prisoners go,' Nowak's coarse voice whispered in his ear.

Kluge felt dizzy, confused. He also felt the muzzle of the carbine running slowly from his waist up his backbone, counting every point of his spine, like his wife's finger used to. His head swam, with memories, fears. Dully, as if from a great distance, Kluge heard the order being issued. Only vaguely did he recognise his own voice giving the command.

The priest reached the scaffold first, hugging the legs of the doctor, trying to take his weight as he collapsed into his arms. Soon there was a tentative smile. The doctor was still alive.

'Now we come to the interesting bit, where we see whether you've got more than thirty seconds left to live,' Nowak muttered. 'You tell your men to lay down their arms.'

'What reason shall I give them?'

'You're the shit-head in charge. I'm sure you'll think of something.'

And Kluge threw himself into the unknown. 'Men,' he began, but his throat was parched. He forced spittle round his mouth. 'Men! Soldiers of the Wehrmacht! Our war in Piorun has come to an end. It is time for us to leave. To return home. To defend our families and our Fatherland.' His voice carried clearly in the cold air to every corner of the square. 'So I order you all'—more spittle—'to lay down your arms. There are weapons aimed at every one of us. Resistance is useless. But there is no need for anyone to die.'

Kluge's soldiers were looking at each other uneasily, unconvinced. Slowly the muzzle of the carbine, which had been hidden behind Kluge's back, was raised until it was pointing very publicly at the Kommandant's temple. A young lieutenant stepped forward, his own weapon raised, ready to resist, only to find himself staring into the barrel of a Sten gun held by one of the underground fighters from the church. As those in the square looked on, the two men confronted each other and for a few seconds neither would give way.

The lieutenant saw in the eyes of the bedraggled Pole only hate and the willingness to die, yet he stood his ground, trying to mirror the other man's emotions and struggling to hide a weakness that he had begun to feel around his knees.

The stirrings that had been rippling round the square now faded to an oppressive silence. Everyone watched, knowing that their own fate lay in the trembling hands of these two men.

Not even the low rumble of distant thunder distracted them, not at first. Yet it wasn't thunder. It was as if the gods were playing skittles in the sky, a noise that swirled around and clung to them like fresh snow, a sound like a thousand hoofs on the stampede, and they were in the path. It came from the east. From the Russians. The front was almost here. Suddenly the young lieutenant's senses were drowning in fear. It was all too much for him. His eyes flickered, his hand sagged, the elastic that had held his courage together stretched until it burst. His pistol clattered to the floor, and gradually the sound was repeated in all corners of the square as Mausers and Schmeissers and even a few obsolete French Lebel rifles were sometimes thrown, sometimes placed with tenderness, upon the cold dirt. Poles from within the crowd immediately

166

snatched them up.

'Very good, Herr Kommandant,' Nowak whispered. 'You see? They think you're a great leader. Next thing you know, they'll be making you the fucking Führer.'

More men were emerging from buildings on all sides—few in number, but all armed, the soldiers of the Home Army.

'You don't have many men,' Kluge declared bitterly.

Nowak chewed his thumb. 'No, not many. But, it seems, enough.'

Soon the men of the German garrison of Piorun, fewer than two hundred in number, were gathered in the centre of the square, morose, subdued, anxious, lined up as though for inspection. Some were so old they looked as though they should have walking-sticks, a few of the Hitler Youth were in tears. One or two of the women of Piorun threw things at them, pieces of bread, clumps of earth, but Nowak quickly brought that to a halt with a wave of his carbine. 'No, my friends, the Germans haven't time for your games. They've got to be going soon. Haven't you heard?' He cupped an ear to the sound of the approaching battle. 'Their Russian friends are only just down the road.' A pall fell across everyone, German and Pole.

'Anyway,' Nowak continued, 'we still have a little bit of business to finish with them.'

'Business? What business?' Kluge demanded.

'Well, you could take your pick,' Nowak responded, and counted off on his fingers: 'There's the beating to death of a young boy. Another dragged from his mother's arms and never seen again. We could deal with all the pilfering and the theft, or the rapes of the young women. So many things. None of them yet paid for—and you know me, Herr Kommandant. Goes against the grain of my trader's instincts not to settle up on things.' He had now come to his thumb, a thick, dirt-encrusted digit with a crudely bitten fingernail. 'But I think we'll put all those to one side, and deal with the matter of the older woman your soldiers set about.'

'You said nothing of this!'

'Oh, forgive me. But didn't I tell you?'

'What?' the German gasped in alarm.

'There's one other reason I've got for hating you, Kluge.' The Pole smiled, all hard lips, bared gums, broken teeth, like a wolf. 'That woman. She's my wife.'

'You said I would live,' Kluge whispered hoarsely, clearly terrified.

'And you will—if you hand over the three soldiers who did it.'

'Please . . . I don't know who they are.'

Nowak eyed the German with suspicion, but the wild flickering in his eye suggested he was telling the truth. He turned to one of his men. 'Bring Mama here.'

And soon Mama Nowak shuffled forward, wrapped in a simple peasant's shawl. She had wooden clogs on her feet. Her husband helped her up the steps of the church to a point where she could look across the entire garrison. A murmur of anger spread through the crowd; several of the other women called out, trying to reassure her. Nowak pointed to the lines of the Wehrmacht soldiers. 'Who were they, Mama?' he asked gently. 'Which ones?'

But her eyes were full of tears and confusion,

and shame. 'I don't know. It was dark and . . .' She shook her head. 'Only one thing I remember.'

'What's that, Mama?'

She beckoned him closer; he leant down, his ear close to her withered lips. She whispered. Then he kissed her forehead. He turned once more to the soldiers. 'Do any of you recognise this woman?'

Silence.

'Three of you vermin attacked her. Did the most terrible things to her. With your guns, your fists, your . . .' For a moment he couldn't go on. What he had learnt of that night, of the sexual indignities they had forced upon his wife, had brought him to a point where he had thought he might lose his mind and, along with it, the sense of purpose that had got him through the long winters in the forest and the pain of watching so many friends die. He swallowed, very hard. 'Anyone want to volunteer? To own up? German honour?'

Still silence.

'One of the men had a scar. Nasty thing. On his arse. That shake anyone's memory?'

Nothing shook, apart from the celestial skittles away to the east.

'Then I guess we're going to have to find out for ourselves.' His hands stiffened round his carbine. He walked slowly down the steps of the church to the first in the German lines, one of the oldest members of the battalion drafted in from the *Volkssturm*. Nowak stared at him. He said nothing, not a word was exchanged, but slowly the grizzled old German fumbled with the buckle of his belt. Fear is an infection. Soon, along the lines of German troops, trousers and underwear tumbled to the ground, accompanied by the mockery of the

169

women, who jeered as the withered members of the Master Race were reduced to insignificance by the cold and their evident fright.

Nowak took his place once more at the top of the steps beside his wife and Kluge. 'You, too, Herr Kommandant.'

Kluge's eyes widened in disbelief. 'But I am an officer.'

'Are you telling me you are responsible?'

Hesitation, confusion, nausea. Then, slowly, the trousers fell.

'*Heil Hitler,*' Nowak mocked, as he inspected the shivering, half-naked German.

Now there was only one German left, a soldier in the middle of the square, who stood to exaggerated attention as his comrades shuffled in humiliation around him. With a crooked and much broken finger, Nowak pointed, and the man was dragged forward to the bottom of the steps. It took only moments before he was exposed and the entire square could see the vivid red scar that had been burnt into his right buttock.

'Now the other two,' Nowak called to the troops. 'Give up the other two, or you'll all get what you gave to my wife.'

The rolling bass sound of approaching thunder seemed to grow, but another sound filled the square: the screeching of the women of Piorun, demanding retribution, not just for Nowak's wife but for themselves. They hadn't all been raped, not physically, but they felt as if they had. War has many ways of stripping a woman of her femaleness, and now they wanted revenge. Few of the Germans had any doubt as to what that would mean. They were disarmed, disgraced, laid bare, humiliated and increasingly terrified, with the sense of order and discipline on which their world depended left lying in the dirt alongside their trousers. It wasn't long before two other soldiers were being pushed and hustled forward, this time by their own comrades. One was little more than a boy.

'What are you going to do?' Kluge demanded, struggling to find his courage.

'You brought along three nooses. That'll be enough.'

The three fusiliers were led to the stools at the foot of the lamppost, struggling and cursing, the boy weeping pitifully, until the one with the scar fell on his knees and began begging forgiveness of the priest.

'God will forgive you, German, and soon enough.'

And they were hoisted on to the shaky stools and the nooses placed round their necks. Their clothing was still at their ankles, the steel studs of their boots scrabbling to find purchase on the polished wood.

Once more, Nowak was whispering with his wife, but she shook her head. Slowly she began to descend the steps of the church, her clogs clicking on the stone like the pendulum of a clock, until she stood before the crowded scaffold. She clutched her tattered shawl around her and looked for a moment into the faces of the three men, saw the fear in their eyes, the snot dripping from their noses; the boy had already pissed himself. Then she remembered all the muck that had dripped down her own body that night, and what they had done with their fists, their pricks, the barrels of their rifles and the rest of it, things she had never imagined could give pleasure to a man, and the nails that had been ripped from her fingers as she had scrabbled desperately to hold on to her own doorpost.

Beside her the priest, her brother-in-law, was praying for their souls. She allowed him to finish. Then, one by one, she kicked over the stools.

The bodies of the three men were still hanging there when the last of the German garrison stumbled out of Piorun.

*   *   *

God, but he's a magnificent beast, Cadogan acknowledged to himself, nodding quietly in reverence. What would I give to get him round a table at the Travellers'? He shows the other two up. Incisive, insightful—*and knows what he wants.* A breath of fresh air. That's the trouble with the others, they give no impression of having thought the thing through. That's why they ramble on so. But not Uncle Joe. He simply bides his time, then drops in a few words to let everyone know what he expects. I've always thought the art of diplomacy was about extracting teeth through the back of the victim's head while giving the impression you were doing him a favour. And Uncle Joe is a master tooth-tugger.

Only trouble is, he's still a trifle crass about things. That nonsense with the lemon tree, for instance. I want a scraping of lemon and he sends the entire tree. Why? To show us that he can do it. All-powerful—and all-knowing. We expect him to spy and snoop on us, just as we do on him, but I'm blessed if we'd ever admit to it quite so brashly.

172

Still, he's made a definite improvement to the cocktails. One up to Uncle Joe.

But what are we to make of Franklin? A cushion, perhaps? Something for the others to sit on, for he seems to be of little greater use. And a very small cushion at that. When he was wheeled in today to start the plenary he began by expressing the hope that it would be only a short session. Winston turned puce. But FDR's grown more frail, he's become almost mystical in his approach, always looking blindly on the bright side, trying to steer away from any touch of controversy, moving matters on as soon as Winston raises his head above the parapet. It's as though he's afraid a good old argument will break him.

It's astonishing how often both he and Uncle Joe manage to tangle God up in their remarks. They say Stalin was a seminarian in his younger days, a bank robber, too, come to that, but even so it always makes you sit up short to hear the leader of the most godless state on the planet beseeching the Almighty to bless everyone. As though he wants to persuade Roosevelt that he's really as sweet as pudding inside. An exquisite routine.

Meanwhile, Winston blows like a great white whale, full of blubber, backbone and grease—and there's been plenty of grease today, most of it spread in Uncle Joe's direction, even when they've been locked in disagreement. Going on about how his heart goes out to mighty Russia, bleeding from her wounds but beating down the tyrants in her path . . . What's he up to?

And Franklin . . . well, if we're talking animals, then Franklin's been flapping around like a turkey at Thanksgiving, and to quite as little effect. Uncle

Joe's been demanding sixteen votes in the United Nations, one for each Soviet republic, but today he arrives, turns one of those little smiles on us and says he's thought about it and accepts the American position. Sixteen votes are impractical, so all he'll want is two or three. Just Russia, Belorussia and the Ukraine. It's a magnificent concession and the President rushed in to welcome it, saying it's a great step forward, but then you see the realisation of what he's done slowly creeping across his face. His eyes go all oystery and panic sets in. He's still left with only one vote himself. So it's Russia 3, USA 1—scarcely the result he wants to take back with him to the Senate, who'll have his balls in a mangle for that. Suppose Averell and I will have to sweep up the droppings, as always. Breakfast tomorrow, I think, so long as we can find a decent omelette rather than more caviar and those blessed mince pies.

Uncle Joe's been brilliant about Poland. Full of praise for FDR's suggestion about bringing Poles to Yalta—he makes it sound as if the whole thing's an American initiative—and then he says he can't find the words to express his sorrow at not being able to achieve it. Apparently, he's been trying to telephone them in Lublin, but they've gone to Kraków or Lodz or Timbuktu, and they're not answering the phone. And as for the Poles on the list that the President suggested, he hasn't got their addresses. Hah! So he trots out his excuses, and FDR sits there nodding, either in agreement or in sleep, it's difficult to tell which.

But to show willing, Uncle Joe announces that he's written a paper on Poland, which he thinks will take in all our wishes but—would you believe this?—it's still being typed! He pulls a face as if he's been up all night clattering away at the keys himself. He really is the most awful brigand; it's one of the reasons I like him so much. And just at the moment Winston spies his chance and is gathering breath to intervene, Uncle Joe suddenly sidesteps and suggests that while we're all waiting we should use the time to clear up any final points about the United Nations! In other words, he's proposing a deal. An old-fashioned horse-trade. He'll let Franklin have pretty much what he wants with his United Nations in return for not pushing Russia too hard on Poland. All fine and dandy, except what the hell does that leave Winston to take home?

Yet Winston's up to something. Been talking all afternoon about the role of France in the post-war world, wanting it restored and strengthened, barrelling on about how the British people would never accept a situation in which France was demeaned and diminished. What utter claptrap. We've devoted a thousand years of British history to getting one over on the French—why, it's a national pastime. And now that Johnny Frog's spent yet another war with his head stuck up his own rump and his hands raised high in surrender, it seems strange that Winston wants to prop him up all over again. Uncle Joe's got the right line. De Gaulle is a wanton *prima donna* with only a handful of troops and not even a pinch of grace. The French deserve him, but damned if the rest of us do. What *is* old Winston up to? I can't fathom him. He's like a man taking a walk with his thoughts, and never quite making it home.

He's about to wind himself up again, launch us

all upon a new tidal wave of emotion, but he's not to get his chance, not yet, at least. The President has turned an unpleasant shade of green and has asked for a ten-minute recess. Is he unwell, or has he merely discovered a brilliant new tactic for keeping Winston quiet?

*   *   *

Words. More words. Blasted words. They had been such a mighty part of his life, the means by which he had carved out his place in the world, his steps to fortune—and throughout his life he had made almost as many fortunes as he had spent. The first shillings had come from his labours as a war correspondent, and since then there had been histories, biographies, commentaries, lecture tours, newspaper articles, even a novel. Words had sustained his ambition, but they had also defined it. They had been the foundation of his politics, the bonds of his friendships, the weapons with which he had fought off the devils throughout those times when all had seemed lost. Words mattered to Churchill, very much, but his words had become superfluous, powerless, irrelevant—even the young Pole Nowak had said so. Nobody wanted to listen. Yet Winston Churchill was too old to change.

As Churchill saw the Russian leader heading for the door, he grabbed the arm of Birse, his interpreter. 'Come with me!' he instructed, and set off in pursuit.

He tracked him down in a lavatory. The Russian leader was occupying himself in one of two wood-panelled stalls with the door wide open. Quickly, Churchill installed himself in the other, leaving

176

Birse hanging around in some embarrassment immediately outside.

Churchill had never sat in such a place. Nothing had been changed. The panelling was of the most intense walnut, the handles huge and brass, the blue-and-white bowl crafted in Delft and several inches higher than normal, as though its user should never be asked to bend as low as ordinary men. A chandelier glittered down upon their labours; even the paper-holder had a tsarist crest embossed proudly upon it. Everything was fitted out with old-fashioned fussiness.

'Birse, are you ready?' Churchill shouted, heaving shut the door of his own stall.

'Yes, sir,' the Scotsman responded, clearly uncomfortable.

'Generalissimo, I have a favour to ask,' Churchill called through the partition.

'Ask away. Favours are permitted among friends.'

'The other night at the President's dinner, you seemed most reluctant to toast the health of my king.'

'We're not much in favour of the health of kings,' the Russian grunted.

'But he is more than a king to us. He's almost a spiritual figure, the head of our Church.'

'Ah, I understand. You speak to your king, and the king speaks to God.'

'Something like that.'

'Well, we Russians have simplified the process. We've cut out the middle man.'

Churchill knew the bastard was smiling in condescension but refused to be diverted. 'All I would ask is that you treat him on formal occasions

177

in the same way as I do your own head of state.'

'What—Kalinin? He's a useless old fart.'

Churchill had seen Stalin's treatment of his head of state during a dinner in the Kremlin. President Kalinin was elderly, some way down the road to decrepitude and largely blind. He had been unable to find his food without help, and had added nothing to the conversation. Yet when he had picked up a cigarette, Stalin had barked at him, 'Don't smoke that. It's a capitalist cigarette!' The old man's face had fallen to his knees and he had trembled so much that the cigarette had tumbled from his fingers to the floor. He was being mocked, but no one had laughed, until Stalin did, and at that precise moment every Russian at the table had joined in, including Kalinin himself.

'Nevertheless,' Churchill continued, trying to push the memories of the needless humiliation from his mind, 'he is the head of your state and so long as he remains in that position I shall treat him with respect. Why, if we were to judge all heads of state on their merit we'd never invite a single one of them to the table in the first place. Apart from Mr Roosevelt, of course.'

'True enough.' Stalin snorted.

'I have a compromise to suggest. When we raise our glasses, rather than toasting kings or presidents, we should toast the heads of state—all three of them. You could manage that, couldn't you?'

'You think the words make a difference?'

'Yes, I do think words make a difference, Marshal Stalin.'

'Won't make your king not a king. And won't make Kalinin any less of an old fart.'

'Words can cement an alliance.'

An epic, primeval grunt emerged from Stalin's cubicle. 'Well, if that's what you want. If that's what it'll take to keep England in the fight, you can have your words and I'll raise my glass and drown your king in vodka every night of the week. Hell, I might even get Molotov to marry into royalty—now there's an idea! A princess, perhaps. I'm sure you've got a few to spare. Some good may come of it. His current wife's a Jewess, and none of that lot likes me. There I am, saving what's left of their race from the clutches of bloody Hitler, yet still they turn on me. Keep talking about how they want a motherland—when they have one right here! Odd. Very odd. Betrays bad thoughts. So, better a princess than a Jewess, eh? Fewer of 'em!' He laughed and pulled with sudden violence at the chain.

The water was still gurgling its way through the ancient system of plumbing when the two leaders found themselves standing side by side in front of a marble washstand, their images reflecting back at them from an oversized mirror that hung in an ornate gilt frame.

'Something else I would like to ask you informally, outside the plenary session, Generalissimo,' the Englishman began, splashing water over his hands while the Russian examined his moustache. 'A difficult matter, something that is beginning to bother public opinion back home. And you know how difficult that can be . . .'

Stalin looked on in utter incomprehension.

'. . . particularly in the run-up to an election.'

'Ah, now I understand! But of course you will win. I have been told.'

'We hear all sorts of rumours about the treatment of women in the countries you are liberating. Like Poland. There is talk of excesses, of women being subjected to all sorts of indignities.'

'Indignities?'

'I feel sure that, man to man, I don't have to spell out the details.'

'If I may also speak frankly, man to man?'

'Of course.'

'Why do you listen to those who chatter like women over the rooftops? I feel insulted you should ask these things.'

'I intend no insult. But I, too, will be asked about these things when I return home.'

'Then tell whichever fool who asks you that they should be ashamed of listening to a viper's nest of lies. Damnable lies for which they will burn. God forgive them, those stinking Polish *émigrés,* for that's where these lies come from. You shouldn't have given them house-room all these years. They take advantage of you, invent these absurd stories and pretend they are the innocent victims, even as their terror fighters in the Home Army are sneaking about massacring Russian soldiers, stabbing my poor bastards in the back while they're liberating the Polish homeland. They want to start a civil war. And you ask me to toss with these men about the future of Poland, to take them into the new Polish government? Well, I'm a simple man and I've got a simple answer to that.' He then uttered a word that Birse found great difficulty in translating, until Churchill told him not to bother. He understood.

'So there is no problem?' Churchill persisted.

180

'I wouldn't call a few unhappy women a problem. Hell, we men can scarcely breathe without upsetting some woman or other. It's the story of life. And of war. Russian soldiers have marched a thousand miles through blood and fire and over the bodies of their dead comrades—so what are we to do? Shoot them every time they take some trifle and have a little fun with a woman? Why, Prime Minister, I hear that even your own son Randolph isn't averse to a little poking around in the shrubbery when he can. No, there may be a few sour-faced old hags in Poland, but they should be on their knees thanking God they're still alive rather than snivelling on their sleeves because some soldier in the Red Army forgot to say please.'

Stalin's tone remained calm, as if he were discussing the functioning of the postal service or the finer points of wheat yields. In the mirror, Churchill could see the other man clearly: the peasant face, the black and irregular teeth, the stern, mirthless eyes. Churchill imagined this face, or a face like it, the face of a soldier, red and sweating, staring into the terrified face of one of his own daughters. Somehow he couldn't see it as a trifle.

'The Poles are all crooked, like fishhooks,' Stalin continued, his voice rising, playing to his audience. 'They'll do anything to drop the good name of Russia in the shit. Why, if they had their way, the next time your wife came to Moscow and I kissed her hand I'd be charged with attempted rape. The Polish *émigrés* will accuse my men of any type of crime—they even accuse me personally. Me! Stalin! Of every sort of wickedness.' Then he

181

laughed, an empty, soulless sound. 'But not buggery, eh? I leave that to your English gentlemen.'

'Those same Englishmen have a vote. It's a right for which they have fought ferociously. I need to be able to respond to those who will question me.'

'Have no worries. I'll make sure you return home with more than enough bones to silence the yapping dogs.'

'I would prefer to give them the truth.'

'Your trouble, Prime Minister, is that you believe in the power of truth. But power *is* truth. You win, history says you're a great man; you lose, and they drop you down the nearest mineshaft. Bury you in new truth. We Russians know it, and if the Poles don't know it yet, they're about to find out. They lost. Didn't defend their country, failed to liberate it. So they must take what they get.'

'Just like your soldiers, taking what they can get.'

The remark might have lost something in translation, or it might have been that Stalin had grown bored with this conversation, for he simply laughed, and left.

With exaggerated care, Churchill finished washing his hands. The Russian hadn't even started.

* * *

There were to be more blasted words. Russian words. Words that would change the world.

When they returned to the great hall to complete their plenary session, it was Molotov who took centre stage. The Russian Foreign Minister, unlike Stalin, wasn't much of an actor, but he had to his credit an impressive list of roles. He was nicknamed Stone Arse by his colleagues because of his impenetrable nature and prodigious capacity for both work and alcohol. In his wire-framed glasses he gave the appearance of being little more than a gentle academic, yet he was very much the hands-on operator. It was Molotov who had planned the destruction of the *kulaks,* deporting and obliterating millions of innocent people long before Hitler did the same. It was Molotov who had given orders that the troops must shoot starving peasants who stole even a handful of their own grain. It was Molotov's pen that had signed the decree permitting the execution of children as young as twelve, and which had endorsed the massacre in the forests at Katyn. It was that same pen that had signed the pact with his German counterpart, von Ribbentrop, and flung the world into war. Now, little more than five years later, he began to tell the others how that same war would be finished.

He told them he had news that would give them comfort, and some they might find disappointing. The good news was that, during the few minutes of the recess, the Russians had finished typing out their proposals on the future of Poland. It would, he assured them, satisfy almost all the points that had been raised, in particular those by President Roosevelt. However, in spite of the repeated efforts of their communications experts, they had failed to make contact with any of the Lublin Poles. It was a pity, but there it was. The chaos of war—and of victory. So he doubted whether there would be time now to summon them before the conference closed. 'We shall have to try to get on

183

with matters as best we can without them,' he announced, without a flicker of irony. The Pole's warning about dirty laundry made little retching sounds in Churchill's brain.

Copies of the new document were handed round for the British and Americans to read. Roosevelt, whose face was still grey, seemed to grow flustered, starting upon it two or three times, only to lose the thread and be forced to return to the beginning, pinching the bridge of his nose as though his *pince-nez* was troubling him.

Surprisingly, for a document that had taken so long in typing, it contained only five points. Points One and Two set out the new frontiers of Poland, east and west, in sixty-six words. Nearly a third of everything Polish was to be handed over lock, stock and farmyard to the Russians, while Poland was to be compensated with a huge chunk of Germany. An entire country was to be moved, like a gypsy wagon, a hundred miles west.

Point Three created a new political system in Poland, and did it in fewer than twenty words. It described the Lublin Poles as 'the Provisional Polish Government'. The paper suggested it would be 'desirable' to add to those Poles from Lublin 'some democratic leaders from Polish *émigré* circles'. And that was it, all of it. And with it, the deed was done, and the control of Poland thrust into the hands of the Leninists from Lublin.

It was a coup—but that particular word wasn't mentioned. Instead, other words were employed, smeared all over the agreement like balm across a burn. Point Four suggested it was 'desirable'—that strange, imprecise word again—for the Provisional Polish Government to be endorsed at an election.

The document said the election would be held as soon as possible, but it didn't say when, or under what rules, or who would be allowed to stand, or who would count the votes. The gaps were so wide you could have driven a brigade of tanks through them, if necessary, and Stalin had more tanks than anyone. In this part of the document, it wasn't what was said but those things that were not said that made the difference.

The fifth and final point merely stated that any questions about the new Provisional Polish Government should be 'discussed'—not settled or agreed or resolved or decided, merely put up for discussion and kicked about a little—by the countries' three ambassadors in Moscow, which would prove as pointless as playing poker with a priest.

There was a subtext, of course. The Russians had already made it blindingly obvious that Poland was being bartered for the United Nations. Look, Franklin, we've got all sorts of suspicions about your United Nations idea, which in all honesty sounds like a playpen for poseurs, but we know how desperate you are for it and we've bent over backwards to help you out. So now we want a bit of leeway in return. We'll accept your system for the United Nations if you accept our system for Poland. That's what it comes down to, your dream of enduring peace and prosperity in exchange for Poland. It's a one-time opportunity, this, you can't afford to miss it. We've built in all the safeguards on Poland you could possibly want—democracy, elections, conciliation, consultation. And if the whole thing upsets that old boar Winston, well—who cares?

And it did upset Winston. The proposed exchange was so lopsided it was almost certain to capsize. For those like Roosevelt, the United Nations was a glorious dream; for others it was more of an hallucination, a talking shop. It would decide nothing, bind no one. But Poland was something concrete. Poland was a step half-way across Europe. Its fate would bind millions and threaten many more. Russia, like its soldiers, was taking what it could get.

Yet Roosevelt read the words as though they came from a different dictionary. He was the last to finish the document, which made it inevitable that he would be the first to speak. And he declared that he welcomed it. It was progress. Oh, he had a few quibbles about some of the language—he disliked the use of the term *'émigré'*, for instance; it reminded him of the French Revolution, he said, but he was sure they could find a better term. And he was most impressed with the Russian view that free elections could be held soon, because that view was entirely in line with his own.

But of Russia's proposal to rip out the heart of the existing Polish political system by referring to the Lublin Poles rather than the London Poles as 'the Provisional Polish Government', the President said nothing. It was as if he had barely noticed, and his silence spoke most eloquent consent. Old Poland was dead.

Roosevelt was clearly flagging. His lower jaw was beginning to tremble. They'd been at it for five hours; time to call it a day, he suggested. And still Churchill was struggling to make a point, to do business today, to put off nothing until tomorrow, for these things were like cement that would harden and set overnight until in the morning they were all but impossible to shift. There was so much he wanted to contest, he had to start somewhere, and start now, so he began with the new frontiers. He reminded them that throughout all their discussions they had never once, no, not once, consulted a map. The proposals would involve the transfer of huge populations as large as any undertaken in the entire history of the world.

'If my computations are correct, I believe there are something like six million Germans between the present Polish frontier and the one that is being proposed,' he said. 'Six million. They can't stay, otherwise there is a danger of stuffing the Polish goose so full of German sausage that she might choke. And yet to lift them physically would be an undertaking as historic as the flight of the Israelites from Egypt and—'

Stalin cut across him: 'They've gone.'

'I beg your pardon?'

'There are no Germans left,' he said, smiling. 'They've run away. Done the job for us.'

Momentarily, Churchill was taken aback. 'That certainly solves some of the problem.'

'And if any have decided to stay, I guarantee we'll change their minds. The Red Army can be most persuasive.'

'I have no doubt of that,' Churchill responded drily, his biblical analogy shattered on the hard rock of Russian reality. 'Six million. Perhaps there's some hidden purpose in this, some pre-ordained balance. I estimate six million to be the approximate number of Germans killed during this conflict. What is taken with one hand . . .'

'The war isn't over yet. Still a lot more killing to be done, Prime Minister. Perhaps another million or two?' The Russian was staring at Churchill and saw that he didn't seem comfortable. 'What's the matter? You have reservations about how many Germans we destroy?'

Reservations? He had any number. He was a warrior, not a butcher, and he had all kinds of reservations about what the Red Army would do, the liberties they would take, the countries they would swallow up and the lives they would enslave. But there was no point in expressing them: Roosevelt wouldn't back him up, wouldn't want a row. He was on his own.

'No reservations, Marshal,' he responded.

'Then it seems we are in full agreement,' Roosevelt interjected. 'An excellent moment to adjourn, I think.'

Inside, Churchill was screaming. But no one wanted to listen.

*   *   *

'How are you feeling, Mr President?' the physician asked.

'Just bully.'

'Then maybe I should call a psychiatrist, too.'

'Just get on with it,' Roosevelt responded wearily, his voice rattling in his throat.

Commander Howard G. Bruenn looked at his patient laid out on the bed and didn't like what he saw. With this patient, it had been a long time since he had liked anything that he saw. The heart shot to hell, the blood pressure stretching to the sky, the arteries closing, the breathing erratic, the weight declining, the blood supply to the brain beginning to choke. But all the President complained of was a blocked sinus. Roosevelt didn't ask about the details of the other matters, and Bruenn was under strict orders not to volunteer any. Yet everyone knew. It was one of the worst-kept secrets in the White House, along with the fact that he was still seeing his old mistress decades after he'd sworn to his wife he would give her up. But nowadays their relationship was entirely innocent, it could be no other way; the President's body was closing down.

Bruenn should have advised his patient in the strongest possible terms not to run for a fourth term as President. The drugs weren't available for the sicknesses he had, and telling him to cut down on his cigarettes and cocktails was like kicking a limping dog. But Bruenn wasn't simply a doctor: he was a military doctor, and as a military man Bruenn knew there was still a war to win, and in wars, some men die. And soon it would be Roosevelt's turn.

'Is there any way you can ease up a little, just for a few days, sir?'

'I asked you to be my doctor, not to play the fool,' Roosevelt snapped, but immediately regretted the harshness of his tone. Bruenn was only doing his job, and it was a job that Roosevelt knew was impossible. 'Maybe if you could get Winston to take a sedative, it would help. He does insist on trying to make speeches all the time.'

'I'm told they are very fine speeches.'

'Winston makes no other kind. But we haven't . . .' a sigh '. . . *I* haven't got time for them right now. Still so much to do.' He was panting, his breathing

189

shallow. 'We're making so much progress, the whole thing is there, so close I can taste it. So, you just keep me going for another couple of days and . . . well, we'll see.'

'In China I'm told that patients only pay doctors when they're healthy. If they get sick, it's a sign the doctor has failed.'

'Then you'd better get yourself straight back to boot camp, Commander. I guess you really fouled up this time.'

'As you say, sir, we'll see.'

Suddenly, the patient let out a breath that rattled and whistled from his frame. 'Just keep me going, Commander—Howard. Please! Not for my sake, but . . .'

'No one's ever going to accuse you of being selfish, sir.'

'Uncle Joe's suddenly started singing all the right notes—at this rate he'll be whistling "Dixie" by the end of the week. It's what I've always dreamt of. A better world, after all this madness is done with.'

'And Marshal Stalin's word is his bond?'

'Damnit, I don't know. And you and I both know I'm not going to be around to find out. But I've got to try.'

It was the first time he had acknowledged that he knew.

Bruenn gazed for a long time into the eyes of his patient. When he spoke, his voice was very soft. 'What would you like me to try to do, sir?'

'Do your best. Just like I'm trying to do. What more can they ask of either of us?'

*   *   *

190

'Bugger off, Sawyers. Leave me alone.'

Churchill sat gazing into the glow given off by the birch logs, a glass in his hand, his blue eyes melting.

'Very well, zur. I'll be back in an 'alf-hour. Put you to bed.'

The servant knew his master almost as well as he knew his own duty. He would leave the old man to deal for himself with the demons that were tearing at him inside, but he would go no further than the other side of the door, waiting, watching, fending off others. At moments like this, a man deserved his privacy.

For the first time in the many years he had served him, Frank Sawyers saw Winston Churchill afraid.

The Prime Minister had spent the evening with Eden and Cadogan trying to thrash out a riposte to Molotov's document, accepting some proposals, amending or ignoring others, trying to stuff the Poles with a little less German sausage and their provisional government with a few more men of good intent. Yet the longer they had argued, the more dense and complex their own document had grown, and the more imposing had seemed the simplicity of the Russian proposal. No wonder it had been so easy for Roosevelt to swallow.

Churchill had sent a message to the President. Said it was vital for them to meet, to consider, to co-ordinate, before Stalin pulled any more rabbits out of his marshal's hat. Churchill had asked as a matter of urgency to see the President on his own the following afternoon. In fact, he'd swallowed his pride and all but pleaded. Dear Mother of Christ,

191

if that was what was needed, he'd get down on his knees and grovel.

But the reply had come back from his old friend that a private meeting would not be possible. The President felt it would be inappropriate—he meant improper—for the two of them to meet at this stage of the proceedings.

It might upset Marshal Stalin.

*   *   *

In liberated Piorun, the three brothers gathered together for the first time in many years. The priest, the mayor and the warrior sat in the darkened inn and savoured the smoke of the fire and their freedom. They ate *zakaksa* and drank some fine old vodka that the inn-keeper had kept hidden. He charged nothing for it: he wanted only to clear his cellar. The Russians were coming. If they arrived and found alcohol, they would drink everything and smash the inn, and if they found no alcohol, they would still smash the inn. Better that his friends enjoy his last bottles than watch it disappear down the throats of beasts.

So they sat and they drank and relived their wars, trying to ignore the sound of the approaching front. And eventually they came round to the events of the day in the square.

That was when they had begun to argue.

They couldn't agree on what to do with the bodies of the three Germans. The priest wanted to give them a Christian burial, but the mayor had grown angry at the thought of them being buried in the same sacred ground as his son. He wanted them burned, all evidence of their existence erased, in revenge—and in case the Germans came back. Yet the warrior had other ideas. He insisted that the bodies be taken to the bridge at the eastern end of the town. They should be displayed there, he said, as a sign to the oncoming Russians that Piorun had liberated itself, and would do the same to all invaders.

And, while they quarrelled, the bodies continued to hang from the lamppost in the square.

Thursday,
8th of February, 1945
The Fifth Day

CHAPTER SIX

'Are you ill, Vyacheslav Mikhailovich?'

Stalin used the informal *ty* to address his Foreign Minister, while the rest of the Politburo had to get by with the more formal *vy*. Molotov was the only one allowed to get close to him. It wouldn't save him in the end, of course, but for the while, it gave him certain liberties.

'I might die, Josef Vissarionovich.'

'I assure you that you will die. The only question is when.'

'Then let it be today.'

Molotov sat at the breakfast-table in Stalin's rooms at the Yusupov sipping fitfully at his fruit juice in the vain quest for *razgruzhenie*—unloading. The previous night had been long and arduous, like all nights in Stalin's company, and Molotov was desperate to allow his system to unwind a little before the next assault. Stalin watched him across the breakfast-table, looking for any sign of weakness and skinning an orange with a single flick of his wrist.

'So, what are the Americans chattering about?'

Every morning the Russian leader and a handful of those closest to him were given transcriptions of what had been overheard in the Livadia and the Vorontsov on the previous day. There might be a shortage of plumbers in the Crimea, but the place was crawling with electricians.

'You haven't read the transcripts?'

'Why should I bark when I have dogs like you?'

Molotov gazed humourlessly through his wire-rimmed glasses. 'You are too kind, Josef Vissarionovich.'

'So it is said, Vyacheslav Mikhailovich.'

'He's running out of time. Apart from his unnatural passion for the United Nations, he wants to make sure we will help him with the Japanese.'

'How much will he pay?'

'He thinks we've already agreed and it's merely a matter of timing.'

'And payment.'

'He hasn't put up much of a struggle over Poland. He'll co-operate elsewhere.'

Stalin was silent for a while, churning over his thoughts. He pulled out his Dunhill and began to break apart his favourite Flor cigarettes to fill the bowl. Not until it was firmly alight did he turn his attention once more to his Foreign Minister. 'I wonder if he's ever going to extract his head from his arse and tell me about the bomb.'

It was his allies' most closely guarded secret. The Manhattan Project. The atom bomb. Churchill and Roosevelt had discussed endlessly when—or whether—they should tell the Russians about their plans, yet Stalin had known almost from the moment the project had started. His network of highly placed spies, particularly in the British Establishment, was superb.

'It's not yet ready.'

'Perhaps they intend to wait until it is ready before they tell us.'

'Or will the first we know about it be when they drop it on Moscow?'

'The President is old and he is foolish, Vyacheslav Mikhailovich. He genuinely believes we may all live in peace after this war is over.'

'The Soviet Union will never know peace, Josef Vissarionovich. There will always be those who wish to pull us down.'

'But not Roosevelt, I think.'

'I am not so sure.'

In any other man, questioning Stalin's judgement was taken as clear evidence of treason, but Molotov was a rare bird, allowed the precious privilege of thinking for himself.

'Well, we shall see. Let's find out how much he's willing to pay for our help in giving birth to this new world order of his. It will be a sign. The more he gives us, the more difficult it will be to take back later.'

'Churchill will give us trouble.'

'Churchill will always give us trouble. Bourgeois bastard. He can't help himself. Hasn't changed.'

'And, according to the chatter, Roosevelt feels much the same. He's refusing to meet on his own with him.'

Stalin sucked thoughtfully at his pipe. 'Then I have a thought, Vyacheslav Mikhailovich,' he said. letting out a long stream of blue smoke.

Suddenly, Molotov was sitting to attention, his pen poised. And no one sat to attention quite like Stone Arse.

'Let's find out if Roosevelt will meet with us again,' Stalin continued. 'On his own. Without bloody Churchill. See how much he wants us. And how much he's willing to pay.'

'Oh, but that is an excellent idea, Josef Vissarionovich. Put him to the test.'

'You know, I think it's about time to throw a bucket of shit over our favourite Englishman.' Stalin smiled. 'And when we do, I want to make

199

sure his American friend is holding it.'

*   *   *

The message arrived at the Livadia soon after Roosevelt had finished his breakfast. Stalin and Molotov wished to see him to discuss the war in the Far East. The note pointed out that Churchill had not been invited: it suggested that the Far East was a matter primarily for the Americans and Russians.

Roosevelt sent everyone out of his study while he smoked another of the Camel cigarettes that Bruenn had forbidden him and considered the matter. Suddenly, he felt stronger.

The Russians wanted to deal, to show a few of their cards, and poker was Roosevelt's favourite distraction. He'd never been known to turn down a game if he had the time. There would be a price to pay for entry to the game with Stalin, always was, and some of the rednecks and retreads back home might say it was too high, but so what? He'd never stand for election again. It wasn't the judgement of voters that mattered now, but that of historians. He lit a new cigarette.

Winston would hate it, of course. But perhaps he'd never find out. The Russians wouldn't blab, and if he kept it close to his own chest, just Harry and a couple of others, didn't tell that old gabblejaw Stettinius . . . Anyway, peace was more important than personality. Time to face up to facts. He'd carried that old English warhorse long enough.

A glow returned to the President's sallow cheek. He was beginning to feel better already.

Nowak the warrior had returned in the middle of the night to his cottage. His wife was still awake, waiting. She stoked the embers in the hearth and gave him a bowl of hot vegetable soup. It was strange to sit once more at his own table after so long, yet there was no time for reminiscence or proper reunion, for as he sipped from his wooden spoon, he told her of the quarrel that had erupted between the brothers.

They had argued about the Russians. Nowak the politician had said that since the Germans had left Piorun, there was a chance the Russians would be reasonable and show them some respect. Nowak the warrior said the rope that had been strung round his neck must have strangled his brother's brain, because the Russians fought without either reason or restraint; they knew only force, and it made little difference to them whether it was a German or a Pole at the end of their bayonet. And there were three types of Pole, the warrior had said, turning a rough eye on his brother. There were those who believed in Poland, those who had betrayed it to the Germans, and those who were about to betray it to the Russians. At which point, Nowak the priest intervened to suggest that their only option was to put their trust in God.

'I'll trust my soul to God,' the warrior replied, 'but I'll swim in the rivers of Hell before I give my country to those stinking Bolsheviks.'

So the three brothers, so briefly united, had gone their separate ways.

Now the warrior sat at his table and gave his

201

wife instructions. She was to kill the cow. She argued that if she did so they would have nothing with which to work the fields in spring, but he told her that there would be no spring: it would be cancelled by the Russians. If she did not kill the cow, the Russians would take it, along with any other livestock and all the seed. What they wanted for themselves they would use, and what they did not want they would sell back to the people of Piorun. Better that we kill the cow and make use of the meat than leave it to the Mongols and Cossacks, he said.

The Nowaks had nothing of value, apart from the cow and a few chickens. But anything she held dear, any photograph or even item of clothing, she was to hide, if she could. The Russians would take everything.

'And what of me, Papa?' she asked.

He kissed her forehead, her torn fingers, and finally her lips. '*Nie kulturny,*' he said, and repeated the phrase until she could say it. *No culture.* Some Russian officers were sensitive to the accusation, he had heard, and perhaps the men under them, too. It might restrain them.

And for an hour he had lain beside his wife in their bed, a bed he had last slept in more than five years before, and he had sung her one of the lullabies they had used with their children and their grandchildren.

Then, as the first thin threads of dawn wove themselves through the winter sky, he had kissed her one last time, picked up his sheepskin and his gun, and left for the forest.

*   *   *

Old men—tired old men—in a hurry.

Stalin was expected and excitement rippled throughout the Livadia. Footsteps paced urgently along the parquet flooring. Americans checked their watches, and grim-faced Russian security men inspected every corner and closet. White-jacketed servants were everywhere, endlessly polishing banisters and doorknobs. Everyone was watching, and waiting.

Four of the six days that Roosevelt had allotted to saving the world had already passed, and although he had come to recognise that he might have to stay for the full biblical seven, there was still so much to do, and so little time to do it. Everything was being done in a hurry.

Like the faithful retriever he was, Stettinius rushed to bring Roosevelt the results of his morning's work. The three Foreign Ministers had been meeting in an effort to sweep up some of the remaining problems on the United Nations. Many things had been settled, but there was still a difficulty with the votes. The Soviet Union still wanted three; the British empire and its dominions, like Canada and Australia, would end up with five or six; and still the United States would get only one. In a flush of enthusiasm on the previous day, Roosevelt had indicated that this might be acceptable, but no other American thought so. Something would have to be done. But what?

Yet in so many other areas the Foreign Ministers had found agreement, on everything except the votes. It was progress, at least. And it was this good news that Stettinius wanted to bring his master at the first opportunity. He found him in his study.

'I thought I'd better report before the Marshal arrives,' he began. 'We've had a most productive morning.'

'Great news, Ed,' the President responded distractedly, as he made a final shuffle through his notes.

'The Russians have been playing ball,' the Secretary of State continued, still a little breathless, 'and I've managed to squeeze a whole number of concessions from them.'

'Excellent.'

'We've reached agreement on everything—'

Then the door had swung open and Stalin was there.

Stettinius had been in the process of saying that they had reached agreement on everything *except* the issue of votes for the Soviet countries, but he hadn't finished, and as he watched Stalin shaking the President's hand he knew he was never going to get the opportunity, no matter how much he hovered and flapped. The leaders were rushing, there was no time . . . As the door swung shut behind him, he heard the two congratulating each other.

'The Foreign Ministers—they've agreed on everything,' the American said.

'On the extra votes?'

'Yes. That, too.'

It was done. The deal agreed. There could be no going back. The door closed on the Secretary of State and his most hapless career.

Inside the President's study, six men were seated—the President, the Marshal, Harriman,

Molotov and the interpreters. They had only thirty short minutes, which included the time needed for translation, but it was all they would need to change the face of the world.

Once more, Roosevelt shuffled the notes that Harriman had prepared for him. They were so simple, made such sense. The Japanese still had four million men under arms and invading the Japanese mainland was going to be one of the most godless tasks of the entire rotten war. So, dear Marshal, we'd like to bomb the crap out of them first, and if you'd kindly let us use some of your Russian bases for our heavy bombers . . .

Of course, my dear President, we'd be happy to help. No objection to bases at Komsomolsk or Nikolaevsk . . .

But they're in Siberia. More than a thousand miles from Tokyo.

Naturally. Anything closer would be inappropriate, the Russian responded. After all, my country is at peace with Japan.

Roosevelt's jaw dropped. But we thought you had agreed to enter the war against Japan.

At which point the Russian shrugged. 'I personally would be happy to support our great American ally,' he said. 'God willing, we could be ready perhaps . . . ninety days after the surrender of Germany?' Molotov nodded coldly in approval. 'But how will I explain to my people why we are jumping from one great war into another? Russia is at peace with Japan,' Stalin repeated. 'They haven't attacked us, threatened us in any way. We've signed a treaty of friendship.'

'Explain to your people . . .?' Once more, the presidential jaw went wobbly. Listening to Stalin on the subject of public opinion was like a crocodile complaining about the screams of the wildebeest he was chewing up for supper.

Harriman jumped in: 'We would assume that the great Soviet people would understand the, er . . . many benefits that would accrue to them as a result of the defeat of Japan.'

'Benefits? And what would they be?' Stalin asked slowly, wiping a finger across his moustache as though he were waiting for a servant to pour soup.

So they began, bartering the support of the Red Army for the pounds of flesh that would be carved from the Japanese bone. Roosevelt was at first surprised: he had taken as given that the Russians would enter the war against Japan and hadn't realised there would be a price to pay, but he recovered quickly and flung himself into the game. The results came rapidly: the Russians knew precisely what they wanted. Territory. The southern half of the Sakhalin islands. The Kuriles. Roosevelt became expansive and threw a vast amount of shipping into the pot that the Russians would be sold on the most favourable terms. And there was the matter of Russian access to the warm-water ports of Darien and Port Arthur, and the railroad near the Russian border that stretched through the infinite reaches of Manchuria.

There was only one small problem. The ports and the railroad were Chinese, and China was an ally in the war against Japan . . .

'I'll have to talk about this to the Chinese,' Roosevelt said, drawing back.

'But that's surely impossible. Talking to the Chinese is like taking a megaphone and shouting at the whole world. Tell them something today, and it'll be common gossip in Tokyo by the time the sparrows start farting tomorrow. We would lose all element of surprise. Why, they might even attack us first!'

'But I've got to talk to the Chinese,' Roosevelt repeated, vaguely.

'Let me suggest, my dear President, that there is no rush. You and I will agree, and we will put our agreement in writing. Then you can talk to the Chinese at your leisure.'

And once more the Russian had shown his extraordinary talent for slicing through the tangle of knots. He made things easy for Roosevelt. So it was agreed. A secret protocol. To ensure that Russia would get all that she wanted in the Far East, whether the Chinese liked it or not.

Of course, there was no way the Chinese would like it, nor many in the US Senate. They would say the secret agreement was despicable, that it violated all the high-minded provisions of Roosevelt's Atlantic Charter and United Nations. They would say it was a betrayal of an ally and a return to the duplicitous ways of the old world. That's what would be said, very loudly, when they heard about it.

Yet Roosevelt was in a terrible hurry. And he was exhausted. He couldn't fight on every front at once. And he was no longer intellectually capable of sorting through all the consequences of what he had done. But there was one point on which his mind was completely fixed. His Chiefs of Staff had told him that without Russian help in the war against Japan, perhaps another two million Americans would be killed or wounded. That

207

would more than double the number who had already suffered. More casualties, more coffins, more widows, more orphans. He couldn't bear all that on his conscience.

'I'll get Winston to agree to it, too,' Roosevelt said. If he could do that, it would cover at least one half of his presidential rump.

'He'll be offended he's not been invited here.'

Roosevelt burst into laughter. 'You're so right. He'll probably want to kill us. But before he does, I'll get him to sign.'

'How?'

'We'll nudge his elbow a bit. Start talking about his own Chinese ports. Ask him when he plans to give Hong Kong back to China—and India back to the Indians, come to that.'

'But he'll never agree.'

'No.' Roosevelt chuckled, removing his glasses and wiping his eyes. 'He'll be so offended that he'll want to make another speech and smother us in outrage. Then he'll sign.'

And, as they both laughed, they began the betrayal of not only the Chinese but also the British.

*   *   *

Adolf Hitler himself had described them as 'scraped-up Russian scum', but the men of the Red Army were coming his way, moving forward in an offensive that the Führer had assured the General Staff would never happen.

These soldiers outnumbered the Wehrmacht almost eleven to one. They had seven times the number of tanks, twenty times the number of

208

artillery pieces and their air superiority was overwhelming, because the Luftwaffe had all but run out of aircraft. Within days, whole German armies were being ripped to shreds, pulverised by ceaseless artillery fire and ground to dust beneath the tracks of innumerable tanks. By early February, there was no continuous front anywhere in the east. The soldiers of the Red Army moved forward in sleighs, in boats, in horse-drawn carts, in trucks, in American Lend-Lease jeeps, and on foot. They were clad in grey-brown padded coats and fur caps, and they came with an insistent battle cry on their lips.

'*Dayosh Berlin!*' 'Let us have Berlin!'

As they came forward, they encountered columns of German civilians fleeing west, back to their homeland. The Red Army didn't stop. They simply fired indiscriminately upon the columns as they drove past. A few less Germans . . .

And then the tidal wave lapped around Piorun, right up to the doorway of the Nowak cottage. And beyond.

Nowak's wife hadn't heard them coming. She looked up from her table and suddenly they were there, standing in her doorway. Their faces were broad, brown, squat. Faces from far away. Her hands were still covered with blood from the butchering, but that didn't stop them spotting her wedding ring. She hadn't hidden it as her husband had instructed; it was part of her, hadn't moved from her hand in thirty-eight years.

It was gone in a second, along with much of the skin of her finger.

Then they came for the rest of her.

It was the moment Churchill called 'the crucial point of this great conference'. It was also the moment when Stalin began openly to bare his teeth, the moment Roosevelt cracked.

Or perhaps 'cracked' was too unkind a word; 'gave up' would be a better description. After all, the President had got most of what he'd come for. The creation of his United Nations was now merely a matter of detail, and Russia would soon be up to its neck in the war against Japan. It amounted to a famous victory, a diplomatic triumph. He'd saved hundreds of thousands of American lives, brought in Russia from the cold, and secured from the ashes of war a world that for the first time in a thousand generations had a chance of living at peace with itself. Not a bad legacy; in fact, a superb one.

Yet there were these other two, Stalin and Churchill, arguing once more about that hole in history they called Poland.

'I'm telling you, the Lublin leaders are very popular with the Poles.'

'I have other information.'

'Then your information, Prime Minister, is wrong!'

Roosevelt could scarcely contain his impatience. He'd met with Stalin in private and within thirty minutes had managed to sort out pretty much the whole of Asia; yet wheel out Winston and even after five days they couldn't settle the fate of one wretched country. Poland. Always Poland. Winston kept coming back to it, like a dog to its own vomit, until it threatened to sabotage everything they'd won so far.

The President had already called one recess for tempers to cool and to enable him to gather his own thoughts and strength. It had changed nothing. Still they argued about the western border. Yet was there so much in it? What damned difference did it make if the border was shifted a few miles one way or another? The Americans had bought the whole of Louisiana and Alaska without this much whingeing. The borders of Poland were like women of the night, forever on the move, and scarcely a matter of much virtue—yet to listen to Winston you'd think he'd buried his grandmother there.

Truth was, Winston didn't like Joe Stalin. For all the smiles and diplomatic gestures, deep down he didn't trust the Russian an inch, and certainly not with the secret of the atom bomb. Roosevelt had wanted to let Stalin know about their plans, for friendship's sake, and said so, but Winston had leapt around like he'd got a bee up his butt. Wouldn't hear of it. Yet Uncle Joe would find out soon enough, and what would he think then, when he realised that such awesome secrets had been kept from him? So much for the Grand Alliance.

God help him, but now they were haggling like fishwives over the make-up of the Provisional Polish Government. Think about it, Winston! *Pro-vi-sio-nal.* Temporary. Something to plug the gap. Until the elections. Elections that they all agreed would have to take place soon. So why did it matter to the bloody man so much? Yet here he was, saying that he'd never accept the Lublin Poles as legitimate, that they didn't have the support of the majority in Poland, that he wasn't about to

211

brush aside the claims of the London Poles or the hundred and fifty thousand brave Polish soldiers who were fighting alongside British forces in France and Italy. Look at him! Waving his arms, stabbing away with his spectacles. And going over the top. Always going over the top. He couldn't resist it, the hyperbole, the chance to throw words around the room, saying it would be 'an act of betrayal', insisting he wouldn't do it, couldn't do it, that if he tried they'd take a rusty blade to his balls as soon as he got back to the British Parliament. Well, bully for the boys back home.

Roosevelt sat back and waited for the flow to pause, for Winston to catch his breath and allow him back in. Yet when the moment came it was the Russian who grasped it.

'All this talk about a government for Poland,' he said dismissively. 'There already *is* a government in Poland. The people of Poland like these men from Lublin. They are brave men, who stayed behind and fought and played their part in the liberation of Poland, who spent their war suffering and making sacrifices, not screwing around in the dark corners of some faraway foreign capital.' Suddenly, both fists beat down upon the table. 'Those men who ran away to London are cowards, by God, cowards!'

Such an outburst of anger was unusual for Stalin and it deeply impressed the others around the table, as he had intended. It was time now to dance to a different tune, to make life simple once more for his old friend, the American President, for when life is simple, old men are blind.

'I ask the conference to forgive my outburst, but I am sure you all understand my passion when I

212

talk of the sacred rights of Russia. And it is the soldiers of the Red Army who have liberated Poland. But I'm not trying to pretend that makes everything easy between us Russians and the Poles. The Poles hate us—yes, hate. That is the word I use. And with good reason. The tsars treated the Poles like serfs, and the country as though it was their own. But . . .' the Oriental eyes wandered around the table ' . . . that was a sin. A sin of the tsars. A sin we shall make good.'

Roosevelt sat, his cheeks hollowed from ever-deeper shades of grey, nodding in hope.

'Almost every yard of Poland has now been liberated. Much Russian blood has been spilt, and it has washed away the past. There is shared sacrifice between us. And now there is goodwill. It is a goodwill that I intend to make sure will last.'

And the fist that had banged the table in anger was now turned to the palm of peace, laid directly over his Russian heart. It had been a most impressive performance, but he hadn't finished. Stalin had a Georgian's eye for opportunity, and one was screaming at him in the form of this ailing American who wanted so very much to believe.

'All this concern about the temporary government in Poland. I understand it, but . . . I am also a little confused. We are the three great liberating powers. Our objective is to release every country from beneath the boot of Hitler. But— what then? I think we are agreed that these countries must be ruled by their own people, not by some foreign power. Although,' Stalin said, turning to face Churchill directly, 'not quite every country, it seems. Not some colonies. At least, not for a while.'

The Englishman forced himself back into the depths of his chair to stop himself squirming in indignation. Poland and the British empire? It wasn't the same thing, not the same thing at all. Yet Roosevelt was smiling, admiring the carefully directed thrust, ganging up with the Russians. Well, it was to be expected. Nowak had warned him.

'And your own armies,' the Marshal continued, 'they have liberated France—well, most of it . . .' another fine piece of swordplay ' . . . and you have put in place a provisional government, your dear friend de Gaulle.' Now Stalin was twisting the blade. 'Perhaps I'm being slow, but I really don't understand the difference. While we wait for elections, we recognise provisional governments. In Poland, in France, everywhere. I don't object to what you have done in France, I understand the need. And I presume there will soon be elections in France, just as there will be in Poland?'

And still Roosevelt was smiling, in relief. Once more, Uncle Joe had given him a simple way out. And that was when he cracked, gave up the struggle and cast Churchill adrift.

'How soon, Marshal Stalin, might there be proper elections in Poland?'

'Why, Mr President, within a month.'

'Excellent.'

Roosevelt looked across the table to Churchill. The Englishman wanted to roar and rage, to denounce the twisted logic and the bogus comparisons, but in order to do so he would have to deny Stalin's word, suggest that he didn't believe in this wretched Russian or his promise of elections, and if he were to do that it would bring

214

an end to everything. To Yalta, to the United Nations, to the Grand Alliance, to everything they'd been fighting for. It would cast the world into darkness, possibly into another still more terrible war, democracies pitted against dictatorship, a new dark age, and they would say that he alone was responsible. It might come to that, but the world wasn't ready for it, not yet. And neither was he.

'Free and unfettered elections,' Churchill heard himself say. 'They must be free and unfettered. Universal suffrage. Secret ballot. The right of all parties to nominate candidates. A government that is representative of all the people. It must be written.'

'We've already agreed on that,' he heard Roosevelt say dismissively.

'And I promise not to take too close an interest in affairs in France,' Stalin said jovially, then moved on quickly to another subject.

So it was done. Churchill knew now that Poland would be lost. He couldn't save her on his own. He had nothing to fight with, except words, and he knew that words alone wouldn't be enough. Poland was about to be buried beneath this table of untruths.

And if Poland was lost, what else might he lose? Win the war, yet lose the peace—the timeless legacy of fools.

*   *   *

'Nie kulturny,' she had cried, 'nie kulturny.' Just as her husband had taught her. But the words had done her no good.

215

The mighty forces of liberation had just about finished with Nowak's wife. Having stripped her of her wedding ring, they had then stripped away her clothes and every last shred of her womanhood. That she had suffered so much before at the hands of Germans did nothing to lessen this fresh onslaught of pain. She was treated as a beast of the field, to be used, beaten, then cast aside when they were done. She no longer felt a woman, no longer even felt human. They had stripped her of every certainty of her long life, except the knowledge that she was a Pole.

When they were done with her, they threw open the cupboards, smashed all the crockery then ripped apart her bed and threw stools through every window. Soon there was little left of her humble home. Then they urinated on the carcass of the freshly butchered cow. Nowak's wife— Maria was her name, although she no longer felt she deserved anything so touchable and intimate as a name—did nothing: she had learnt that to protest or to cry out would only increase her suffering. They lit a fire of straw in the middle of the room in an attempt to smoke out any other woman who might be hiding within her pitifully small cottage, but when none came, and the room was well ablaze, they departed, leaving her with nothing but fragments.

Her torment was neither isolated nor casual. She suffered far less than others.

There were only a few *Volksdeutsche* left in the Settlement outside Piorun, those who were either too old, or too frail, or too stupid to have left earlier. There were some who, even now, still believed. The Russians found one family in a

216

farmhouse on the outskirts of town: a husband and wife, a son aged twelve, and daughters of sixteen and ten, along with an elderly Polish maid and her husband, the handyman. The Poles were allowed to leave when it became clear who they were, fleeing into the February drizzle that had begun to fall. The father and son were ordered to kneel on the floor while every stitch of clothing was ripped from the mother and girls. Soldiers pinned them down, spreading their arms and legs, while the officer inspected them. Then, while the father and son looked on in horror, he entered the mother and the eldest daughter in turn, toying with them at first, but growing more brutal, enjoying the terror that filled their eyes and the screams that burst forth from somewhere deep inside.

The youngest of the family, the daughter of ten, was still clutching a doll when the officer turned to her. He took it from her hand, and smashed its head on the floor. Then he laughed and reached for her.

It was at this point that the father found himself. He knew he was going to die, and preferred death rather than to watch his child being raped. He threw himself forward, catching his guards by surprise and hammering his head into the face of the officer, breaking his nose. It stopped the bastard laughing. A shot rang out, the father slumped, but he was not yet dead, for as the officer grabbed at his hair and wrenched back his head, the eyes still flickered. The officer stood, shouted, and the father was dragged out through the door by two of the soldiers. And still the captain stood, for he was waiting. He was listening for something.

Then they all heard it, a sound so appalling and

217

piercing that it seemed no longer to be human. It was a noise like that of a stuck pig, driven insane by pain and the desperate longing to be dead. The mother groaned, and fainted. She would never know what had happened to her husband, could not see him leap up from the mire of melting slush and mud that had become freshly mixed with his blood, and tear frantically away, doubled over, clutching at the fresh and gaping wound where, moments before, had been the part that made him a man. Local people say that, if you stand on that spot in winter when the wind blows through the trees, even today you can hear his screams.

Once the officer had finished with the woman and her two girls, the rest of them had their way. The mother never regained consciousness.

Poland was being liberated.

*   *   *

'It has been a good day, Josef Vissarionovich,' Molotov said, as the black Packard drove them the few miles back from the Livadia towards the palace at Yusupov.

'Yes, a damned good day, Vyacheslav Mikhailovich.'

'I think we have the bastards!'

'Perhaps,' Stalin replied. 'A little more patience. Still a few details to nail to the floor.'

'We should've demanded more,' Molotov continued, his enthusiasm rising. 'The Americans want us in their Japanese war so badly they'd skin their own daughters for it.'

'By God, you're a pig of inexhaustible appetites, Vyacheslav Mikhailovich.'

'I'm grateful for your confidence, Josef Vissarionovich.'

'What more could we have asked for? They've already handed over railways, ships, ports, credits, Sakhalin, the Kuriles . . .'

'And Poland. They've as good as given us Poland.'

'It has never been theirs to give or take.'

'Given *in* to us on Poland,' Molotov hastily corrected himself.

'They quibble only so they can save face back home.'

'Pathetic. Toss them a few words about elections and they go belly-up like spaniels.'

'Have a care, Vyacheslav Mikhailovich. Remember, I have given them my sacred word,' Stalin warned. 'And you know I always keep my word.'

'Of course, Josef Vissarionovich.'

'It's just that, sometimes, I change my mind.'

And their laughter brought tears to their eyes.

'We should have asked for their atom bomb,' Molotov said, when they had grown quiet once more.

'No, no, we can't do that. Even to hint we know about it would betray the whole of our intelligence network in the West.'

'But we shouldn't need to ask, Josef Vissarionovich. They talk of alliance and friendship, yet still they deceive!'

'What do you expect? You think their hearts will turn to sugar simply because they've got a bomb tucked in their pockets? Roosevelt whimpers on about this new world of his, and how all three of us will be its policemen. But he seems willing to rot in

219

Hell to make sure only two will have a truncheon.'

They fell silent for a moment, staring into the gathering darkness as the headlights picked out the sentries at their posts along the road.

'I fear they mean to use it against us, Josef Vissarionovich.'

'Not Roosevelt, I think. He's too befuddled, deceived by his own dreams. But look at him, how long can he last? Every day he steps closer to his God. No, it's not him we should worry about, but what will follow.'

'And that black bastard Churchill.'

Stalin snorted through his moustache. 'Every day I ask myself how much longer we will be forced to suffer that man.' The Packard was turning into the driveway of the Yusupov, the engine whining as it shuddered its way down through the gears. 'Yet there's another way of looking at it,' he continued. 'Perhaps he's part of some divine plan. Think of it, Vyacheslav Mikhailovich, maybe we owe him a debt of gratitude.'

'I can't see a single reason why.'

'For sending his armies to Archangel all those years ago in the hope of crushing the revolution. Why, without Churchill and his ham-fisted invasion, the Red Army might never have learnt how to fight.'

'For some reason—which I feel with great intensity, Josef Vissarionovich—I doubt that you intend to make him a Hero of the Soviet Union.'

'But you're wrong!' Stalin contradicted him with a laugh. 'I intend to show my gratitude this evening, to them all. At dinner—with hospitality that'll be worthy of Peter the Great himself. I want to drown them in kindness. I'll be the perfect host.

220

Toast their heroism, the size of their manhood, the breadth of their wisdom. Then we'll go on to toast their generals, their womenfolk, their pets, their catamites, even that weakling of an English tsar. Wash away all their worries.'

The car had drawn to a halt, the door was open, a blue-capped NKVD major was offering a starched salute.

'I want to stuff Churchill and Roosevelt with so much gratitude that they'll stagger away into the night and scarcely know where they are. And then, Vyacheslav Mikhailovich, in the morning, when they are dull and dim-witted—that's when we shall bury the bastards!'

*　　　*　　　*

A wave of tension, even crisis, wafted along the parquet-floored corridors of the Vorontsov. The 'trifle' had gone missing. This was the informal name given to the gifts that the British brought with them on their diplomatic wanderings to hand out as tokens of gratitude to their hosts. At Yalta the trifle consisted of two silver cigarette cases, four cigarette lighters, a silver powder compact, six silver propelling pencils and various other items. It comprised almost the entire monthly quota of luxury goods from Dunhill in St James's, and every single bit of it had disappeared. That morning the pieces had been in a desk drawer in one of the offices; by the evening, they had been liberated. No one had any doubts that the outstretched hand had belonged to one of the many Russians who were in constant attendance and who barged in and out of the rooms without knocking—

chambermaids, cleaners, sentries, electricians, even plumbers. Yet no complaint could be made to the Russian authorities. It would have been insulting to their hosts, and it would doubtless have ended in tragedy with some poor innocent bathroom attendant dragged off to face a firing squad. The prospect didn't make for a sound night's sleep, so the British decided they would have to resolve the problem on their own. It placed Sir Alexander Cadogan in a mood that was several steps beyond foul.

The diminutive diplomat was feeling the pressure. As the conference drew closer to its deadline for conclusion, the supporting staff members like Cadogan were condemned to spend their nights poring over the ambiguities and imprecisions arrived at during the day by the High Ones and turning them into something solid. This was a task of Herculean order, since it required Cadogan not only to find agreement with Russians and Americans but also to secure some sort of understanding among his own team, yet every man seemed to be a lawyer who could spot nothing but loopholes and loose ends. Cadogan sought harmony and found only confusion. All in all, it was beginning to turn into a bit of a flap.

His temper wasn't helped by the fact that he had only just discovered he'd been pushed off the invitation list for Uncle Joe's grand show that evening at the Yusupov. The invitation list was littered with assorted admirals and ambassadors, even Sarah was going, but for him, the man who was responsible for squeezing meaning out of all their diplomatic manure, there was to be no place at the table.

And now the wretched trifle had gone missing. The heels of Cadogan's hand-stitched shoes made sharp clicking sounds of displeasure along the polished corridors as he went in search of someone upon whom he might offload his unhappiness. He found just the man, lurking in an alcove near the Prime Minister's rooms. A workman.

'What are you doing here?' the Englishman demanded. The workman's eyes were shifty and he shuffled uneasily from foot to foot: he was clearly hiding something, perhaps even the missing gifts.

'I come to see Mr Churchill.'

'Don't be ridiculous, man. Let me see your bag.'

But the workman refused to co-operate. A struggle quickly broke out for inspection rights to the bag; voices were raised, a woman's head popped out from a nearby doorway to find the cause of the commotion. It was Sarah, dressed for dinner. And then the Prime Minister's door opened.

'No need makin' a fuss. I'll deal wi' this, Zur Alex,' Sawyers said softly.

'I think he's stolen something, Sawyers.'

'Wi' all respect, Zur Alex, I doubt that. I can vouch for him.'

'What the hell's going on here? You know him?'

'I do. So does Mr Churchill. An' he wouldn't be wantin' a fuss.'

'Who is this man?'

'I can't tell you.'

'You most certainly can.'

Sawyers stood his ground. 'Then I regret I'm not goin' to, zur.'

'I . . . I . . .' The diplomat reddened and rose on to his polished toes, trying to redeem his authority,

223

but failed. 'Well, I never. I really never did!'

He had known Sawyers too long to doubt him, yet he resented being left out of things once again. This place was beginning to exasperate him beyond measure. Cadogan's world was one of decisions, of clarity and, yes, of dinners. And he wasn't getting any of that here. But his world was also one of order, and a mountain of untidy problems still waited for him back at his desk. He hadn't time to make the fuss he thought he deserved. 'I don't know what the bloody hell's going on here, Sawyers, and I don't care for it. The world's gone mad, you know. Mad! Quite blindingly mad!' He threw the last thought over his shoulder as he stumped away.

Sawyers hustled Nowak inside the Prime Minister's door. Sarah followed.

'Now, Mr Nowak, wi' all due respect, you can't just come and—'

'I need to see Mr Churchill. It is very urgent,' the Pole interrupted. He was agitated. Beads of sweat were clustered above his eyebrows.

'But you can't,' Sarah said. 'He's not coming back until after the dinner tonight.'

'But I must see him.'

'Simply not possible,' she insisted.

'I must!'

'Calm yourself, Mr Nowak,' Sawyers said. 'No point in gettin' all bent out of shape.'

'I risk my life to come here. I do not need lecture from a servant!'

Sarah laughed as the Pole's working-class clutch began to slip.

'Your father did not laugh when he promised to save my life.'

224

The smile was immediately smothered.

'Your father is man of honour. Yet others are not. They seek to betray him. And if I do not see him tonight, there is nothing anyone can do to save him!'

'Sorry, zur, but you can't be seein' him, not tonight. He's not here.'

'Then Mr Churchill is lost,' the Pole cried, and slumped to his knees. 'And if he is lost, I am, too. Everything is lost . . .'

*   *   *

Churchill had gone directly from the afternoon's plenary session to the Yusupov. There had been no time to return to his own quarters to wash or change or, as it happened, to see Nowak. When Sarah arrived at Stalin's villa to join her father in the early evening, she found him in a corner with two Soviet generals, deep in discussion about the campaigns of Napoleon. For the moment, he had succeeded in slipping the leash that tied him to Birse, the interpreter, and was conducting the conversation in pidgin French.

'Papa,' she greeted, touching his elbow gently.

He neither turned nor faltered in his monologue, ignoring her.

'Papa,' she repeated, more firmly, squeezing his arm.

'*Ah, ma petite burrito. Excusez-moi, messieurs les généraux,*' he muttered in his execrable accent, nodding to the two men. Sarah led him to a corner beside a large pot plant.

'Well? It's been a bloody day, Mule, absolutely bloody. Can it get any worse?'

' 'Fraid so, Papa. Your Polish plumber's been to the Vorontsov. Quite desperate to talk to you.'

'Ah . . .'

'Gave me a message. He says to remind you that you're a man of honour and have given him your word.'

'I am also a man with an unfinished drink.'

'And he says there's something you've got to know. Apparently, Stalin left from here in something of a hurry earlier today. Went straight to the Livadia, where he met with the President. In private.'

'What?'

'It was a sudden change of plan, he says. All the guards running around like headless chickens for a while. Our Pole felt certain you didn't know.' She didn't explain, as Nowak had done, that the Russians had been joking about it: 'What do you get if you go behind the back of Winston Churchill?—An opportunity!'

'Stalin? And Franklin? Are you sure?' he gasped, incredulous, as though in physical pain.

'Molotov and Averell, too. No one else.'

'But . . . dear God, why?'

'Polish didn't know the details. Only that it was to talk about Asia.'

There are moments in a man's life when his world begins to turn on a different axis. In most respects it appears the same world, but its sky holds a new guiding star. And it changes everything. If this tale were true—and Churchill was enough of an old dog to lick his paws before springing to conclusions—but *if* it were true, they were trying to cast him aside. To carve up Asia for themselves. A continent where Britain was master

226

in many households—in India, Burma, Malaya, Singapore, Hong Kong, to speak nothing of Australia and New Zealand. Yet now they were trying to *force him out.*

Roosevelt had never made any secret of his loathing for empire, and he made no exception for the British. At their first wartime meeting in Newfoundland, Churchill remembered how the American had made clear his ambition that the war would do away with 'eighteenth-century colonialism'. He had talked of European nations riding roughshod over colonial peoples, even come close to comparing British rule in India with Fascism—oh, how those words had whipped across Churchill's cheek. Roosevelt never forgot that the roots of every American were republican and revolutionary: now he saw the chance to squeeze the British empire dry. The bloody, bloody man!

If it were true.

Yet the melting sensation that suddenly flowed inside Churchill's gut told him it was so. He felt as if he'd just found his wife in bed with his own brother. Desolated. Betrayed. And if Franklin could betray him over empire, he was capable of betraying him on almost anything. Perhaps it was already happening.

Churchill was a fighter. He'd not stopped doing battle since the day of his birth when he'd bumped his head on the floor of that cloakroom in Blenheim while his mother had looked on and screamed in surprise. That was when he had started screaming, too, and he'd not stopped since. He didn't know any other way, could never tell when the time had come to shut up and give in. But now Churchill knew that something terrible had happened. He had lost. There was nothing he could achieve here at Yalta that Roosevelt and Stalin between them couldn't, and almost certainly wouldn't, undermine. The consequences in Poland and in so many other places would inevitably be abominable.

And yet . . . Winston believed with every breath and every beat of his heart in what he was fighting for—Britain, of course, but not just that. There was so much more, something wider and deeper that went beyond even loyalty to one's country. Strange, elusive virtues that grew like seeds in dark places, like Truth, Hope, Family, the freedom for a man to think his own thoughts and sing his own songs. These often started life as scrawny stems, yet no matter how hard they were beaten down and left for dead, they kept coming back, often uncertain but ridiculously insistent, until eventually they burst through with such power that no man could tame them, not even one like Stalin. It might take the better part of for ever, but so long as the world turned and the sun rose, their time would come.

And in that struggle, the most powerful weapons of all were words. For Stalin, words meant nothing, and even Franklin was no great respecter of words. He often said that words meant only what he could make voters believe they meant, something elastic that might be stretched round every street corner from Poughkeepsie to the Pacific coast. Yet for Churchill, words were secure, solid things that couldn't simply be bent until they broke. And when the great clash of military machines was over and the noise of battle had faded from the field, and men and women could raise themselves once more

228

from the dirt, that was when words would be heard once more, and words might yet decide their fate.

The battle for Poland was lost. It was time for the war of words to begin.

And the time to start had already arrived. Stalin was striding across the room, ushering them into the dining-hall. There were to be many different recollections of what followed that night, but everyone was unanimous that it was an evening of exceptional abundance. Stettinius said he recalled twenty courses and forty-five toasts, but he might well have lost count. Most did. They were up and down from their chairs to raise their glasses so frequently that much of the food was eaten cold, yet there was so much of it that a few abandoned platefuls made precious little difference. The official transcript has preserved only a fraction of those toasts, most of which were so grandiloquent that they left the translators sweating to find language fertile enough to convey the right meaning. So much was said that night, but what was actually meant would be argued over for decades.

The evening was to be remembered in quite contrasting lights. To some, particularly the Americans, it seemed like the high-water mark of the alliance, the occasion when hearts and minds came together in common cause. The mood was later described by Hopkins as one of 'extreme exultation'. Yet there were other views. One of the British military commanders who sat and sipped through it all described it as nothing more than 'insincere slimy sort of slush'.

The tone—whatever it meant—was set by Churchill, who insisted on offering the first toast.

Almost as soon as they had started, he rose, glanced over his spectacles at those seated along the table, and called them to order.

'Mr President, Marshal Stalin, I hope you will be kind enough to indulge me a moment.' The voice came as though sieved through gravel. 'It is no exaggeration or compliment of a florid kind when I say that we regard Marshal Stalin's life as most precious to the hopes and hearts of all of us.'

Stalin's face had at first been wrinkled in curiosity, but now a look of amusement and appreciation dawned. The mood quickly became infectious.

'There have been many conquerors in history, but few of them have been statesmen'—cries of approval began to ripple around the table—'and most of them threw away the fruits of victory in the troubles which followed their wars. I earnestly hope that the Marshal may be spared to the people of the Soviet Union and to help us all move forward to a less unhappy time than that through which we have recently come.' He held out his pink, fleshy hand towards the Russian, his other hand grasped at his lapel. 'I walk through this world with greater courage and hope when I find myself in a relation of friendship and intimacy with this . . .' he hesitated, seeming to search for the right word, but only in order to add to its emphasis '. . . *great* man, whose fame has gone out not only over all Russia, but the world.'

Fists were pounding on the table in agreement, making the cutlery ring like chimes.

'I raise my glass'—everyone jumped to their feet, apart from Roosevelt and Stalin himself—'to Marshal Stalin!'

'To Marshal Stalin!' they cried.

'Drink it down!' someone instructed jovially, and the long, long evening had begun.

When Churchill resumed his chair, they all applauded him. He smiled modestly, nodding in appreciation.

Then Stalin rose to his feet. 'I propose a toast, too,' he began, in his soft voice, chopping up his sentences to assist the translators. 'For the leader of the British empire.' He nodded graciously towards Churchill. His eyes were catlike, washed of any emotion, but the words overflowed. 'The most courageous of all prime ministers in the world. Who embodies political experience with military leadership. Who, when all Europe was ready to fall flat before Hitler, said that Britain would stand and fight alone against Germany—even without any allies. I know of few examples in history where the courage of one man has been so important to the future history of the world.' He raised his glass. Once more they stood. 'To the health of the man who is born once in a hundred years, and who bravely held up the banner of Great Britain!' They applauded. Churchill sat with tears welling in his eyes, staring in gratitude at the Marshal.

'I have said what I feel,' Stalin explained, 'what I have at heart, and what I know to be true.' Then he drank, and all followed.

And even before they had sat down, Molotov was demanding their attention with yet another toast, to the three British military commanders present, wishing them success. Then it was Stalin's turn once more, walking round the table to clink glasses with Roosevelt, praising the selfless devotion of a country that had come to the aid of

231

the entire world even though it had never seriously been threatened. And everyone was in on the act, raising toasts on all sides. The tables groaned with small mountains of caviar, trays of sturgeon and steaming slabs of sucking pig, while waiters rushed around ensuring that the crystal glasses were never wanting for vodka and whisky.

Roosevelt, sitting wearily at the end of the table, tried to dilute his drink with water, but the tidal wave of alcohol quickly overwhelmed his meagre defences. 'Pour it in the pot plant, Sis,' he advised his daughter forlornly.

Stalin toasted the three women present—Sarah, Anna, and Kathleen Harriman, and Kathleen replied, using a little of her stilted Russian. Stalin hurried round the table to clink glasses with her; Molotov followed, as though attached to his leader by a piece of string. They drank to hospitality, to victory, to heads of state and to the common man, to the indefatigable interpreters, to the Soviet armies that had broken the back of the German war machine, to the generosity of the Americans and the persistence of the British, and still the toasts kept coming. Roosevelt raised one; he rambled a little as he fought to capture the mood, extolling his belief that all those around the table had come together to form one family and one hope for the future of mankind. Syrupy stuff, too sickly sweet for some. The following morning, one member of the British delegation wrote that 'FDR spoke more tripe to the minute than I have ever heard before, sentimental twaddle.' Yet, as with all the rest, it was greeted with an outpouring of adulation.

They were still there at midnight. That was how

they made the peace. There were those at the table who were visibly wilting, dozing, so drunk that they were unable to rouse themselves even for Stalin. The sense of order with which the dinner had begun descended into confusion and occasional incoherence as small groups talked among themselves, every man with one hand on a glass, the other diving beneath the table to defend himself against the fleas that seemed to have declared war on every ankle.

Then Stalin was once again on his feet, although to some eyes he seemed a little unsteady and his grin distinctly lopsided. 'I know, I know—I talk too much,' he began. 'Like an old man.' Howls of protest came from the Russians, but in avuncular fashion he waved them down. 'Shut up, you fools. I want to drink to our alliance.' And they went quiet.

'In our alliance, the Allies should not deceive each other.'

'Hear, hear,' Churchill growled; Roosevelt, too, nodded his agreement.

'Perhaps this is naïve,' Stalin continued. 'Experienced diplomats may say, "Why shouldn't I deceive my ally?" But I am a naïve man. I think it best not to deceive my ally, even if he is a fool. And one of the reasons our alliance is so firm is because it's not so easy to deceive each other. So that is what I drink to. I drink to that!' He threw back his head and finished off his glass in a single flourish.

Sounds of agreement came from all sides, but those who cheered him failed to realise they had been listening not to words of celebration but of warning. As Stalin sat down once more, he bent to whisper in Molotov's ear: 'And still the bastards carry on deceiving us, even when we've got them as

233

drunk as fishwives. May they burn beneath their own atom bomb.'

Then it was the turn of Sarah. It was unclear even to her whether what she said was intended to be a toast or merely part of the increasingly chaotic conversation, but she raised her glass and offered her few fragments of Russian to the man opposite her: *'Dalte grelku, pozhalsta*—May I have a hot-water bottle, please?' she declared in triumph.

'You do not need a hot-water bottle. You have enough fire in you to warm the coldest heart,' Lavrenti Pavlovich Beria declared. The notorious head of the NKVD was making his first and only appearance at the conference. He hadn't been needed at the plenaries: he wasn't the negotiating type.

'Spasiva—thank you,' Sarah replied, giggling.

And suddenly the balding, bespectacled security man had grabbed the flowers from a vase on a nearby side table and, with a bow, offered them to her as a bouquet. 'Please. In the spirit of co-operation between our two countries, allow me to express my admiration, and show you the extraordinary view from the terrace.'

'I'm not sure that I should.' She laughed, looking dubiously as the flowers dripped water over his shoes. 'But is it true that if I don't you can have me locked up?'

'With a single flick of my fingers,' he declared.

'Then, in the interests of the alliance, perhaps I'd better.'

He bowed once more, offered his arm and began gently to guide her out of the room. Her father, deep in conversation, hadn't noticed, but little escaped the all-seeing eye of Comrade Stalin.

Just as Sarah and Beria disappeared, Stalin raised his glass yet again. 'To the faithfulness of our daughters,' he declared, and drank.

As Churchill and Roosevelt joined him, another Russian voice spoke up and a blast of gruff laughter erupted from the Soviets.

'What was that? What did he say?' Churchill asked Birse, his Scottish translator.

'I . . . didn't quite catch it, sir,' the Scot replied awkwardly.

Suddenly Churchill's senses were up. 'Birse, you're neither a young man nor a fool. Tell me.'

'It was . . . a joke, sir.'

'Then, pray, allow us both to enjoy it.'

'The Marshal raised a toast to the faithfulness of your daughters . . .'

'Which you translated very effectively.'

'I'm rather afraid the other gentleman added, "If not the daughters-in-law."'

'Ah. I see. Thank you, Birse.'

Pamela, of course. For a moment, Churchill closed his eyes as his mind wandered far away and to an earlier, more innocent time when his children were young and no one talked of war. When he opened them again, he found Harriman staring at him, his cheeks flushed with guilt. The American looked quickly away.

*   *   *

Back at the Vorontsov, at the far end of the darkened room, the two men, one middle-aged, round and pink, the other young yet painfully gaunt, sat in front of the fire toasting bread on pokers.

235

'Didn't think you'd know how, zur, you bein' an aristocrat, like.'

'I am no longer aristocrat, Mr Sawyers. And since I stopped being aristocrat, I have learnt many new things.'

'Here. Try a bit of this cold meat on it. Can't stand that caviar muck.'

'You are very kind.'

'It's me job.'

'No, Mr Sawyers, you are very kind.'

'Well, then, what do you say we have one of Mr C's whiskies to wash it down?' He fetched the bottle and two crystal tumblers.

'Will he not object?'

'Why, Mr C always objects. About everythin'.'

'He is unkind?'

'No, not really. It's all show wi' him. He's just impatient and bloody stubborn. Thank the Lord.' Suddenly, Sawyers stuck out his lower lip and spoke in a voice remarkably like that of his boss. '"Sawyers—you're a bloody fool. A complete waste of house room. For the life of me, I can't imagine why I ever employed you in the first place. Wasn't for your looks, that's for certain. Still, suppose my daughters are safe with you. Now, bugger off and get me a drink."' Sawyers burst into a fit of giggles. 'Truth be told, zur, he's the best damn' boss I ever had.'

'You don't object? To being a servant, rather than a colonel?'

'Me? No. Wouldn't swap my job for a field marshal's baton.' He poured two exceedingly large measures. 'Second most important man in the country, I am. Why, if it weren't for me, they'd all still be waitin' for D-Day, with Mr C stuck in his bedroom shoutin' that he couldn't find his trousers.' He burst into laughter once more.

'Mr Sawyers, *na zdrowie*. To your health.'

They sat for a while with their toasted pork sandwiches and their thoughts, staring into the red embers of the fire.

'Tell me about her, zur, your little girl.'

Nowak looked into his glass, swirled it as though to excite the memories. 'Katarzyna. Her name is Katarzyna Maria Krystyna Irena Raczynski. After her grandmothers. And after that, there is so little to tell. One moment I was there and she was so very small and beautiful, next moment I was gone, ordered off to cavalry.' His hand wandered up to touch the pocket over his heart, as though checking for something.

'You have a photo of the little girl?'

'No, not any more. It was impossible to keep anything in camps, dangerous, too. But I imagine it always, here'—he touched the pocket over his heart once more—'and in my mind. On Sunday it would be—no, *will* be—her sixth birthday.'

'Then I drink to the young lady's health, zur.'

'Thank you. But, please, do not call me "sir". I think after war that all such things will be gone. In war, ordinary men die just as well as aristocrats. And more often. It is another thing I have learnt.'

'Do me out of a job, you will. Another slice of toast?'

'*Dziekuja*. Thank you.'

They busied themselves in silence for a while. Sawyers cut more cold pork, then wrapped the rest of the joint in paper and, without asking, placed it in the plumber's bag.

The Pole bowed his head in gratitude. 'Where

do you come from, Mr Sawyers?'

'Me? I'm a country boy. From Cumberland. That's up north. Hills and dales, and a lot of lakes.'

'My homeland is very flat. With forests.'

'Home's a long way away.'

'For both of us.'

'We'll get you back there, to your little girl. I promise. And, more to the point, so does Mr Churchill . . .'

*   *   *

The dinner at the Yusupov continued. It was indulgence without respite. They might just as well have poured the vodka out of buckets and dragged in the sucking pigs on a truck. Toasts raced round the table pursued by plates of dessert and vast bowls of ice-cream. Glasses were spilled, trousers stained, tongues grew slurred. Then came more toasts. Churchill's eye wandered further down the table, taking in the panorama of flushed cheeks and straining collars until it snagged upon the figure of Roosevelt. God, the President looked awful. Ashen, slumped in his chair, smile fixed, movements almost mechanical. And it was at that moment that Churchill realised what this dinner was all about. The purpose was not so much enjoyment as exhaustion—the exhaustion of Roosevelt. He was sick, he was tired, and now he was going to find it harder than ever to resist the demands of the Russians. In a man so frail, keeping him up this late was as good as spiking his milk, and in a game so vital it was nothing short of fixing the result.

There was no time for reflection: it was instinct

that drove Churchill to his feet, smacking the side of his glass with a spoon. 'Mr President. Marshal Stalin. Friends,' he began, as they turned towards him. 'At the end of this extraordinary dinner'— well, someone had to send them home—'in addition to proposing a vote of thanks to our host, I would like to offer one final toast. I must say that never in this war have I felt the responsibility weigh so heavily on me, even in the darkest hours, as now, during this conference.' And he was off. Grand, overblown phrases, unrehearsed but unforgettable, tumbled forth like acrobats into a circus ring. 'The crest of the hill . . . the prospect of open country . . . comrades in arms . . . toiling millions . . . falling into the pit.' His tone was sombre, and the gaieties of the previous moments were gone. His voice grew ever more emotional. 'We now have a chance of avoiding the errors of previous generations and of making a sure peace. People cry out for peace and joy. Will the families be reunited? Will the shattered dwellings be rebuilt? Will the toiler see his home? To defend one's country is glorious, but there are greater conquests before us. Before us lies the realisation of the poor—that they shall live in peace, protected by our invincible power from aggression and evil!'

The American Secretary of State later wrote: 'I was immensely impressed while Churchill was speaking, with the way his attitude had changed on the future of the world. At Malta, he had been extremely discouraged and distressed, but in his toasts this evening at Yalta, he manifested real hope that there could be a world of happiness, peace, and security.' That was Stettinius's view, but almost everyone knew the man was a naïve bloody fool.

Churchill finished by toasting them all, and what he called 'the broad sunlight of victorious peace'. They cheered him. Then they left.

As Churchill himself was leaving, he found Harriman at his side, touching his sleeve, the guilt still lingering on his cheeks.

'Winston, I can only apologise,' the American said softly. 'I've never wanted to cause you embarrassment.'

'No need for apology, Averell. You are, and you will continue to be, a most dear friend, not just of Pamela but also of mine.'

'I can't tell you how much those words mean to me.'

'But I intend imposing upon our friendship.'

'Anything.'

'Averell. I need to ask you. Did the President meet privately with the Marshal this afternoon?'

Silence sometimes speaks with a most eloquent voice. Harriman's silence screamed at Churchill as the American Ambassador, trapped between friendship and duty, wriggled with indecision. 'Forgive me, Winston,' was all he could manage.

'Nothing to forgive. You have done your duty. But, as the Marshal himself said, it's not so easy to hide things from each other.'

'I seem to have nothing to say to you this evening except that I'm sorry.'

'As am I. And I fear the sorrows of the whole world will not be slow to follow.'

In his distraction, the Prime Minister didn't notice that Sarah had failed to reappear.

Churchill kicked open the door. It was past one o'clock. Still Sawyers stood beside the glimmers of the fire, waiting for him.

The old man threw his hat into the corner and, in spite of the evening's excesses, grabbed the proffered glass.

'A long day, zur. Another one tomorrow.' It wasn't so much a question or a statement as a gentle warning. Churchill's eyes were raw, inflamed, not merely tired but exhausted. Every morning since they'd arrived, Sawyers had seen the bedclothes tossed and unsettled, the sign of a troubled night. Too many fears, too much strain, too much strange food and, evidently, too much alcohol. The old man needed to harbour his strength rather than try to drown his sorrows, but instead of heeding his servant's warning, he drank. He sat in silence beside the fire, scowling, cradling his glass as though it were a chalice, while Sawyers stooped to release the laces of his shoes.

'The Pole was here again,' Sawyers said.

Still nothing.

'Says he wants to know how we're goin' to get him away.'

'But we can't,' Churchill said softly.

'What?'

'Even to try might be to ruin everything. To throw away our last chance.'

The servant stiffened. 'But you gave him your word, zur.'

'Matters have changed.'

'Not for him they haven't!' Sawyers was growing bewildered, even as the master turned impatient

241

with his apparent defiance.

'You don't understand, Sawyers.'

'Quite right, zur. I don't. One minute you're givin' a man your word of honour and your hand upon it, the next . . .' He trailed off. He couldn't finish—couldn't seem to finish anything. One shoe lay by the hearth, but the other remained still firmly tied to Churchill's foot. Sawyers had had as much practice at hiding his feelings as any servant, yet he felt a connection with this Pole; after all, it was he who had found him, who had been the first to hear his secrets. Sawyers also possessed a working man's straightforward understanding of right and wrong, and what was going on here wasn't just wrong, it was rotten.

'So what's goin' to happen to him, then?'

'None of your business.'

'It most certainly is.'

'Then to Hell with you, Sawyers. Haven't I got enough without—'

Suddenly the door burst open. It was Sarah. She stood at the threshold, trembling, struggling to hold back tears.

'Mule!'

She flew across the room and buried herself in her father's arms.

'What has happened, my kitten?'

'That bastard Beria. He . . .' Whatever followed was lost in sobs.

Churchill stroked his daughter's fine burnished hair. It was ruffled and damp. Then her face was up, the blue eyes she had inherited from him burning with defiance. 'He took me outside to show me the view. But I should've known—there isn't any bloody view, not at night. So he talks to me in his fractured French, all stuff and nonsense about the statues in the gardens and the walks down to the sea, and all the while he's leading me further away from the house.'

'My dear,' her father wailed.

'Then he tried to kiss me. That fat loathsome slug tried to kiss me. I did what I thought was best, Papa—didn't want to create a fuss, embarrass you, so I simply said, "No, thank you." But he wouldn't listen.'

Churchill groaned in despair.

'He started to touch me. Wouldn't let me go. Kept putting his hands on me and . . .' She rubbed her own over the intimate parts of her body to show him where. 'He's an evil man, Papa. Twisted. Not used to anyone saying no to him. Takes whatever he wants. I swear to you, these people are animals.'

'I know, I know . . .'

'I started to move away. He grabbed me. Held me. Pinned me to a tree. For a moment I thought he was going to . . . His eyes were sick, Papa, his face all twisted. This wasn't anything new to him, I could tell. That man is capable of anything, absolutely anything! But then I reminded him who I was. *"Je suis la fille de Churchill!"* I said. *"Churchill!"* That made him hesitate. Then he sort of smiled, and let go. So I ran.'

Tears were cascading down her father's cheeks.

'I ran all the way back to the villa, as hard as I could go. But when I got there—you'd gone.'

It sounded like an accusation, and he felt ashamed, as though it were his fault, for he had forgotten all about her. 'I am so sorry, Mule. So dreadfully sorry.'

243

'Oh, it's all right, Papa,' she replied, trying to summon up a defiant smile. 'You know I can take care of myself. "*Je suis la fille de Churchill!*" and all that.' She dabbed away at her eyes. 'Anyway, I've got a lot to look forward to. Like watching that miserable maggot squirm when we tell Marshal Stalin.'

The groan her father gave made it seem as if he had been physically wounded. 'But we can't, Mule, we simply can't.'

She stepped back from his arms to look at him, her brow furrowed. 'What do you mean we can't, Papa? We must!'

Slowly, as if it took him every ounce of energy, he shook his head. She backed away another step, and another, until she was standing beside Sawyers at the fireplace.

'If we accuse Beria,' Churchill said, 'there will be uproar. The entire conference will be ruined.'

'But you're my father.'

'Please try to understand, Mule. I have other responsibilities, not just to you but to an entire empire of souls. And if we are to pluck anything from the disaster that is being created at Yalta, we must do absolutely nothing to upset the Russians or give them any excuse to break their word.'

'But . . . what about your word as a father?'

'And your word you've been givin' to Mr Nowak?' Sawyers joined in.

'Can neither of you understand how important this is?'

They were glaring at him. He took a step towards them, but faltered, seeing the resentment boiling in their eyes.

'I feel so utterly wretched. My heart is bleeding

244

for you, Mule. And for the Pole. I don't think there has been a moment in my long life when I have felt more torn. Yet when the world turns round and remembers this week at Yalta, I suspect they will look back on a picture of failure and abject betrayal. And they will need to know who was responsible, who was to blame for casting aside this one opportunity for peace. Otherwise, all the bloodshed and sacrifice will have been wasted. That's why I have had to say so many things I did not mean and offer a smile to men who deserve nothing but our eternal scorn.'

'So tomorrow you will shake Beria's hand?'

He said nothing, afraid to answer.

'Will you, Papa?' Sarah insisted.

The words came slowly, as though they were being torn from him one by one. 'If it is necessary.'

'You would shake the hand that . . .' Her own hand went to her throat, then dropped slowly to her breast. 'Politics, Papa, is that what this is all about?' Sarah whispered, incredulous, bitter. 'You'd trade my honour simply to give yourself an excuse?'

'Even if you never come to understand, it is something I must do.'

'But what about the poor Pole?' Sawyers demanded.

'And what about sodding Beria?' Sarah screamed in fury.

Friday,
9th of February, 1945
The Sixth Day

CHAPTER SEVEN

It was supposed to be the last day, but even the impatient Roosevelt realised they had to give it just a little longer.

Cadogan and Eden came to Churchill's room late that morning, seeking an audience. He was still in bed. The Prime Minister's sleeping habits were a source of both amazement and irritation to his collegues, who had long been used to his breakfasts in bed, yet at Yalta he had surpassed himself, often not getting up until after lunch. Not idleness, of course, but eccentricity, exhaustion and age. Oh, and excess, buckets of it, particularly the previous night.

Sawyers shuffled past the sliding door to the bedroom to tell his master of his colleagues' arrival.

Soon a voice was raised, clear for all to hear: 'Tell them they can go bugger themselves!'

'Would that be each other, or individually, like?'

'What are you blathering about, man?'

'Why, buggery, zur.'

'To hell with you, Sawyers. Get 'em in here!'

The sight that greeted his principal aides was typical. Churchill resembled a walrus wrapped in pink silk and propped against a pile of pillows, cigar stuck firmly in mouth, breakfast on a tray, papers spilling from the eiderdown. It prompted irritation in both the visitors. They were all toiling hard—harder than Churchill himself, working longer hours, digesting considerably more paper and consuming far less alcohol. Yet he lay abed while they stood and waited on him. A little too imperial, for some tastes.

'What news? What news?' Churchill barked. The diplomatic bag from London with all its messages and golden nuggets was taking up to four days to arrive, and Churchill grew increasingly impatient. He always hoped for some excitement, some new bulletin from the front where British troops were preparing to cross the Rhine, something to make Stalin just a little less smug. But the front he had to deal with was here, in Yalta, which at times made him feel as though he'd much rather be back in the trenches of Flanders. At Ploegsteert, he remembered, you could spot a rat at a hundred yards. And shoot it.

'Things going pretty well, I think,' Cadogan began, his moustache and upper lip flexing like a hamster. 'Making good progress. Few hurdles still to jump, of course, but Ivan's proving surprisingly co-operative. Giving ground.'

'On what?'

'Why, many things. The United Nations, for instance. Accepting only three votes.'

'Tell me, Alec, how many other countries are going to get more than one vote?'

'That's not the point,' Eden intervened protectively.

'No, you're right. The point is that Stalin doesn't give a damn about the confounded United Nations. So long as it remains nothing more than a talking shop, he'll pay it no more heed than he would a brothel. He'll take advantage of it when he's in the mood, and will pass it by on the other side when he's not.'

'He's been surprisingly conciliatory,' the Foreign

Office mandarin protested.

'It is not a mark of conciliation, Alec, when a highwayman holds you up at gunpoint and takes only half your money.'

'Not gunpoint,' Cadogan corrected. 'Not the right analogy at all.'

'Tell that to the Poles.'

'But we'll get a pretty good settlement for them.'

'We'll get nothing for them, Alec.'

'Elections?'

The cigar was waving, glowing, then being stabbed forward like a bayonet. 'Ballots my balls, Alec! I understand Marshal Stalin himself is elected. By a hundred per cent of the vote.'

'May we all be so fortunate,' Eden muttered, as he brushed an imaginary crumb from his waistcoat.

'Damnit, if I'm to be judged on what I have achieved for the Poles, I shall deserve to be hurled from office and dragged naked through the streets.'

Eden wrinkled his nose in distaste.

'We've got to push for observers,' Cadogan interjected, as always the practical thinker. 'Make sure the elections are free and fair.'

'And maybe by the time they hold the elections those blasted Poles from Lublin will have arrived.' Churchill snorted.

Eden examined his Prime Minister with care, looking for a sign that might explain his mood. Exhaustion? Illness? Or the previous evening's indulgences? 'Did the Marshal say something last night to upset you, Winston?' he enquired.

'Everything he said last night upset me. Everything until he said goodbye!'

'I thought he showed up with his pockets

251

bursting with charm. Never seen him in a more benevolent mood. Particularly pleasant about you, I thought.'

'He must think I'm as dull-witted as Franklin.' Immediately, Churchill bit his lip. He might be allowed his private thoughts about poor, dear Franklin, but it wouldn't do him an ounce of good to spread them abroad. 'I'm sorry, gentlemen, but I'm grown sick with worry. We are constructing a new world out there, and I feel we are so very alone.'

'You doubt the Americans?'

'Two years—Franklin has given us two years. Then he says they'll be gone. Back across the Atlantic. And we shall be left with Stalin and the Russians.'

'But the Marshal was so generous in his praise last night. You heard him. A world without deception.'

'Talk? Surely he'll talk. Talk till the cows come home and the birdies all sing in their bower. Oh, and he'll be as gracious as can be, so long as he gets what he wants. But words mean nothing to the Marshal. He offers them as freely as an eager youth offers his loyalty to a pretty woman. But in the morning it's a different day, he is gone and the words all forgotten.'

'I'm not sure you're being fair to him,' Cadogan responded, wondering why the old man was resorting to so much sexual innuendo, and putting it down to a wandering mind. He didn't know about Sarah.

'Perhaps you are right, Alec. I cannot look into his heart. But what I do know is this. That in two years' time we may be at his mercy with nothing

252

but a wasteland from the white snows of Russia all the way to the white cliffs of Dover. Our future, our very life as a nation, lies in the hands of those weak, tattered states that stand in his way. Poland. France. Even Germany. So everything we do, every moment of our time here and every fragment of our endeavour, must be put towards the strengthening of Europe. Everything beyond that is secondary, and that includes his Benighted Nations and the war in the Far East. There is almost nothing I wouldn't trade in Asia to keep a stronger foothold in Europe. So let it be Europe.'

'Even Germany?'

'Germany will be divided but it must not be dismembered. We've already lost Poland. Can't afford to fall back any further.'

'You want to save Germany?' Eden asked, incredulous.

'I want that we should save ourselves. Stalin wishes for mass killings and Germany destroyed, ripped into many parts and made to pay reparations that will reduce it to pasture and perpetual serfdom, while the President . . . well, he simply doesn't care. Germany has broken so many American hearts.'

'I still believe you're being too pessimistic about Poland,' Cadogan said. 'After all, they're getting a new government, free elections, universal suffrage. All guaranteed. It may not be as bad as you fear.'

'You think I am old, Alec. That I lie awake at night in terror of demons and hobgoblins . . .'

Cadogan offered a Delphic smile.

'We offered Poland guarantees before,' Churchill growled. 'In 1939. Don't remember Marshal Stalin paying them any more attention

253

than Adolf Hitler.'

'You're surely not comparing the two,' Cadogan protested.

'There is a difference. I've never had to shake Hitler's hand.'

'Uncle Joe's our ally, Prime Minister.'

'And, in his own strange, twisted fashion, a great man. If it hadn't been for him and the millions of men who have died under his command, we might not have pulled through. We owe him that. But you must never for one moment forget, Alec, that the only thing that binds us is our common hatred.'

'Of Germany.'

'No, of Hitler. I don't hate Germany. I want to use it.'

'Against our ally?'

'Understand this. So long as Russia remains our ally, I shall offer her all the public respect that goes with that most valued status. And Marshal Stalin, too. I shall not question his word or doubt his honour, not in public, and I will not provide him with any excuse to turn on us. But what if it all goes wrong? What if Stalin dies or changes his mind? What if we discover we have grasped a viper to our bosom? What then? We shall need to be able to rely on something a damned sight more solid than Comrade Stalin's goodwill. So this is what I want you to do, Alec. Make sure we have an agreement that's as tight as a duck's arse. Fashion it so solid that not a chink of light can pass through. Let's not leave any ground for obfuscation or ambiguity— oh, I know it's your life, all this diplomatic prose that leaves a meaning as loose as a monk's morals, but I want the entire world to know what was done here, and what was agreed. Let us use the language of freedom, and ensure it's fashioned so robustly that it can tie a noose round the neck of anyone who ignores it. I want a document that can stand up in court.'

'And what court would that be?' Cadogan demanded breathlessly, his tone flooding with scepticism.

'The court of public opinion. It's the only court that can ever try such a case. But when the trees have been blown down in the coming tempest, when the great cities are levelled and the whole of Europe is nothing but flat, scorched earth, when there is no hiding-place left to us, we may have little else with which to defend our freedom.'

As Eden and Cadogan left, the Foreign Secretary suggested they take a walk in the garden where the warm breezes would blow away their words from prying ears. They were standing beneath one of the magnificent cypress trees, looking out over the sea, hands clasped behind their backs, before Eden spoke. 'Some little performance, that.'

'Breathtaking, Anthony.'

'What do you think?'

'Honestly?'

Eden nodded, forgiving in advance any sin of indiscretion.

'Winston's overcooked it as usual. In danger of spoiling everything.'

'You think he's wrong about the Russians?'

'We don't have to love them, for God's sake. But we can surely fix something up with them.'

'But what if he's right, if they change—'

'But that's precisely what the United Nations is about, Anthony. For when things go wrong.'

In spite of their circumstances, Eden lowered his voice, drawing back his lips in distaste. 'And what do you think of the other issue?'

'Winston? I think he may have lost his grip on the realities.'

'You've turned against him because he doesn't agree with you.'

'No, that's unfair. I've grown displeased with him because he doesn't even bother to read the papers we put to him. Just sits in bed and dreams bad dreams like the silly old man he's become. So much better if it were you.'

'But it's not.'

'No, not yet. But before too long. He was writing another of his histories in there today, Anthony, writing it before it's happened and making sure of his place in it all.'

'If we succeed, he claims the credit . . .'

'And if we don't, he's got a few florid words on some little piece of paper with which to defend his honour. But we've seen that game before.'

Eden made no reply. Although he was the politician, he had little stomach for the bloody business of turning on his friends.

'It's gone to his head, all this conspiracy nonsense. Either that or it's the buckets of Russian champagne he's been pouring down his throat,' Cadogan continued. 'It's got to him at last. Rotted the mind.'

'Perhaps.'

'But I take my hat off to the Marshal. He's been playing a blinder. I love the way he sticks pins up everybody's backside, then gets them to pay him for pulling them out again. He makes Winston look so—well, old. And Franklin is so woolly and wobbly. They simply don't compare.'

'What do we do?'

'Look, if it's good enough for the Russians and the Americans, who are we to stand in their way? We'll only get trampled. Winston's spent his entire life standing out against the crowd. It was magnificent in 'forty and 'forty-one, of course, but this is a new world we're building, Anthony. History is being made here at Yalta, and you and I should be part of it. Best leave Winston to his bad dreams. And after our election . . .'

'Ah, the election. Everyone seems to be worrying about elections.'

'The people must have their way.'

'Strangely enough, I rather think that was the point Winston was trying to make . . .'

*   *   *

Stanislaw Nowak, the mayor, wandered through the streets of Piorun at first light. Some semblance of order had returned: the shock troops of the Red Army had moved on, replaced by other troops who lacked the glazed, impenetrable eyes, the bared teeth and the desperate need to despoil everything in their path. But if they were gone, their legacy was inescapable. All along his route he found burnt-out houses that were still smouldering, sending up sour-smelling ribbons of soot into the sky.

No one said anything to him, no one complained, no one wished to rekindle the horrors of the previous hours. Their eyes said it all. They were alive. For them the war was over. It had to be enough.

Notices had been pasted on doorways and corners all around the town. They were addressed to any German civilians who might still be in Piorun, instructing all male citizens between seventeen and sixty years of age to report to the police within forty-eight hours, 'to render labour service behind the front lines'. Nowak knew what that meant. They were to become slaves, just as five years earlier the Poles had become slaves for the Germans. They were told to bring with them two changes of underwear, one blanket, one straw sack, identification and food for ten to fifteen days. Nowak felt a foul taste forcing its way into his mouth. He doubted whether there was a single German male left alive in Piorun to comply. And as for the women . . .

The notice was signed: 'The Military Commander'. Nowak found the signature offensive. He was the civilian authority in the town, and although his head ached furiously and he had no clear purpose in mind, he knew that he was the one who should be trying to bring some sense of normality to the people of Piorun. If only he could remember what normality was.

A silence hung above the streets. The rolling thunder of battle had already moved on, further west, and there were few signs of the people of Piorun, his friends and neighbours who would normally fill these spaces and bring them to life. Those he did see made him feel all the more helpless: an elderly woman, her back stooped by her many years, bending to pick up the fragments of glass that littered her doorway, another weeping as she sat on a doorstep that had no door. He glimpsed empty faces at empty windows, exhausted eyes peering from the shadows, a young woman drawing back in terror at the sight of a man. Even the dogs slunk away as he approached, his feet crunching on shards of glass as though he was walking through crisp snow.

He turned the corner into the town's square. He found two trucks parked opposite the church and a military guard posted at all four corners. The trucks, he noticed, were American, manufactured by Dodge. He tried to avert his eyes from the bodies that were still hanging from the lamppost. His lamppost.

As Nowak stepped forward he was stopped by the guards, who demanded to see his papers. Their voices were harsh, their eyes flooded with suspicion. Their hands hovered near the triggers of their guns, the muzzles pointed directly at him. Yet eventually they were satisfied and he was allowed to pass. He made no objection to their behaviour: he had grown accustomed to such indignities in the past few years, and he walked slowly on towards the doorway that led to his office. Outside he found yet another set of guards. More suspicion, more interrogation. He stood patiently as they rifled through his papers, telling himself that such things did not matter. As he waited in the shadows behind their shoulders, he saw something he couldn't at first understand. On the broad stairway that led up to the mayor's office, a Russian soldier was squatting, his pants down. Then the man started to relieve himself. It was clear he was far from being the first to do so. The stench in the stairwell was appalling. Then the guards allowed him through. As he climbed the creaking, urine-soaked wooden steps, he put his sleeve to his nostrils and wiped his eye.

At the top of the stairs, he was surprised to hear sounds of activity coming from his room. He found a soldier in his chair with his boots propped on the desk, smoking an American cigarette. He was wearing the uniform of a Russian major. A bottle of vodka stood on the table, on the spot where Nowak had kept a miniature red-and-white flag of Poland.

Reluctantly, Nowak knocked. 'I am the mayor,' he said.

Slowly, the soldier rose to his feet. 'And I am Major Morozov. I am the Political Officer here. Welcome, comrade.' His Polish was excellent. He came round the table to shake Nowak's hand. 'Please. Be seated. Would you like a drink? A cigarette, perhaps? It is a pleasure to meet you, Mr Mayor.'

Nowak, disoriented by the warmth of the greeting, declined the drink. He hadn't eaten for more than a day and a slice of bread would have served him better, but he accepted the cigarette, hungrily drawing down its smoke to quell the anxieties that were churning inside him.

The Russian sat down once more. 'I am delighted that you have come. I was in any event going to make contact with you. I would be most grateful for your help.'

Nowak nodded.

'But first—if I may?—your identity papers.'

Wearily, Nowak handed them across once again. The Russian examined them, then produced a sheet of paper on which appeared to be typed a list of names. 'Ah, yes,' he muttered, 'Nowak. It seems you are a most important family in these parts.'

'We are not important people. I am the mayor. That is all.'

'But you have a brother who is a priest, and another . . .' His finger ran down the list of names, but he didn't finish the thought. 'You see, Mayor Nowak, we have many friends in the Polish community, and we have asked for their help in identifying those who will be useful to our task.'

'Your task?'

'I am only here to help. Until such time as I can hand over to Polish authorities. Let me assure you, we have no intention of trying to impose ourselves upon Poland for any longer than it takes to defeat the enemy.'

'I am glad we were able to expel the German garrison before the Red Army arrived.'

'Ah, yes. Most interesting. It seems you have some very capable people here.' Once more the eyes ran over the list. 'But you will understand the need for all weapons to be handed over immediately. I'm afraid to say that in some parts of Poland there have been outrages, bandits who have attacked the Red Army from behind our lines. That must be stopped, of course. But soon there will be a new Polish government, and we shall be gone. You will soon be mayor once more, Mr Nowak!'

From somewhere near at hand came the sound of a burst of gunfire, but it didn't last for long.

'May I be frank with you, Mayor Nowak?' the Russian continued. 'We wish to help in the rebuilding of Poland, but in turn I hope you will help us. You know, most Poles are like you—loyal, decent, democratic, and I salute them. *Pobeda!*' He downed his glass of vodka and wiped his lips with

261

the back of his hand. 'They will be the ones who will run the new Poland. But there are a few who are Fascists, who collaborated, betrayed Poland to the Germans. And partisans, too, who intend to betray Poland to other enemies.'

'What other enemies?'

But the major ignored the question. 'I would like your help in identifying these traitors before they can do more harm.'

Nowak sucked deep on his cigarette. Now he regretted having turned down the vodka. Behind the major's head on the bare wooden wall hung framed photographs of all the mayors of Piorun during the twenty short years of Polish independence before the war. Piorun didn't much like change: there had been only three. He wondered whether there would ever be a fourth.

'I need your help in making a register of all those who live in Piorun,' Morozov continued. 'Every household, every family. That will be easy for you.'

'Why do you need such lists?'

'Because after liberation comes organisation. But we rush ahead, perhaps too fast. First, we must celebrate. This evening. Celebrate liberation!' He slapped his hand upon the table, causing his glass to jiggle. 'You will summon all those in the town of importance—the doctor, the policemen, the schoolteachers, all those types of people. Anyone who has standing in the community. We want the best people in the town to come to the inn. You will arrange it. How does that sound, Mayor Nowak? At eight o'clock. Before curfew.'

'Curfew?'

'Just for the time being. Until things are settled.'

The major was standing: the interview was over. 'I'm sure I can rely on you, Mayor Nowak.'

The mayor rose wearily from his chair, trying to figure out the meaning of these people who shat on his doorstep then invited him to a feast. The world was moving too fast for Stanislaw Nowak. He gazed out of the window of his office. The young alders were coming into bud, but he could still see clearly across the square to the church. So much had happened here, so much suffering endured, so many tears had washed their way through this little town. Yet perhaps the worst was past and they could begin to paste the fragments of their lives back together again. He would help: it was his duty. Yet suddenly the mayor stiffened in surprise. Bodies still hung from the lamppost, but he had been mistaken: they were different bodies, just two of them. Men he knew. Poles. They had signs around their necks. One said 'Faszista', the other 'Partizan'. They were hanging side by side.

The new regime had begun its celebrations early.

*　　　*　　　*

Poor, dear Franklin.

Churchill really did love the man, *loved* him, for his warmth, his generosity of spirit, for the ships and food and planes he had sent in those darkest hours, for being there when he was most needed. He was an exceptional man, and Churchill felt extraordinary pain as he watched his friend struggle and suffer, protected on every flank by his ever-present advisers. It was like watching a once magnificent cathedral whose walls had begun to crack and crumble, propped up by flying buttresses.

Churchill gazed in sadness as his friend struggled with a cigarette. His fingers were trembling like the wings of a butterfly. And his mind was fading, too, losing its hold as surely as a great oak is stripped of its leaves by a wind in autumn.

Churchill's doctor, Moran, had told him how it was, how the blood supply to the senses slowly lost its power, how the brain would demand more oxygen and be denied, and would begin to drown. And as he drowned inside, he would struggle, grow more frantic, lash out, even at old friends. Not his fault. The President had recently been overheard complaining that he was exhausted from spending 'the last five years pushing Winston uphill in a wheelbarrow'. He didn't mean it, of course, and Winston couldn't blame him, at least not all the time. It was the decay.

It had been another day, another lunch, another flaccid excuse for not seeing Churchill on his own. During the lunch, Churchill tried to reignite his friend's concern for the Polish elections, even quoting from the Declaration of Independence: *'We hold these truths to be self-evident, that all men are created equal, that they are endowed by their Creator with certain unalienable Rights . . . That to secure these rights, Governments are instituted among Men, deriving their just powers from the consent of the governed.'* They were words that would surely inflame any American about the plight of the Poles, and Churchill could recite them by heart, yet to Roosevelt they seemed as obscure as Ancient Greek. He simply changed the subject.

He could sustain nothing, not a story, a speech, a joke—not even, come to that, a deception.

He loved the man, but the question arose, how far could he trust him? Churchill had spent so much time worrying about whether he could trust Stalin, yet had given no thought at all to how far he could still put his faith in Roosevelt. The question hadn't even entered his head, until now, until that bloody Pole had arrived and dragged in all those doubts. But Franklin had changed, wasn't the same man and, as heart-wrenching as he found the whole situation, there was no longer any avoiding it. He had to put his old friend to the test. Trial by trust. He cradled his glass in both hands, staring across its meniscus, and sighed deep inside.

'Germany will soon be done for,' he declared. 'Before the grey mists of autumn fall, the armies of Narzidom will have been wiped out. The last of their aircraft will have been torn from the skies and their ships and submarines swept from the seas. Then we must turn our eyes to other challenges. To the East, the Orient, where lies our other great foe.' He looked around the table at his American hosts, who today included the American Chiefs of Staff. 'In the last three years it is you, my friends, who have borne the lion's share of the struggle against them. You have pursued the forces of Nippon from island to island, from one savage encounter to another, and done so with courage and phenomenal tenacity. And while we British have been wholeheartedly engaged in Europe and the Atlantic, in the Pacific you have fought on largely on your own. Yet the times are changing, and soon the forces of the empire will be in a position to stand ever more firmly with you. The instant the war in Europe and the Atlantic is done, I formally propose to send the capital ships of the Royal Navy to the Far East so that together, side by side, we may deal out the final, deadly blows.'

He had made another little speech. Offered help. And he could see the slow windmill of Roosevelt's mind turning, trying to grasp the meaning of what he had said. A friend would simply have asked what he wanted, but Franklin . . . oh, dear, he was hesitating. You could almost see the cogs of his mind trying to turn. What lay behind this offer? Was Winston trying to interfere once more, to stake a claim to the running of the war in the Far East? To grab new glory—and grab back his old colonies? And what did it all mean for the deal with Stalin? As the sails of the windmill continued to turn, they cast a shadow over the Englishman.

Roosevelt wouldn't commit himself. He turned to his colleagues, and they tumbled over themselves to offer excuses. Fleet Admiral King was the first to speak. The sour-faced naval chief had never made any secret of his impatience with the British. He was a man who still seemed to think his country was fighting its Revolution, that this was Yorktown rather than Yalta and that redcoats hid behind every bush. He didn't want to listen to any plummy accents, he didn't want to share any of his coming glory, and he certainly didn't want the Royal Navy. So he explained that it would be too difficult to integrate British forces at this late stage; it would take up too much of their time. Yes, other Americans added, it would be too little, too late. They were turning Winston down. Turning away the Royal Navy that had given so many lives to the war against Japan, a British fleet that, in one terrible afternoon just three days after the attack on Pearl Harbor, had lost the *Repulse* and the *Prince of Wales* and left a thousand men at the bottom of the sea. And these bloody Americans had the nerve to say that the British contribution was too little, too late!

Roosevelt, his friend, his ally, the man he loved, was hiding behind their excuses. He muttered about the need for further study, for delay, for putting things off. The man who had crawled up Stalin's backside to ensure the Russians got involved in the Far East was trying to push aside the British.

'It would be a glorious day,' Churchill continued, through teeth now so firmly gritted that they ached, 'if not only the Americans and British but also the Russians—all three of us—could unite to finish off the Japanese.'

It was a trap. And Roosevelt stumbled. Wasn't quick enough on his feet to avoid Churchill's outstretched leg. Before he realised what he was doing, he had as good as admitted to what had been going on, but still he would not trust his friend with the truth. 'My sense, Winston, is that the Russians would be more than happy to do so. I've had an exploratory chat with our mutual friend. He seems happy to co-operate.'

'Then we should bind him in now! Strike while the pulse for action still races. Agree all the details of our combined command while we are here at Yalta.'

'That's not possible.'

'And why not, pray?'

'I can't. I haven't got the time,' Roosevelt said

lamely. 'I've got to leave Yalta no later than tomorrow.'

'But surely your countrymen and the Congress would understand your being away just a few hours longer. A small delay, a day or so, to bring together the most mighty fighting force the Orient has ever seen, so mighty it might yet shake the Japanese into surrender simply through its existence?'

'I can't. I've made commitments. I have to be elsewhere,' the American replied doggedly.

'Forgive me, Franklin, but what could be more important?'

'Got three kings to see. Farouk. Ibn Saud. Haile Selassie. I've arranged to be in Egypt the day after tomorrow.'

And yet another sordid little secret had tumbled forth from those tired lips. The Middle East was a region that had long been the historic preserve of the British. This was the place of General Gordon and of Lawrence, of the battles of El Alamein, Tobruk, Benghazi and Sidi Barani and, above all, of the Suez Canal, the imperial lifeline that connected Britain to the colonies and dominions beyond. This was the spot where, nearly fifty years earlier, Churchill himself had fought and almost been killed in the last cavalry charge the British Army had ever made in anger, at Omdurman. It was a place of so many battle flags, so many British graves, so many vital interests. So what the hell was Franklin up to in the Middle East? And why hadn't he thought it necessary to let the British know he was going?

Poor, dear Franklin was betraying him. Perhaps not deliberately, perhaps for no better reason than his growing incompetence and infirmity, yet in the end the cause didn't matter. Betrayal was still spelled the same.

*   *   *

Sawyers was pressing Churchill's trousers. It was what he did when he was upset, some mindless activity that would drag away his tangled thoughts to a world of order and neat creases. He enjoyed the sizzling steam that rose up to warm his cheeks when he placed the iron upon the damp tea-towel and the way in which old, crumpled wool was suddenly rejuvenated with a turn of his wrist. If only he could do the same to Churchill.

Sawyers had never doubted his master, not until now. Oh, of course the man could behave unspeakably: at times he had the manners of a schoolboy and the temper of a castrated boar, and his language could get as ripe as one of Mrs Landemare's fruit cakes, but he'd never before doubted the man. Sawyers's loyalty wasn't a sham but as deeply ingrained as the polish on the Prime Minister's hand-made shoes. Yet something had gone amiss.

Perhaps it was all this foreign muck they had to eat, the cold, fatty pig that was forced on them even for breakfast, or the pepper vodka that was only marginally more approachable than horse liniment. Or perhaps . . . Sawyers hated to admit it, but the old man was getting—well, just that. Old. Seventy. He kept saying he'd never expected to live that long, that he would die young, like his father who'd closed his innings at forty-five. Perhaps that was why he insisted on living every day as though it were his last and drinking every bottle to its end.

269

Yet the flame always consumes its candle, and it was beginning to show. He no longer bounced out of bed in the mornings, or even after lunch. He had trouble putting on his socks, often developed a temperature, wouldn't travel without a doctor. The old man had grown brittle, begun to lose his edge. It showed even in his speeches. The age had passed when the world hung on his every word, and now time-servers like Cadogan saw him as little more than—what was the phrase he was using at the moment? A silly old man. Still head and shoulders above the rest, but not what he was. He had given too much of himself, and there comes an end to every man. Worn away by war.

As the butler pressed down still harder with the hot iron, he couldn't tell whether the drops of moisture that were gathering on his cheeks were condensation or tears.

He pressed another pair of trousers, but it didn't help. The issue was still there. Winston Churchill was about to break his word. He'd given it to the young Pole, along with his hand, but now he had all but forgotten. And that wasn't right. That young Pole had a fine spirit—he stood up for himself and had been taken away from his family for far too long. Anyway, the butler felt a peculiar sense of ownership of this problem that had come walking through their door swinging a wrench and a length of old lead pipe.

And it wasn't just Churchill's problem. For the Old Man to give his word was something that concerned everyone connected with him, and breaking it would bring shame on them all. Young Nowak had said it was a matter of honour. He was right. Anyway, in Sawyers's view, Winston

Churchill's word was bigger than any one man. When it came down to it, it was bigger even than Winston Churchill himself.

He knew the boss would regret it, would look back on what he'd done—or not done—as a moment of weakness, just as when he'd ignored what that oily bastard Beria had got up to with Sarah. That was the moment when Sawyers had known the Old Man was *off song*. What father would do that? Not Winston, not in normal times. He loved Sarah so. And what would Mrs C say when she found out? The edge of her tongue could gut a fresh salmon at fifty feet. But it wasn't the Old Man's fault: there was simply too much distraction and exhaustion around this place for anyone to withstand.

It was at times like this that he needed his friends. Didn't have many friends, not here, not anywhere, come to that. Deep down he had always been a bit of a loner, like Sawyers. And if Sawyers felt a sense of ownership of the Pole, his sense of loyalty to Winston Churchill was inexhaustible.

So he wasn't going behind the Old Man's back: he was simply going to do something for which, later, the Old Man would be grateful.

Or perhaps not. On second thoughts, he might just blow a fuse, as he so often did when he thought others were interfering, so better simply to do it and do it quietly. No fuss. No fury.

Sawyers weighed the iron in his hand, a splendidly solid sort of thing. Ideal for the purpose he had in mind.

He wiped his cheeks and headed for the bathroom.

They had all gathered in the courtyard of the Livadia. There had to be an official photograph to show the world—and particularly the Germans—that the three were as one. They sat in chairs, the Russian in a military greatcoat that seemed a trifle too large for him, Churchill with a lamb's fleece hat on his lap, and the President swathed in his cloak, looking gaunt, terribly infirm, almost transparent. It was a dark day, chillier than before, and it seemed to soak into Roosevelt's bones. His hand trembling, he sat quietly, his eyes casting around for the comfort that he couldn't find inside.

By the time they had returned to the warmth of the crackling log fire and their round table inside the ballroom, general impatience had taken control of the field. This was Roosevelt's sixth day, he was exhausted and wanted to be elsewhere, and Stalin, too, had grown bored with it all. He knew what he wanted: it was merely a matter of taking it. Only Churchill had any lingering determination to carry on arguing for his interests, but no one was paying him much heed. It's what happens when a great flame begins to dim. It casts an ever-weaker light, and men no longer fear to walk in its shadow. That's what was happening to Winston. And to the British.

They were talking about Poland—yet again—and Stalin decided that the moment had come to put an end to all these words and time-wasting, yet when he spoke, his tone was gentle. His shoulders kept shrugging, he waved his pipe in the manner of an old man sitting on his porch.

'Gentlemen, my friends, I sense we are going

round in circles because there may be some element of doubt at this table about the intentions of the Soviet Union. Let me put your minds at rest. We have no intention, absolutely no intention, of interfering in Poland's internal affairs.' He let the phrase stand for a moment to allow it to set, like a pudding. 'Those matters are for the Poles, not the Russians—or, indeed, if I may say so, the Americans or the British. I think we've all agreed she will have a parliamentary system, a democracy much like . . .' he spread his hands as though trying to catch raindrops '. . . that of Belgium and Holland. Yes, exactly. And any talk of trying to sovietise Poland is stupid.' He gazed slowly round the table, smiling like a doting grandfather. But this was Stalin, and no one was in any doubt that he was confronting them, challenging anyone to defy his word. At last his eyes came to rest on Churchill. And the smile grew broader.

Churchill had no doubt as to its meaning. *Defy me, Englishman, if you dare! With every fibre of your being you think I'm lying, that I don't mean a word of what I say, but do you have the balls to call my bluff?*

This was no longer negotiation but a scene held together solely by old men's fermenting pride. It was a test of wills, man to man, eye to bloodshot eye, a tug of war, and Churchill knew that, on his own, he no longer had the weight to resist. Yet for a while, he held the other man's stare. It was an interesting analogy, he thought, the one with Holland and Belgium, two countries that had been used as doormats by other powers, but it was an analogy he couldn't pursue. He was a statesman, Stalin was his ally, he couldn't simply stand up and declare that the Russian was lying. All he could do was to raise an eyebrow and repeat: 'Holland and Belgium?'

'Certainly.'

Laboriously, as though in an amateur drama, Churchill wrote the two names in large print on his notepad and underlined them, preserving them for the historical record.

That irked Stalin. The sugar in his voice was replaced by sarcasm. 'After all,' he declared, 'it's not as if we're one of the imperialist powers wanting to gobble up our weaker brethren. But that's another point we may come to.'

'What do you mean?' Suddenly, Churchill's head was up, alert. 'What do you *mean*?' he repeated. He was greeted with silence. Was this another stitch-up, another deceit they were about to inflict upon him? The Pole had said they'd been overheard talking about the empire. Churchill hunched his shoulders and glowered round the table. His glare jolted the hapless Stettinius into action: he was trying to be helpful, the fool, so he started to mutter something about how it had been discussed that the United Nations should take a look at the issue of dependent territories.

He never got to finish. A growl of almost canine quality emerged from the Englishman. It was partly the weariness of it all, and the humiliation of not getting his own way. They were all doing deals behind his back, even Cadogan and Eden, he suspected. No one listened any more. But they were going to listen now, because Churchill began to shout. To rave. He grew choleric, purple at the gills. He banged the table, a full two-fisted tantrum, and he bloody-well roared. 'Colonies! You mean colonies! But I'll not have it!'

274

Roosevelt was trying to intervene, flapping his hand, but it was like waving tissue paper in a thunderstorm.

'I will not have one scrap of British territory discussed in this way. We've fought this war longer than anyone, fought for freedom, for humanity, we've done no crime to anyone and we shall not be put in the dock in order for other nations to wring their hands in hypocritical horror at the most successful and civilising empire this world has ever known!'

Stalin rose in his seat, as if to walk away. So did Churchill, but only to confront him on equal terms. Still Roosevelt waved his tissue paper.

'We were the only nation at this table not to be kicked into this war. We stood up for principle, fought for honour. And we ask nothing from this war—nothing!—except to retain that honour for which we have fought. No territories, no loot, no new bases, no new borders, no shabby secret deals. Nothing but honour!'

'Winston, Winston, we don't mean your colonies,' Roosevelt blurted, but the words were lost in the gale.

'Never! Never! Never! Never!' Churchill shouted, turning on the President. 'If you mean to squeeze us out, I have nothing more to say, not here. But out there'—he pointed to the wide world that lay outside the tall ballroom windows—'out there I shall object to such perfidy as long as I live.'

'Winston, we'll sort it out,' Roosevelt wailed, while Stettinius rushed to make assurances that his proposal was never intended to cover the British colonies.

'Then I want it in writing,' Churchill snapped. 'I

want it written that it excludes the British Empire.'

They tripped over themselves to offer him their assurances, and slowly the volcano subsided. And while they all recovered from the onslaught, an American aide named Alger Hiss quickly typed up a memorandum that gave Churchill everything he required, on that point, at least. So, what Winston had failed to get with reason and argument, he got with bloody temper.

Yet the performance had been more than simply vanity and temper. Churchill had seen Roosevelt cave in on almost every point since they'd arrived in Yalta, wilting under any form of pressure. But Stalin, what of him? The Russian was a master at giving it out—you could see that from the catamites around him who picked up a pencil and scribbled every time he opened his mouth, if only to yawn. But how good was the Russian at taking it? Did he remember what it was like to be at the receiving end? When had the Leader of All the Russias last been confronted by someone who looked him straight in the eye and spat at him? There was an advantage in being British at moments like this, for neither the Russian nor the American were parliamentarians; they had little experience of standing only feet away from opponents who attacked your morals, your memory and even at times your miserable manhood. Could Stalin take that? Churchill had decided it was worth giving it a go—after all, as he later told Sarah, he had bugger-all to lose—and he had got the assurances he required on the colonies. But he still had fish to fry.

So, when the foaming tidal wave of the Englishman's wrath had once more receded and

276

they were allowed back on to the beach to pick over what was left, it was inevitable that they would trip over the remnants of poor Poland.

'It seems to me,' Roosevelt began, and with evident relief, 'that we're pretty close to a full agreement here. Only a few words and phrasings to get right, drafting matters, really. We're almost there. Elections. A broad-based government.'

Stalin was about to interject for the umpteenth time that it already had a broad-based government when suddenly he stopped in surprise. Something had startled him. Churchill was smiling. And what the hell did he mean by that?

Churchill was talking about the broad-based government as being a temporary phenomenon, an ornament, but an important ornament. Until the elections. An ornament? Like his ridiculous bow-tie? All these endless rivers of rancour they'd had to cross over the last few days had been for nothing more than a useless, pointless ornament? And he was prattling on about 'Marshal Stalin's usual patience and kindness'. The Russian knew there was a trap here somewhere, but was damned if he could spot it. He began tapping the table with his pipe, a sign of anxiety, as though he were expecting to be pounced on yet again. But Churchill was covering him with honey. Praise for the Red Army and their success in liberating Poland. Congratulations for the decisive manner in which the Marshal had suggested that early elections might be held in a month, and how much he had done to ensure that the President could return home and face the eight million Poles living in the United States with honour.

And for the first time it appeared as though

277

Churchill and Roosevelt might be standing side by side on the issue. Had Churchill given in? Or run rings round Roosevelt? It seemed as if they were both more interested in words—and ornaments—than substance. That was why Stalin had agreed to give anti-Fascists a couple of *ornamental* posts in the new government, because no matter what the words said it would make no difference: the Lublin Communists would still have control. That was why he'd agreed to elections, because the result was already ordained. And if the only thing Roosevelt and Churchill required in return were sugary words to take home as sweets for the kiddies, it was no skin off the Marshal's nose. Except—damnit—Churchill was now asking for a commitment to international observers who would ensure that the elections were free and fair. Stalin stiffened. It was a phrase too far.

'I think we couldn't guarantee that point,' Stalin interjected, sniffing.

'But why not, pray? It is surely within the spirit of everything we have agreed.'

'I think that's right, Marshal,' Roosevelt said. 'The elections, like Caesar's wife, must be above suspicion.'

Stalin smiled at the President and chuckled. 'Caesar's wife was only above suspicion to her husband. Between you and me, I hear she had other interests, too.'

But his gentle humour was not enough to push aside Churchill. 'Yet her reputation for purity kept her husband happy. And all we seek is to establish the good reputation of the Poles and their election.'

Further round the table, Roosevelt was nodding

in agreement—or was he simply falling asleep?

Stalin wouldn't accept observers. They would get in the way, make life difficult, perhaps even question the authenticity of the elections and the legitimacy of the government that was going to win them. He couldn't have that: it would ruin everything. So he cursed beneath his breath, offered a smile, breathed out plumes of tobacco smoke and played for time as he searched for the riposte. Then it came to him, like a bird to seed, and he beamed even more.

'I find myself in total agreement with the President and the Prime Minister,' he declared. 'The purpose of the elections and everything else we've agreed is to preserve the good reputation of the new Polish government. Unblemished. Like the faithful wife.' He stroked his palms across the tablecloth as though smoothing away wrinkles. 'But what would people say if we sent observers? What would they say if we sent observers to pry into the fidelity of your wife, Mr President? Or Mrs Churchill? Their presence in the closet would do nothing but arouse mockery and suspicion. It would be an insult—yes, an insult. So the Poles will never accept such a condition.' He shook his shaggy head, but he couldn't help catching the eyes of the Englishman, which were gazing at him, cold, blue, full of understanding. He knew.

And Stalin moved on quickly, raising his hands theatrically above his head. 'But on everything else—*Ia sdaius!* I surrender!'

'Then I think, my dear Marshal, that I shall let you in on a little state secret.' Roosevelt smiled. 'I believe I've got just about everything I came for on this matter.'

From the other side of the table, Churchill said nothing but sat and stared, snagging at Stalin's eye, letting him know. The Marshal stared back, claiming victory. But very slowly, and with an expression just less than a smile, Churchill shook his head.

Oh, but this Georgian bastard was a master! He was no spring chicken—his hair was thinning, the jowls sagging, the shoulders growing ever more stiff—but still he could be the master of the moment. In adversity he never lost his nerve, had skilfully avoided the trap Churchill had set for him. Perhaps if there had been an ounce of humanity and compassion in him, he and Churchill might have become friends, or drinking partners, at least, but instead . . . Stalin would get Poland, but Churchill was one step closer to getting most of the language he wanted in the final communiqué. It was what he had to fight for now. And he particularly liked the analogy with Belgium and Holland. When the time came they would form threads of the rope with which he might yet hang the Marshal's reputation, like a crow on a country fence.

*   *   *

Stanislaw Nowak trudged discontentedly through the streets of the town he loved. He had been born here, and all he had ever wanted was that he should die here, in good time. He had harboured ill-will towards no man, and sought little but a patch of earth no bigger than his neighbour's on which he might be left to scratch a living for his wife and sons. He'd never had the learning for the

Church or the initiative for enterprise like his brothers, yet he had riches of his own. His neighbours had given him their affection and trust as the leader of their small community and that, for a while, had made his life seem almost perfect. Then the war had arrived and now his sons were dead, his wife was so very different and he was no longer certain of very much at all. Piorun had been crushed by tanks built in the Ruhr and had now been liberated by tanks built beyond the Urals, and perhaps he should be grateful for what the Russians had done, but it was said that nothing good ever came from the east. On the other hand, the war had done away with the old truths, perhaps all truths, and if the Russians wanted to invite him and his friends for a celebration, there had to be some good in it.

Earlier that day the townsfolk had gathered for a thanksgiving mass, and he and his brother had stood at the door and kissed everyone as they had entered the church. His sister-in-law hadn't turned up, neither had a few of the other women, and all sorts of lurid rumours were flooding around, but he paid them no heed. There were so many whispers about what was going to happen, about frontiers and governments and the like, but when he had been asked he always replied that no harm would come to them, not with America standing four-square behind Poland.

Yet, as he settled on his knees and gazed up at the carved wooden statue of St Casimir, the country's patron saint, confusion drenched his senses and brought tears to his eyes. The future belonged not so much to the holy Casimir as to St Marx and St Mammon, and in the battle for

281

supremacy that would be fought between them, people like him would count for nothing and places like Piorun would be changed beyond recognition, turned into a collective farm or a car factory. And all he had ever wanted was Clara, his cow.

After the service, he'd gone looking for his sister-in-law but her house was empty. Someone said they'd seen her walking towards the bridge, dragging a suitcase behind her bound by a leather strap that was his brother's old army belt, but Stanislaw discounted that. She had no reason to leave, not now, not when the worst was over. But on the way back he had passed the house of the doctor. The door was open and its window smashed, and a group of Russian soldiers were drinking what looked to be his rubbing alcohol and picking through objects in the street. A chair. Clothes. The bathtub. Medical instruments. Radio. The doctor's telephone. One of the soldiers kept shouting into the phone and waiting for an answer, and when none came he eventually lost patience with it and smashed it against the wall. Of the doctor himself, there was no sign.

Stanislaw was bewildered, he didn't know what to think, but the years of Occupation had taught him not to think much at all and never to share his thoughts. To survive you had to be silent, to look the other way, or end up sleeping on pine needles in the forest like his brother. And that wasn't necessary any longer, was it?

Stanislaw continued his trudging. It was almost dark. The creaking pump handles were falling silent, the doors being drawn shut and bolted, the geese ruffling their wings one last time. As he approached the inn, he could hear music coming from within: someone was playing a mazurka, and suddenly a little of the warmth of the old days crept back. A military guard stood outside and saluted, presenting arms as he walked in. And inside, the inn was crowded and bathed in unaccustomed light. He found the postman, the schoolteacher, a couple of farmers, the owner of the sugarbeet factory, all the important men of the town, along with Russian officers. The fire was roaring. At one end of the room a table was laden with bread and sausage, behind which the Soviet and Polish flags had been intertwined, and the inn-keeper was rushing around serving vodka while his red-faced wife wound up the gramophone. It was almost as he remembered Marian's wedding feast, held in this same room all those years ago . . . Perhaps, after all, things would turn out right. For a moment, Stanislaw Nowak began to find the glimmerings of happiness once more.

Then Major Morozov was approaching, shaking his hand, calling him comrade, checking his list of names and telling him he was the last to arrive. He and all his friends were ushered over to the table at the end of the room, given glasses, invited to eat. Yet as he turned to thank his host, Nowak suddenly felt as though he was standing on that unsteady stool beneath the lamppost once more, with a noose round his neck and the breath being tugged from his body.

For guards had suddenly appeared, guns had been drawn, the gramophone kicked over and the inn-keeper's wife slapped into silence.

'Comrade Nowak,' Morozov was saying, 'I have the pleasure to inform you and your colleagues that you are all under arrest.'

'Arrest? But why? *Why?*' he shouted. 'On what charge?'

'Charge?' Morozov repeated curiously, playing with the word like a cat with a piece of string. 'Why, you choose, comrade. Whatever you like. We'll make sure it fits.'

And the Russians had roared with laughter as they pushed the Poles towards the truck that was waiting outside the door.

*   *   *

Sawyers had just stoked the fire and made sure there would be a welcome for Churchill at whatever time he returned, when the door opened. The butler stood back and gasped.

Water was creeping across the bathroom floor and the plumber had come to clear up the mess. Come to sort everything out, Sawyers hoped, and not just the leak. To get everything back as it should be. And now the plumber was standing in the doorway, toolbag in his hand, wiping dirty hands on his apron.

But it wasn't Marian Nowak. They had sent a different plumber.

*   *   *

Nowak had been playing cards with some of the other men, squatting on the steps of their barracks in the weak afternoon sun and sharing a packet of Chesterfields that one of them had liberated from the Livadia, when they came. The trucks arrived with no warning, but what should they expect? The

NKVD never gave warning. Today they simply turned up and told them to gather their belongings. Apart from what they were wearing, it amounted to no more than a change of shirt and underwear and their bag of tools for most of the workmen. Then they were ordered into the trucks.

There was no hostility, no alarm, nothing but an edge of boredom. Another day in Paradise, with guards, trucks, much grumbling, flapping canvas, men in shambling queues waiting to climb on board. An officer stood by with a clipboard, counting heads, shouting for them to hurry. Just like Katyn.

'Where are we going?' Nowak asked.

'Going?'

'Yes, where?'

'You're going home, you halfwit. To Moscow.'

'But the conference.'

'Almost over. Time to go. For everyone to go.'

'But . . . I can't. I've got to fix Mr Churchill's plumbing.'

'Fuck Mr Churchill's plumbing. And fuck Mr Churchill. So get your arse on board. What are you looking so shifty about? It won't kill you.'

But it would. Not today, not immediately, but they would ship him back to Moscow until the time came when his deceptions began to unravel and all those lies he had told would line up to denounce him. Then they would kill him. A bullet to the back of the head. That was the Soviet style.

They would murder him because he had lied, cheated the system.

Because he had made fools of them.

Because he was an awkward bloody Pole.

And, above all else, because he knew about

285

Katyn.

He had cheated Stalin once, but few got away with it a second time. As they pushed him on board the truck, his hand went to the pocket of his tunic, the place where he kept his daughter's memory. The daughter he now knew he would never see again.

Saturday,
10th of February, 1945
The Seventh Day

CHAPTER EIGHT

When he came into the bedroom, Bruenn found the President already dictating to a secretary. With only a murmur of greeting, he sat down near the head of the bed while the President continued with his work. Roosevelt ignored his cardiologist, didn't even divert his eyes, but slowly a bony wrist was pushed across the covers.

Bruenn bit back his frustration. He'd given his patient explicit instructions to take it easy that morning and allow no visitors before eleven. It was as close as a lieutenant commander could get to giving his Commander-in-Chief a direct order, but it had proved a complete waste of breath. The man was so damned stubborn! Bruenn had noticed how his patient was also beginning to have trouble concentrating. The struggle over this last week had seemed to drain the President. The face had become an anatomical diagram, without an ounce of flesh, the bones showing clearly through stretched grey skin that had turned to parchment. And, as the doctor placed his fingers on the other man's wrist, he noticed that the irregular, stumbling pulse was back: the congested heart was having difficulty finding its rhythm, like a marathon runner whose legs were buckling. His patient was desperately unwell.

Then Stettinius and Harriman entered, locked in a discussion that was slowly turning to argument.

'Morning, boys,' the President greeted them, struggling to lift himself up and wave his free hand.

'Looks like you've all got me surrounded. No chance of escape now, and just when I was planning to go for my morning run.' Another face appeared at the door. 'Hah! But here comes the cavalry. Morning, Harry.'

Hopkins came in. Stettinius and Harriman both looked drawn and tired from the effects of a long night's haggling but Hopkins appeared even more played out. He was still in his dressing-gown, breakfasting on cigarettes, and was clearly intending to return to his bed. Yet of them all, it was Roosevelt who appeared most frail.

'Mr President!' Bruenn muttered in warning.

For the first time that morning Roosevelt looked directly at his doctor, only to look away again.

'So, gentlemen, have we and Uncle Joe got ourselves an agreement?'

It was the naïve, unworldly Stettinius who decided to rise to the bait and reply, little realising that it would leave him exposed as a target for the others.

'It's been a struggle, sir, but apart from a few minor drafting details, I think we're done on most things. We've got agreement to hold the inaugural meeting of the United Nations in little more than a month. In San Francisco.'

'Bully.'

'And we're very close on Poland, except . . .'

'Ed?'

'Well, our British friends are being a real pain about the drafting, picking over words like they were panning for gold.'

'That's old Winnie up to his tricks.' The President sighed. 'Can't push past a dangling participle or a split infinitive without jumping up and down like he's sat on a porcupine. Told me yesterday he wouldn't stand for it being called a "joint communiqué", says it makes the whole thing sound like a Sunday roast.'

'A matter on which he is an acknowledged expert,' Hopkins chipped in.

'Mr President, I think we've got most things we wanted on Poland,' the Secretary of State continued earnestly. 'A more broadly based government. Free elections—'

'In a month?' demanded the President, levering himself up from his pillows and remembering Stalin's promise.

'They're to be held as soon as possible. That's what we've agreed. But no observers, Uncle Joe's boys won't budge on that.'

'Doesn't that rather defeat the entire object of the exercise?' Harriman interjected, picking up the threads of their disagreement.

'Only if you consider that the Russians have no intention of keeping their word,' Stettinius responded, 'in which case, what's the point of anything?'

'Look, if we've got the Marshal tied into the United Nations and the war against Japan, we're going back home with ninety-five per cent of what we came for,' Roosevelt muttered, sinking back on to his pillows.

'That's exactly what Stalin wants us to believe,' Harriman replied. 'We think we've got an agreement, then at the last minute he drops some whole new condition into the pot. We thought we had a deal on the Far East, then late last night, Molotov insists that we guarantee Russia's "pre-eminent interests" in the region and agree that all her claims must be "unquestionably fulfilled". The precise wording he wants used.'

'Damnit, we paid for that horse already,' Roosevelt muttered.

'Looks like we've got to raid the bank once more.'

Roosevelt sighed. 'Still, "pre-eminent interests . . . unquestionably fulfilled". Only a couple of phrases. Could mean almost anything. I don't think we go upsetting the applecart over a few words, do we?'

Stettinius turned to smile at Harriman, claiming victory, while Bruenn's brow creased with concern. The President's pulse rate was up, and he hadn't even got out of bed.

'And I think I may have a solution on Poland,' the President continued. 'Uncle Joe says he won't sign up to observers because it might look like a slap in the face for the Poles. But if he'll accept in private how important some sort of scrutiny is to us, I can't see it's necessary to make a great public fuss over it. Hell, otherwise we could be stuck here another week just bickering about punctuation. I'll have a quiet word with the Marshal later today, make sure he understands.'

'Somehow I think he understands perfectly well already,' Harriman said disconsolately.

It was at that point that Bruenn jumped in. His fingers were still clinging to Roosevelt's wrist. It was clear his patient had lost the ability to fight— for anything. One infection might finish him off. 'May I ask, Mr President, just how long you think it will be before the conference finishes?' he asked quietly.

'You anxious to get home, Commander?'

'I'd rather we were both in our own beds, sir.'

'Well, we'll leave just as soon as I can get these gentlemen to stand in line with each other and give me a piece of paper to sign. Which will be . . . ?'

'Another day at most!' Stettinius replied enthusiastically. 'Today, perhaps. Why not?'

Bruenn noticed Harriman roll his eyes in dismay, while Hopkins lit another cigarette and began to cough. Everything was dragging on too long, the exhausted leading the infirm. Time to bring it to an end.

Roosevelt sensed his cardiologist's unspoken warning. 'Well, let's hope that Marshal Stalin finds some pressing distraction on the Berlin front,' he said, 'and if we can keep Winston thinking about his Sunday roast, then maybe we'll all be allowed to go home.'

*   *   *

Eden was beginning to think that the Old Man was doing it deliberately. It was bad enough being forced to report to him while he was propped up in bed, but he drew the line at this steam-soaked bathroom. How was he supposed to conduct a serious conversation while watching the Prime Minister scrub his back? It was so wretchedly demeaning. He stood beside Cadogan, sensing the creases in his trousers dying with every passing minute and growing increasingly irritable.

'The Americans have been going behind our backs, Winston.'

There was a parting of the waves, and the Prime Minister appeared. 'I know.'

'They've been talking to the Russians about the

293

Far East, cooking up a deal. I've got it all here, in a detailed note.' Eden waved an increasingly damp-stricken piece of paper.

'Seen it. They were kind enough to send me a copy. For signature.'

'Well, we can't sign. Can't possibly. What they're proposing goes against every principle we've been fighting for. Openness. Honesty. Consent.'

Well, Churchill wasn't entirely sure that that was what they'd been fighting for all these years, but Anthony was something of an idealist and deserved his illusions.

'This is a disgraceful piece of subterfuge on our Chinese allies,' the Foreign Secretary continued.

'Not to mention the empire—Sawyers, where's the bloody soap?'

'I suspect you're sittin' on it, zur,' a disinterested voice replied, drifting through the open doorway. Churchill scowled: Sawyers had been out of sorts all morning.

'We think you should raise it at the plenary,' Cadogan joined in.

'But what's the point, Alec? As you say, our friends round the table have already agreed to it. What on earth can we do on our own?'

'Open his eyes to the implications! Get them to think again!' Eden protested, searching for the handkerchief he kept tucked up his sleeve in order to wipe his brow. 'It's a repudiation of the Atlantic Charter and makes a mockery of every principle behind the United Nations. This is old-world diplomacy at its worst!'

Churchill wiped the suds that were drifting down his face to peer up at his colleague. 'My dear Anthony, you are absolutely right in your analysis, but utterly wrong in your outcome. We can't get them to change their minds at this late stage. And China is so very far away. There are too many other fronts on which we still have to fight, fronts closer to home.'

'What fronts?'

'Poland. The election observers. It may not be too late.'

'The Russians have come up with a new proposal on that,' Cadogan interjected. 'Instead of sending in observers, their duties should be taken on by our ambassadors.'

'And the Russians, as ever, take us for fools!'

'It seems . . . worthy of consideration,' Cadogan said, bureaucratic, hesitant.

'Alec, it's about as half-witted a proposal as could be devised. Ambassadors? What ambassadors? We won't have any until we recognise the Lubliners as the official government. By which time it's all too bloody late! The horses bolted! The virgins plucked! Too. Bloody. Late!'

'I'm afraid the pass has been sold, Winston. Stettinius has already agreed.'

The blue eyes stared, almost pleading, Churchill trying by simple force of spirit to change what he had just heard. Then he whispered a single word: 'Bugger.' And thumped the sides of the bathtub in anger.

'Sawyers, get me a drink. I need to think!'

The Old Man submerged himself once more beneath the water. Only two pink wrinkled knees protruded above the suds. He stayed there for a very long time.

*   *   *

295

The convoy of trucks taking Nowak and the rest of the workers from the barracks had spent several hours crashing though the gears as it meandered its way along the rising road that led up to the railhead at Simferopol. The woods on either side were often thick, the roads rough, their progress slow, but there was no chance of escape. There were guards on every truck—not that the workers were prisoners: they were citizens and guests of the Soviet system, but there were always guards. It was the manner in which things were done.

Simferopol had once been an elegant town, before the war, built on a small scale with graceful boulevards, but now it had been taken over by suspicious soldiers and sad-eyed people who dragged their lives behind them on carts and in battered suitcases, stopping only to stare or to sell what they had for a few copecks. Everyone was on the move, and everything was for sale. When the convoy at last reached the railway station, those on board hoped they'd find a few moments to haggle for a little fruit, or bread and sausage to get them through the journey, but there was no opportunity: as soon as they arrived they were counted out from the backs of the trucks, and counted on to the carriages of the train.

Counted. Like sheep. No one checked to see who they were, no names were required, they were simply part of a tally that would keep the officer's arse out of trouble. So many on, so many off, and the same number signed over to the next officer down the line. On the journey down from Moscow one old waiter had suffered a convulsion and stopped breathing, but they wouldn't let him off, not even when he was dead. That wasn't part of the regulations. There wasn't a place on the list for any sort of absconder, no category for the 'gone missing' or 'given up'. No one would take responsibility for him, so the dead man had travelled with all the rest, propped in a corner, on his own, for two days.

Now they were going back. There were no facilities on the train that pulled out from Simferopol, no water, not even a toilet. All they had was a hole that had been hacked through the floorboards in the corner of the carriage. And there was no room, a hundred men crammed into each carriage meant for seventy, on a journey that would last at least four days. That first night they had slept wherever they could, squashed together on the rough wooden benches, on the floors, in the corridors, even in the luggage racks, grumbling, pushing, stepping over slumbering bodies. As the hours passed the old steam engine jerked and jolted its way a little further north, making frequent stops for reasons that were never apparent to those on board. And with the passing of those hours, Nowak began to lose a little more of what was left of his hope.

Guards squatted on chairs at each end of the carriage, and the Pole had seated himself where he could keep an eye on the one nearest him. He knew that at some point over the next few hours he would have to risk it, jumping off, even if it meant collecting a broken ankle or bullet, because the only chance of survival lay back there in Yalta. But the guards were always wary. Throughout the night he waited in vain for some moment, some distraction that would provide an opportunity, but none came, and with every mile that crawled by, he died a little inside.

It was not until the morning, when those on board began to stir, that he thought the moment might have come. Men were standing, stretching, scratching the sleep from their eyes and their crotches, chatting to each other and to the guards, distracting them. Nowak joined the throng, moving down the carriage, nodding at the guard, asking him when they'd stop for food, getting nothing back but a shrug, until someone else had asked the guard if he had any tobacco for sale, and Nowak had slipped past. Suddenly he found himself alone. He was at the door of the creaking carriage, his fingers on the window pull, about to take a deep final breath.

But he had chosen his time with appalling luck. At the very instant he pulled at the window to reach for the outside handle and throw himself from the train, it entered a tunnel and everything was cast into confusion. He couldn't see, couldn't move, just stood there, choking on smoke, the noise of the train pounding in his ears like a drumbeat.

Then the light from the low wintry sun was pouring back in, blinding him, and when he was able to see again he found the guard standing nearby, staring at him. 'What are you doing, comrade?' the guard shouted, above the noise that was spilling in from outside.

Nowak cursed. The train had moved from the tunnel directly on to a bridge that spanned high above a ravine. If he jumped now, even if he managed to avoid the bullet that would certainly follow, the fall would kill him. He stood undecided,

298

the wind whipping through his hair, wanting to let go, to throw himself through the door and fly like a bird, to find for himself a taste of freedom one last time in the few seconds before he died.

And a final kiss for his daughter. Little Kasia. Instinctively, his fingers went to the pocket over his heart, brushing over her face, tracing the tiny profile of her nose, stroking the curls and her sweet, innocent lips. Yet, even now, if there were still the smallest spark of hope . . .

'Nothing, comrade,' Marian Nowak replied, turning. 'Just a breath of fresh air.'

* * *

Stanislaw Nowak's guards asked no questions and answered none, either. Every time he demanded to know why they had arrested him, they beat him with rifle butts and hard leather coshes. When they had beaten him into unconsciousness they threw him, along with the other leading citizens of Piorun, into a concrete cell and soaked them with a hose, then left them there for the night. In February. By morning, none of them had much appetite for making further enquiries.

It wasn't until around midday, when they were pushed and kicked and jammed into cattle trucks, that they found the answer to one of their unspoken questions. As the train set off, the sun began to peer fitfully from the grey sky and shine through the cracks in the plank wall. From the fall of the shadows, they could tell they were travelling east. That was when they knew.

They were going to the gulags.

*   *   *

The seventh afternoon of meetings. So little time left, but time enough for one final, tumultuous, cheek-flushing, artery-tightening row. It was just as Churchill had planned it even as he emerged from his bath.

He had come finally to accept that there was little more he could do to save Poland. The fate of that nation lay in Russian hands and nothing could change that, no matter how long he stayed submerged beneath the suds. He knew he would have to give way. Take a step back. But only as far as Germany.

So he rose from his bath and declared that he felt rather like the defenders of Berlin; he would do anything to hold back the advancing Russians, otherwise they might never stop.

'Do you really think they intend to occupy the whole of Europe?' Cadogan sniffed.

'I've no bloody idea,' Churchill replied, dripping water across the floor. 'But the French tried it with Bonaparte, and now the Germans have had their go with Hitler. It's probably the Russians' turn.'

'I don't quite see it as a board game . . .'

'It's not. Lose this one and you don't get to play another round next weekend, Alec,' Churchill said. 'So I want us to lay down a few tank traps. Before this afternoon's plenary, I want you to put it around that I'm having trouble with the War Cabinet back home. Sound a little disloyal. You can do that, can't you?'

'But . . . why?'

'Spread a little rumour. Suggest . . .' he began towelling himself down '. . . that my colleagues have telegraphed in a state of some excitement . . . desperately anxious not to repeat the mistakes made after the last war . . . all but forbidden me to sign any agreement that would be too financially beastly on the German people. Leave it a little vague in detail, but you must make it as firm as you can in spirit. Suggest that the rats back home are gnawing away behind my back.'

It wasn't a million miles from the truth. As the end of the war approached, so did an election, and the solidarity that had bound together Churchill's coalition government was already crumbling under the onslaught of peace.

'But, Prime Minister, I'm not sure I quite understand,' Cadogan protested.

'Alec, if we cannot dam the red tide in Poland, we must do so elsewhere. So we have to persuade our allies that there is a point beyond which they will be unable to push me, no matter what. And that point lies in Germany.'

Eden joined in, gazing at the ceiling rather than confronting the sight of his Prime Minister climbing into a large pair of silk drawers. 'But, my dear Winston, we're about to carve Germany into pieces.'

'Only one of those pieces will be Russian. Remember that, Anthony. And in the years to come, even a reduced Germany might give those in the Kremlin pause for thought.'

'You want to revive Germany—before we've finished crushing her?'

'If that is what it takes.'

'For what?'

'For the future.'

'Winston, are you telling us that they shouldn't

be punished? Not at all?'

'No, merely that in the process of retribution we should be careful not to punish ourselves. Let's strip them of their Nazi leaders, shoot and hang a few of them as an example, and then pray that we shall be able to harness the strength of her people for good.'

'I admit to being a little bewildered, Prime Minister,' Cadogan said. 'It seems such a volte-face . . .'

'You think I'm making all this up on the spot?'

'Well . . .'

'Of course I ruddy well am! But things are moving too fast. The Americans offer as much resistance as an old lettuce leaf and we're in dire need of some help. If we leave this conference with Poland occupied and Germany utterly destroyed, there'll be nothing between us and the Red Army besides the French, and the only thing they'll fight for is another man's wife.'

'Well, if that's what you want, Prime Minister,' Cadogan said primly, 'for me to be disloyal. I'll try.'

'Splendid. Just for the afternoon.' He splashed on a large amount of cologne as he inspected himself in the mirror. 'And you, Anthony, my dear. You hate this deal they've done on the Far East.'

'It's nothing less than rancid.'

'I agree. But I'll sign it. I've got no choice. Don't let that stop you making your own views perfectly clear.'

'I couldn't possibly disagree with you in public.'

'Well, give it a go. They'll only think you're flexing your muscles and pushing for my job. Another sign that my Cabinet's growing out of control.'

'Winston!'

'I know, ridiculous thought. I've never had a more loyal lieutenant. So,' Churchill turned from the mirror, 'you'll do it.'

'Well, if you insist. But I have to say, it goes against the grain . . .'

*   *   *

There was a mood of confusion at the Livadia, almost chaos. Men stood in small huddles, conferring in corners, their heads bowed, whispering, bickering, growing frustrated, doing deals. Time was running out. As the three leaders sat at their table, smoking and sipping tea, their advisers would rush back and forth, pushing pieces of paper at them that reflected the details of both the new-found agreements and the enduring disputes. And there were still plenty of disputes. The acrimony was spreading round the table like spilt milk. Eden was halfway through a denunciation of the Far Eastern deal, which he likened to the ancient practice of pillage—he didn't call it that, he was too restrained, too diplomatic, but left them in no doubt that his view was shared by a large number of his cabinet colleagues back home. Britain shouldn't put its name to such a discreditable document, he said, but Churchill, looking weary and a trifle embarrassed at such outright dissent, said he would, anyway.

'Got to get on with things. Got to,' was all he could offer by way of explanation to his lieutenant.

' 'Fraid so, Anthony,' Roosevelt added, trying to console the exasperated Englishman. 'Got to move on. Can't hang around. I'm leaving tonight.'

His words exploded like a thunderclap in the middle of the table, leaving most of them stunned. The President clearly hadn't realised the impact that such a declaration would have on the others.

'Tonight? But you can't. You . . . you simply cannot,' Churchill responded with heat.

'I've got commitments to several kings, Winston.' Not to mention a throbbing headache, a faltering heart and the desperate need to rest for a month.

'Franklin, I must beg you to think again. You can't set three dusky princes of the desert above what we are trying to achieve at this conference.'

'I agree with him,' Stalin added, having kept his ear very close to his interpreter all through the exchanges, anxious not to miss any nuance.

And others joined in, reminding him that there was still much to agree, many details to check, a final communiqué to sign. 'And, Mr President,' Molotov added, 'you have worked so hard for unity around this table. We are so close. One more day—just one more day—it might make all the difference. Bring everything together.'

So, with a sigh, Roosevelt capitulated, in spite of Bruenn's most earnest pleas. He agreed to stay just one more day—and once again, had been bullied into changing his mind. Throughout the conference, he hadn't stood out against the combined opinion of two other men on anything.

Then the storm began, quietly at first. An aide distributed a note that had been typed in both English and Russian. As it was shuffled round the table, it began to rustle like leaves in a cold wind. As they read it, heads came up, sensing trouble, and a gale arrived that threatened to blow everything apart.

Germany.

The three leaders had arrived at the conference with no clearly formed view as to what they wanted to do with the nation that had brought down so much suffering upon them all twice in a generation. Roosevelt, true to his romantic view, saw it reduced to a collection of tranquil, almost medieval rural principalities, while Stalin saw it primarily as a quarry from which to plunder whatever he could. And Churchill . . . Churchill had changed his mind. In their earlier discussions he had gone along with the proposals for wholesale destruction of the old enemy and the slaughter of its leading villains, but vengeance had never been part of his personal creed and now his mind was turning from punishment for past sins to what might lie ahead—and he cared little for what he saw. Germany ripped apart. The heart sliced out of Europe. Russia tearing at the carcass.

What the Russians intended was spelt out in the note. They were insisting that reparations be set at twenty billion dollars, and that they should get half of that enormous sum.

'That cannot be,' Churchill said.

Slowly, Stalin turned his yellow eyes upon the Englishman. 'I will accept nothing less.'

'And I will never sign such a paper. I cannot. I have a telegram from my Cabinet in London practically instructing me not to sign.' He knew they had heard the whispers put round by Cadogan and Eden.

'You would hide behind others?' Stalin sneered.

'We cannot consent to the rifling of the German

Reichsbank without limit,' Churchill insisted, with Eden nodding in support.

'There is a limit! Twenty billion dollars!'

'But we have no idea whether such a sum is possible—whether there will be that much left. It is a figure plucked out of the air.'

'We have calculated!'

'How can you calculate what will be left once you have finished—how many houses will stand, how many people will survive in the cellars and the forests, how many factories will have roofs and how many machines will remain unsmashed? It would be folly to squeeze the fruit until all the pips had squeaked and been utterly squandered.'

'You would deny Russia her rights?'

'Not at all. Whatever is sensible to take, Russia should have the lion's share. But have we learnt nothing from the last war? We tried to bleed Germany white, and we got nothing but Nazis.'

Roosevelt had been sitting silently up to this point, hoping for the storm to blow itself out, but instead it was growing. There was a danger of it causing widespread damage. 'The facts aren't simple—or often helpful,' he interjected. 'Truth is, after the last war, most of the reparations paid out didn't come from German pockets but were taken out of American loans, which were then defaulted. It wasn't Germany who ended up paying. No, it was Uncle Sam.'

Stalin sprang from his chair and stood behind it, as though it were a barricade, pounding the back in fury. 'Now I see it. You have sided with each other against me. You wait until the very last minute to deny Russia her rights. You quibble about twenty billion—our share won't cover a fraction of our losses, yet you would deny us even that!'

'No, Marshal, no,' Roosevelt said. He was shaking his head, in genuine anguish. Yet when Stalin turned to glare at Churchill he found nothing but an expression of steel.

'Ah, but I have made a discovery,' Stalin continued, stabbing his finger in accusation at the Englishman. 'You, Mr Churchill, no longer want to crush Germany. Oh, all those defiant words we remember of a few years ago, but you've changed. You have a new plan. Why won't you be honest? You don't want to punish Germany, no—you want her to become prosperous and fat once more, as a milk cow for British business.'

Churchill's face coloured. He threw down his glasses and he banged the table in anger. 'I will not listen to such accusations!' he shouted. 'No one has fought Nazi Germany longer or harder than we British. I am more than content that Russia should have first consideration on any compensation we may seek from Germany—yes, half of everything— but I will not sit here and listen to Britain being accused of greed. And I will not sign!'

'Gentlemen, gentlemen . . .' Roosevelt sighed, praying for an outbreak of sweet reason. 'Surely there must be some means, Marshal, of finding an agreement that gives you what you want, gives you justice, without getting stuck on this figure of twenty billion.'

'But it was your own Secretary of State, Stettinius, who only yesterday evening agreed to it!' Stalin stormed. 'Look, I have it in the minutes.' He waved a piece of paper like a prosecutor with a signed confession.

Roosevelt swallowed hard. 'I'm sure that was an

expression of our sympathy, Marshal, rather than a commitment.'

'If that's so, then it is sympathy that has vanished with the dew.'

'Marshal Stalin, if you would be kind enough to sit down,' Churchill said, 'I will be happy to repeat my undertaking that Russia should have first claim on whatever is extracted from Germany, and half of the final total. It is simply that until we know the circumstances better I cannot agree to a set figure. I have orders from my Cabinet.'

'Orders? I thought you said they were no more than instructions.'

'Sadly, I am not a dictator. I, for one, must do as I am told.'

'And it is so very difficult, Marshal, to put a precise figure on . . . well, the value of manpower.' Roosevelt sounded almost ashamed, as indeed he was. Germany had taken Russians as slaves for hard labour in their factories and mines, and now it was to be the Russians' turn. Forced labour. Nothing would stop them. There was to be no emancipation, no freedom from slavery. The best the American would get was to ensure that the victims of this terrible policy weren't described as slaves in the final protocol, so that his shame should not be made public.

And yet, as much as the President metaphorically squirmed and fidgeted, he was still arguing, still resisting. Stalin realised he wasn't going to get all that he wanted, not here, at least. 'We shall take twenty billion as a starting point,' he said, 'and get our officials to sort out the details later.' Then he sat down.

A starting point. Not a finishing point, only a

308

starting point. A linguistic loophole, but it was enough. Churchill and Roosevelt nodded, and officials scurried off to put textual flesh on this meagre bone.

Churchill sat back in his chair, inwardly content. If the three of them couldn't sort out this problem in a week, there was a damned fine chance that their underlings would have trouble sorting it out in a lifetime. Germany might not be raped—not all of Germany, at least. There was a chance.

And now another piece of paper was floating round the table—God, was there no respite? He reclaimed his spectacles and read. Poland. And his sorrows flowed again. Meanwhile, that contemptible maggot Molotov was at it once more, proposing yet further changes to the agreed text, perhaps already trying to extract revenge for the setback on reparations. '. . . so I would like to suggest,' he said, reading from a scribbled note, 'on the matter of the new eastern boundaries, that it might be useful to refer to "the return to Poland of her ancient frontiers in East Prussia and on the Oder". To emphasise the historical justification.'

'Ancient frontiers?' Roosevelt asked. 'How ancient? How long ago were these places Polish, then?'

Molotov swallowed. 'A very long time ago,' he replied slowly, his expression totally deadpan.

'Awkward precedent. Why, Winston, maybe on that basis you'd want your American colonies back?'

'No, thanks, Franklin. Too troublesome by half.'

Stalin joined Churchill and Roosevelt in their laughter, while Molotov quietly screwed up his little note.

The train travelled fitfully, ever onwards, and away. The only sustenance they had during the day was a little rye bread and the dark, strong black tea that was served to them by sweating *babushkas* and which they drank through pieces of hard sugar clamped between their teeth.

As dusk was falling, the train pulled into the outskirts of a substantial town. It was not allowed to go any further: an unexploded mine had been discovered beside the signal box, a present from the departing Wehrmacht who had left this place less than a year before. Sappers were busy disposing of it, and while they did so, nothing moved, and the schedule of arrivals and departures, always tenuous at best, was thrown into further chaos. For the moment, Nowak and the others were going nowhere. They were allowed on to the platform to stretch their legs, and they were soon surrounded by a small army of women selling food and drink, and items of tobacco, and serving more tea from steaming samovars. No one had any idea how long they would be staying.

Nowak had taken little interest in the course of these events. He had no appetite, and he had lost all hope. They were now too far away from Yalta for him to make it back. Even if he had taken the risk and slipped away from the platform in the growing darkness, he had no idea of where he was and there was nowhere for him to go. It was over.

All around him there was noise. Guards shouted instructions as men and women haggled for food and station hands went around with huge spanners banging away at wheels. The engine continued to belch plumes of steam, and someone began to play a mouth-organ. The confusion grew as another train drew in on the far side of the platform. More men poured forth; another convoy, filled with construction workers, headed south, to the port of Sebastopol.

That was when Nowak saw him. The man was no youngster and everything about him sagged: the stomach, the shoulder, the spirit. He seemed to prefer his own company, or perhaps it was simply that he had no friends. Nowak approached. As he got near he could smell the sourness of alcohol and onion on his breath. The hands were dirty, uncertain, heavily calloused, and trembled as he sipped his glass of tea. They were a drinker's hands. 'Got any cards, comrade?'

The shallow eyes turned slowly in his direction. 'What if I do?'

'We could be here all night. Fancy a game? *Durak*, maybe?'

There was no suspicion in the eyes, no joy, no warmth, nothing much at all, until they saw the large bottle of vodka that Nowak had just bought from one of the *babushkas*. Suddenly the man wanted nothing more than to play cards. With fingers that seemed to creak with stiffness the stranger scoured through his pockets, only to come up with a miserable collection of coins and small notes. He held them out and shrugged apologetically.

'Don't worry, friend,' Nowak reassured him. 'I want to kill time, not your pocket. Let's sit.'

So they found their way to an end of the platform where the jostle of the crowd was less intense, and in the gloom they sat propped against a brick wall. As the night drew on, they played and they drank, except that Nowak played badly and drank almost nothing at all.

'You play like an old woman.' The stranger chuckled, winning yet another hand.

'Just luck. It will change.'

But it didn't. Soon the stranger was brimming over, not only with winnings and with vodka but also with contentment. He celebrated by finishing off the bottle.

When the call came to return to the trains, the stranger was in a sleep so profound that he heard nothing. They had to search for him. Even when the guards kicked him and screamed at him, he scarcely stirred, and when they threw him back on to the train he had precious little idea what was going on. And by that time Nowak was nowhere to be seen.

He was already miles away. He had satisfied the guards, fulfilled all their requirements, been counted on to the other train in place of the drunk and kept their tally filled, and now he was heading in the opposite direction.

South.

Back towards Yalta.

*　　　*　　　*

The conference in the Crimea was drawing to its close. The participants had reached the point of exhaustion where matters were settled, even though they knew things weren't right, simply because they feared the consequences of lingering, although Cadogan proved to be something of a terrier and continued to pursue his prey with determination. A damned fine ratter, Churchill called him.

The Prime Minister played host for the final dinner. They gathered at the Vorontsov, but only after a squad of NKVD goons had flushed through the place, locking doors, peering behind walls and into cupboards, like seaside landladies checking that the guests weren't stealing the towels. This was not done gently, and they were so thorough that some of those staying and working in the Vorontsov were forced to walk round the outside in order to get to their rooms.

Stalin set the tone for the evening. He strode up the steps of the palace pursued by a host of security men, to be greeted at the door by Sawyers. A comical wrestling match ensued as the servant tried to assist the Marshal off with his greatcoat.

'What, Englishman? You want to steal my coat?' the Russian demanded gruffly. Only belatedly did he laugh and place his red-striped Marshal's cap on Sawyers' head. Throughout the evening he would miss no opportunity to leave a tiny barb in any Englishman who crossed his path. A parting gift.

Then poor, dear Franklin arrived slumping in his wheelchair and surrounded by oversized, square-jawed young men in trilbies. It made him look so frail. Churchill gave his guests glasses of champagne and invited them into the Map Room. It was where he and Stalin had started at Yalta, and it was noticeable that in the ensuing week the lines of battle in the east had moved inexorably closer to Berlin. Less than fifty miles to go before the Russians would be kicking down the doors of the Reichstag. Meanwhile, the forces under Eisenhower's command were still gathering themselves a world away, stuck on the far side of the Rhine. For all the pieces of paper that had been pushed back and forth during their week in the Crimea, this map was the one that truly mattered.

From his wheelchair, Roosevelt waved languidly at the scene. 'You know, gentlemen, some years ago my wife was asked to go and open up a school in the country. When she got there she found a large map of the world stuck on the wall. On it was this huge blank space. It stretched all the way from the Pacific to the plains of Europe, and when she asked what it was, she was told in a hushed voice that it was the Soviet Union—but the teachers were not allowed to mention it. It was forbidden even to talk of its existence. That was during my first term as President. I am delighted, Marshal Stalin, and more than a little proud, to see how far our nations have come.'

Quietly the two men raised their glasses to each other, leaving Churchill to stare at a map that, within a few years, had gone from a total blank to a huge red stain spreading across the world, like blood on a bandage. And that was how it was to be for the rest of the evening: Stalin bluff and combative, Roosevelt nostalgic to the point of turning maudlin, and Winston Churchill.

'You see,' Stalin said, thumping his finger into the map, 'Germany is the heart of all our problems. And I shall have to return home and explain to the Russian people that, in spite of all their sacrifices and all their pain, they will get no compensation, no reparations, because the British

314

say so.'

'Never been my point. Never will be,' Churchill growled. 'You can go home and tell the Russian people what you want. Won't change the facts, Marshal.'

'Boys, boys,' Roosevelt cut in, trying to act the uncle, even though he was the youngest.

But Stalin wasn't finished. 'There are rumours in Switzerland, Mr Churchill, that you might want to do a deal with Germany. Make a separate peace, once they've got rid of Hitler.'

'I have to tell you, Marshal Stalin, that I have no experience of doing deals with Hitler. If I were even to think of it, be assured I should come to you first, to gain from your own considerable experience in the matter.'

They stood smiling at each other, both wondering whether to push the button that would ignite the evening beyond repair.

'As for such ridiculous rumours, we Britons have a marching song from the last war that I think adequately reflects the position of His Majesty's Government. God bless him!' He started singing, in a bass voice that was cracked and deeply flawed: 'Keep right on to the end of the road, keep right on to the end . . .' Then he turned on his heel and led them into dinner.

It was an intimate affair: the numbers were small, only nine including the interpreters, since many of the senior officials and military men had already left Yalta to return to their duties, with instructions to make all those lines on Churchill's maps move a little faster.

'I have ordered a roast of beef,' Churchill announced, as they took their places.

315

'Splendid,' Stalin offered, in both congratulation and expectation.

'It is the fare of kings!' Churchill added, with a chuckle. 'Enough of the republican fare you've both been serving.'

'The Central Committee may insist I lose my appetite.'

'Nevertheless you must drink,' Churchill responded, rising once more to his feet and holding his glass aloft. 'To the three heads of our three states.'

Stalin was also on his feet. 'To the three heads of our three states,' he echoed.

'Yes, to President Roosevelt'—Churchill nodded in the American's direction while Stalin grunted in approval—'President Kalinin . . . and His Majesty the King!'

'To the three heads of state,' Stalin repeated once more.

And honour was satisfied.

But Churchill remained on his feet. 'It is also my honour to propose the health of Marshal Stalin. It is a toast I have drunk on several occasions, but this time I drink it with a warmer feeling than on previous meetings, not because he is more triumphant but because the great victories and the glory of Russian arms have made him kindlier than he was.'

Kindlier than he was? A clumsy suggestion, which left Stalin wondering when he had shown kindliness to this man, and worrying that he might have been too soft in the negotiations.

But Churchill was still speaking. 'I feel that, whatever differences there may be between us on certain questions, the Marshal has a good friend in

Britain. I hope to see the future of Russia bright, prosperous and happy. I will do anything to help, as, I am sure, will the President.'

From his wheelchair, Roosevelt nodded like a rag doll, while Stalin was left asking himself what Britain could offer Russia that he hadn't already taken.

'There was a time when the Marshal was not so kindly towards us'—that phrase again—'and I remember that I said a few rude things about him, too. But our common dangers and common loyalties have wiped all that out. The fire of war has burnt up the misunderstandings of the past. We feel we have a friend whom we can trust, and I hope he will continue to feel the same about us.'

Stalin beamed. Of course he'd always feel the same about this old imperialist and his tawdry little island. Some things would never change.

'I pray,' Churchill concluded, 'we may live to see his beloved Russia not only glorious in war, but also happy in peace.'

The Englishman drank deep and resumed his seat. Stalin leant across the table. 'Are you glad now that you and your armies didn't kill me all those years ago?'

'I hope one day I shall have the pleasure of seeing you driven down the Mall in London, my dear Marshal.' Preferably in chains.

'Careful, Marshal,' Roosevelt warned, not fully comprehending what was passing between the other two, 'or Winston'll start singing again. It's the British secret weapon. There is no known antidote.'

And cheerfully the Englishman hummed a few bars of 'The Roast Beef of Old England'.

'You know,' Roosevelt began, settling back in his wheelchair, 'I'm left in amazement and no little awe at how much we three have learnt from each other—and about each other. It's like . . . well, in the United States there's an organisation that goes by the name of the Ku Klux Klan. It has a ferocious reputation. It takes its stand against many things—Catholics, Jews, Negroes. And there I was once in a small southern town as a guest of the local Chamber of Commerce. On one side of me sat a Jew, on the other side was a man who, by his name, was clearly an Italian Catholic. So after we had got to know each other a little, I asked them if they ever had any difficulties with the Klan. "Why, no," they cried, "we're both members! It's all right, you see, because everybody in the town knows us."' The President laughed quietly at the recollection. 'I think that's what has happened here, in the Crimea. It's the key to sweeping away all prejudice—getting to know each other.'

The inanity of the observation struck Churchill like a thunderbolt. It left him waiting for a witty punchline, something that would turn the story round, give it relevance. But no, that was it, and all of it. The President was that far gone.

'I suppose we are like the Three Musketeers,' Churchill muttered, struggling to find some response that the President wouldn't find hurtful. 'All for one—and one for all!' He raised his glass again. He was going to need it to get through this evening.

'That leads me to another thought, gentlemen,' Roosevelt continued, his brow creased in deep thought. 'I wonder—what you've just said, Winston, I know it's a little late to raise it, but the

318

voting procedures in the United Nations. It's not all for one and one for all, is it? We've given the Marshal three votes, and the British Empire in total has even more . . . The United States has only one. I apologise for not thinking about it before but I wonder . . . would you agree to allowing the United States three votes? To match yours, Marshal? It might make things so very much easier with public opinion back home.'

Stalin looked at the American. He seemed so helpless, leaning weakly in his wheelchair, and his plea was so pathetic that it had to be genuine. This was the man who had done more than anyone to ensure the creation of a world organisation: it was his child and would be his legacy. Yet here he was, down on his metaphorical knees, begging for a little extra help. Up to this point, Stalin had perceived the United Nations as being little more than an Anglo-American brothel in which everyone would set about screwing each other while they whispered sweet words in their ears and made all kinds of pretence, yet Stalin hadn't cared. Let them talk, words were free, an old man's sedative. But for the first time, Stalin was coming to understand that Roosevelt was entirely sincere in his belief that they were ushering in a new world system dedicated to reconciliation, rhubarb pie and choir practice every Christmas. The man was a fool, a doddering old fool, and it was Stalin's firm view that fools should always be encouraged.

Stalin took out a handkerchief, blew his nose, appeared almost close to tears. 'I will lend my weight to your appeal, Mr President, and wish God's blessing upon it.'

'And you, Winston? Sometimes I wonder if you

are capable of understanding how much this means to me. You have in your veins the blood of so many generations who are accustomed to conquest. But we are here at Yalta to build a new world, one that will know neither prejudice nor violence, a world of justice and equity. Will you help me in this . . . this *little* matter of a couple of extra votes?'

Churchill wondered if he were dreaming. Here was a man extolling the virtues of equity and equality while at the same time demanding that the United States be given three votes. Three—why three, for pity's sake? Why not forty-eight, one for every state? Rise up, Rhode Island, and be counted! Awake, Alabama! Onward, Oregon! And while they were about it, perhaps the Ku Klux Klan should provide the doormen and lift operators. 'My dear Franklin, I am sure my feelings on the matter precisely match those of the Marshal.'

'Then, gentlemen, I'm a happy man.' And with that, he seemed to deflate into his chair.

'One day the entire world might be one huge and happy family,' Stalin offered, smirking slightly.

'One day,' Roosevelt whispered, 'even Germany might be a member of the United Nations.'

'Germany,' Stalin returned, 'will do as she is told. As Germans have always done.' He forked a huge pile of roast beef on to his plate. 'They are a queer people. Like sheep, but led by rams. I remember before the October Revolution that we all thought the main uprising wouldn't come in Russia but in Germany. We were wrong. There can be no revolution in Germany—do you know why? Because they would have to step on the lawns.' He was piling spoonfuls of sturgeon on to his plate alongside the beef. 'But maybe we Russians are no different. I remember a tale about how, after the battle for Stalingrad, one of our men was leading back a large number of German prisoners and on the way he killed all but one. When he arrived at his barracks with the prisoner, they asked him what had happened to the others. "I was just carrying out Stalin's orders," he said, "to kill every German to the last man. And here he is!"' The generalissimo exploded in mirth and thumped the table, full of self-congratulation.

Roosevelt felt it was time to change the course of the conversation, yet his mind kept being pulled back to the same point. 'Will you come to the opening ceremony of the United Nations, Winston?'

'If I can. It depends upon so many things,' the Englishman replied, gazing in wonder at the confection of food on Stalin's plate. 'First, I may have to endure the rigours of an election. It is possible that this may be the last time we three shall ever sit together.'

'What?' Stalin demanded, with creamed potato lurking in his moustache. 'They'd never get rid of you. Who better than the man who led them to victory?'

'Regrettably, it seems that the ordinary Englishman is no match for the German or Russian when it comes to taking guidance on these matters. We have two parties—three, even—who will contest the election.'

'One party. One party!' Stalin insisted. 'So much better.'

'Electorates have no memory,' Churchill continued, sounding morose. 'Every day dawns fresh for them, with all its promise of novelty and new fashion, and they remain ever hopeful of imminent seduction. To be tried and tested is taken as a grievous fault, to be old even more so. It may be that I am thrown out of office.' He sulked for a moment. 'Tell me, Marshal, what happens when a politician is thrown out of office in Russia?' Yes, tell me, you black-hearted bastard, tell me that. Men like Trotsky and Kirov and Rykov and Kamenev and Zinoviev and Bukharin and Lakoba and Ordzhonikidze and a hundred others, many of them women. Those who were your colleagues and friends and became rivals, and are now nothing but bones.

'Why, they disappear,' Stalin mumbled between mouthfuls of fish, 'from public life. But you seriously think you might lose the election, Prime Minister?'

'I like my politics like my beef. Well done. Yet the taste in my country seems to be for their political fare to be a little pinker. But never bloody red.'

'But what will you do—if you lose?' Stalin asked, his tone still incredulous.

'Why, I shall do what each one of us is doing. Seek to secure my place in history.'

'And how will you do that?'

'By writing it.'

And they all burst into laughter, perhaps the first genuinely shared expression of warmth they had shared throughout the conference. So they sat, and talked, and exchanged stories, the Dreamer, the Dictator and the Democrat, until it was time for them to go.

In the hallway, as they departed, many of the British staff were lined up to say goodbye and

Churchill called for three cheers for his departing guests. Roosevelt waved his thanks, and Stalin gave a stiff little bow. Sawyers helped him on with his greatcoat but appeared to be in a sombre mood. The Russian said something to his interpreter, Pavlov.

'The Marshal wishes to know if you have enjoyed your time in Russia,' Pavlov said.

Sawyers summoned up a servant's smile. 'Up the Revolution, I say.'

'He wishes success to the Revolution,' Pavlov whispered to his leader.

'And up yours,' Sawyers added.

'Success also to you personally, Comrade Stalin,' the interpreter continued, hoping he had managed to capture the meaning of this servant with the few words and strange accent.

*   *   *

Hour upon hour, mile upon mile, the train rattled over the sleepers, heading south. Not to Yalta, but its route would at least take it through Simferopol. Near enough. Nowak tried to make himself invisible, feigning sleep, his cap pulled low over his face. All the while he kept an eye open for landmarks he might recognise, things he might have seen only the day before, but it was pitch dark.

He sat in the corner of his carriage, waiting for the moment when someone would come and denounce him as an impostor, but no one did. The head count was in order. It was enough.

He had no plan, but once more he felt a flicker of hope. So he sat on the hard wooden bench and waited for Fate to play its hand.

Sunday,
11th of February, 1945
The Last Day

CHAPTER NINE

First light. The faint silver threads of dawn. Most of the men on the train still slept, even the guards, anaesthetised by drink and the rhythmical chant of the wheels. Mile after mile, the train rattled and swayed its slow way south.

Nowak had no plan, no information as to where he was and no idea how long the journey would take. All he had was the hope that the train would take him somewhere near Yalta, where he knew his fate would be decided, for that was where Winston Churchill had taken his hand and given him his word. His strange servant, Sawyers, too. Now, for Marian Nowak, there could be no going back.

He knew he was a man who counted for little in this world, whose life or death mattered to no one, except perhaps a little girl lost somewhere a lifetime ago in Poland. This had become a world in which men were no longer individuals but had become nothing but statistics, to be nodded on and off trains or work details and on to casualty lists. But Marian Nowak wasn't yet ready to die.

The elderly guard at the end of the carriage stirred, scratched himself. Nowak caught his eye. 'When do we next stop for food, comrade?'

The guard shrugged and spat through the latrine hole. 'Maybe we don't.'

'But we must eat.'

The guard stood by the hole and, with unsteady fingers, fumbled with his belt. 'When we get to Sebastopol. Perhaps midday.'

'So soon?' he asked, struggling to quell the

mixture of excitement and terror that was rising within him.

'What's so soon about it? Look,' he nodded out through the window, 'we'll be pissing in the station at Simferopol any moment now.'

The train was slowing, swaying as it passed across the points.

'Will we be stopping here?'

The guard ignored him as he set about his business.

Nowak stood. 'My turn next,' he suggested, as he passed by and moved through to the end of the carriage. He stretched, trying to force life back into sleeping limbs. Slowly, he pulled down the carriage window and took in the blast of fresh, cool air. The brakes were squealing, beginning to bite. As Nowak leant through the window, he looked back into the compartment to where the old guard was squatting and struggling, his rifle leaning against the wall several feet away. That was when Nowak reached for the handle and threw himself off the train.

*   *   *

Churchill stood in his shirtsleeves at the open window, looking out to sea where gulls were twisting and turning through the warm air in their relentless pursuit of the shoals of fish.

All morning he had been distracted, rising unusually early, yet with no apparent purpose. A message had arrived from the President inviting him to share a drive through the grounds of the Livadia while the advisers finished preparing the final drafts, but Churchill had sent his regrets. All

328

week long he had sought a private audience, to the point of humiliation, but now his pride wouldn't allow him to accept. 'Too late. Much too late.'

Now the dolphins had also found the sardines and were joining in the attack. The water was being churned silver as the fish crowded ever closer together in their futile bid to escape. More carnage.

Sawyers was at his elbow, collar and bow-tie in hand.

'What about our Pole?' he asked quietly.

Churchill continued to gaze at the attack that was pouring in upon the defenceless fish. 'And what about Poland?' he whispered hoarsely. 'Never has so much suffering settled upon the world as it does at this moment, Sawyers.'

'I don't understand your job, zur. You're about to sign a peace agreement, yet you're misery itself.'

'Oh, but I shall smile as I sign, Sawyers, with a face that will crack with delight. For if I am sad, they will know they have won.'

'They?'

'The forces of chaos. And that's half the secret, not letting the other bastard know when he's won. Giving yourself a chance, another day to fight.'

'Never surrender.'

'Something like that.'

'There were a time when you didn't have to pretend.'

'Was there? Was there really?'

He went back to studying the sardines.

*　　　*　　　*

The fall sucked the breath from his body. He

329

screamed at his limbs to move, but they wouldn't respond, didn't hear his calls, and for a while he wondered if he'd broken something. But slowly, as though in a dream, he found that he was running, dragging his leaden limbs behind him. He didn't look back. Behind him he could hear menacing noises—the slowing train, angry steam, tortured brakes, reluctant windows being forced open, shouts, a whistle being blown. More shouts.

He stumbled as he ran, his body still protesting from the fall, his feet catching in the long grass. At one point he tumbled, and when he picked himself up, he couldn't remember where he was—Warsaw? Katyn? He had done so much running. Then he heard a familiar sound, one that seemed like the crack of a breaking branch, followed by the hiss-zip of an angry hornet as a bullet forced apart the air somewhere above his head. Soon there would be a swarm of them. Thank the Virgin that the guards were mostly old, not front-line troops, as slow with their trigger fingers at this time of the morning as they were with the buckles of their belts.

He had faced gunfire many times, but this had none of the exhilaration of attack, staring at the enemy, knowing that one of you was about to die. Instead he was running like a rabbit, his arse bobbing in the air, knowing that his was the only body that might be dragged off the scene. As he ran, he felt his veins turning to ice, his muscles binding up in anticipation as he waited for a bullet to tear its way through his back. Would he feel it? Would he be aware of the flesh being torn from his body and his life oozing out through the gaping hole? His throat was parched. He very much wanted to be sick.

Ahead of him and to the right, a few hundred yards away, stood a small farming cottage on the outskirts of Simferopol, and beyond that other buildings and outhouses. In the open fields he was nothing but a free target and he desperately needed to make it to the clutter and chaos of the town. The train had now halted, its brakes howling in protest, and behind him he could hear the sounds of the gathering pursuit.

He focused all his energies on a window in the old mud wall of the cottage. It kept his head up, his legs pounding, even though his heart wanted to burst. More hornets. As he drew near, a small cloud of dust erupted from the wall, leaving behind it a dark, unpleasant hole. Soon there were more. He stumbled again, concentration broken, and for an instant he thought he might have been hit, but his lungs were still screaming and his feet smashing into the ground. Every part of him hurt. Then he was behind the wall of the cottage and found himself on a track that led to the shelter of more buildings.

Only then did he stop for a few precious seconds to suck in lungsful of air that proved to him he was still alive.

*   *   *

Churchill picked up his pen for the second time in as many minutes and dismembered it, checking that it had sufficient ink in its reservoir. Wouldn't do to run out of ink, not when you were signing a warrant of execution.

They were gathered for the last time in the ballroom of the Livadia Palace, indulging in the

331

small-talk they all abhorred, waiting. There was much scurrying in the wings. Fevered last-minute whisperings. Everything smothered in tobacco smoke and nervous smiles.

Churchill gazed around 'this bloody place' and checked his watch. Twelve. Too early, by half. Throughout the night their advisers had been testing their endurance and the meaning of words, redrafting, retyping, giving what they hoped was final form to the document—although, in fact, there would be two documents. The first was the Protocol. It would reflect what they had agreed, yet its paragraphs would be piled high with caveats and conditions because the President of the United States was forbidden by his own constitution to enter into formal treaties: that was the exclusive prerogative of the US Senate. So for the sake of such formalities the Protocol was larded with words that were deliberately soft and supple, recording their 'conclusions' rather than talking of them as commitments. And to offer themselves a further layer of protection, the Protocol was to be signed by the Foreign Secretaries, Eden, Molotov and Stettinius. It was almost as though the leaders wanted to keep their fingerprints off the knife.

The leaders would sign the second document. It was a communiqué or report—the press release of the proceedings, if you like—which was more polemical and overflowed with ambition and exhortation. It talked of their 'inflexible purpose', of the 'restoration of rights' and of 'a world order under law, dedicated to peace, security, freedom and the general well-being of all mankind'. Mighty stuff. Yet this, too, would not be binding.

Ah, but there was also to be a third piece of paper, one that would be written in words of steel and would bind them like shackles: 'The Agreement on Terms for Entry of the Soviet Union into the War against Japan'. In a single page it gave Russia everything she wanted, the islands, the ports, the railways. Everything. It also ordered the American President to obtain the concurrence of the Chinese on every one of these matters. And so as to leave no shred of doubt it went on to state: 'The Heads of the three Great Powers have agreed that these claims of the Soviet Union shall be *unquestionably fulfilled* after Japan has been defeated.' So, Stalin was to get the language he wanted, too.

These documents were warrants of execution, not just for Germany and Japan but for innocent countries like China, Poland, and many others in the further reaches of Europe. Churchill thought it might even involve his own execution, too, when it came to the election. Yet still he would sign, and smile.

Then the advisers, like Oriental minions, were shuffling forward with their gifts. The final drafts. The small-talk evaporated as slowly, painfully, silently, they began to read.

They all saw different things. Roosevelt lingered on the first paragraph of the protocol summoning the conference that would create the United Nations: 25 April. He read it twice, three times, with a feeling of excitement inside that he hadn't experienced since he was a young and predatory man. He noticed his hand was trembling as it hovered above the paper. In less than three months the dream would be flesh and even as his

333

own flesh fell apart he knew now that he was on the verge of the sort of immortality that is bestowed only once in a hundred years or more. George Washington had created a new nation, yet Franklin Roosevelt was creating a new world. Not bad for a man who couldn't even get himself out of bed.

A few feet away from him, Stalin was skimming. He had little interest in the United Nations and the other helpings of pious prose: it was the section on Germany that claimed his attention. The three powers were giving themselves the authority to do almost what they willed with her. They would disarm Germany, demilitarise and dismember it, rip the country apart, words that would allow them to wreak vengeance on it almost without limit, but the dramatic phrases couldn't hide the fact that they still hadn't worked out the details. And he lingered long over the provisions for reparations. They were specific about the figure of twenty billion, and that Russia should get half of this, but these figures were said to provide only 'a basis for discussion' and 'one of the proposals to be considered', and the British—may wild dogs snap at their testicles—had made a point of reserving their position. For a few moments the Russian wondered whether, even at this late stage, he should throw a fit of temper and demand further changes, hold them to ransom, but he had grown tired with the haggling. He was a dictator, but there came a point when even he had to accept some limits, if not to his authority then at least to his physical endurance. Stalin was sixty-six years old, he was tired, and he very much wanted to go home. Anyway, Russian troops would be sitting on a huge chunk of Germany, including some of her finest industrial cities, and they would take whatever he told them to, no matter what the paper said. So he shrugged, and decided to sign.

And Churchill wept for Poland. Oh, there were many words of comfort with talk of the government being reorganised on a more democratic basis, with 'the holding of free and unfettered elections . . . on the basis of universal suffrage and secret ballot'. But he knew that in all probability this damsel of democratic virtues would soon be turned into a whore who would be made to bend over a Russian barrel.

There were still a few drafting points that the advisers hadn't been able to settle, a touch here, a suggested tweak there, but they were minor matters. They were almost done.

'I don't know about you gentlemen,' Roosevelt said, 'but I see little point in struggling further with these matters. I suggest we get it typed up as it stands. Marshal?'

Stalin looked up, ran a finger across his moustache, exposed his yellow teeth and nodded his assent.

'Prime Minister?'

The agreement was like an oak with disease eating away at its core. One good wind and it would be gone. But there was nothing to be done: punctuation wouldn't save poor Poland. So Churchill looked up from his text and he, too, nodded.

'Then, gentlemen, let's do it,' the President instructed.

*   *   *

335

He couldn't hide in Simferopol. Armed goons were everywhere. Anyway, there was no time. Sawyers had told him that Churchill expected to leave Yalta tomorrow, on Monday, as early in the day as possible, and that was more than fifty miles away. He had to be there by nightfall, and somehow he didn't think the Russians would be in a mood to provide a taxi service.

And they wouldn't give up. They had no idea why he was running, no specific idea, at least, but the fact that he was running was enough to persuade them he was guilty of many terrible crimes, including the most terrible crime of all. Dragging them into it. He had placed them in danger. If they arrived at their destination with a wrong headcount there would be hell to pay, demotions to endure, punishment duties to fulfil, and perhaps even worse. While others were bleeding their way to Berlin, they'd been handed a cushy number where the greatest threat to their lives was being bored to death. They couldn't afford to throw away such a privilege, so they very much wanted this bastard back on board, and alive or dead really didn't matter.

It had been a long chase for Nowak, over all these years, but now it was coming to an end, one way or another. He'd run with his luck and used it up, every drop. Simply by fleeing he'd let the bastards know he had a guilty secret, and it wouldn't be long before they uncovered it. And when that happened, they wouldn't bother taking him back to Katyn before they did for him. He would simply disappear, just another useless Pole, not enough even to make a statistic.

But it wasn't over, not quite yet. He could still run, summon up the energy to pound his feet into the dirt and the cobbles, even though the pain was forcing its way up through his ankles and knees and into his guts. He had to keep running. But for every guard he could outpace and exhaust, he knew there was another—ten others—to take his place. Nowak couldn't run for ever, and he hadn't the time to hide. He had only one option: he had to escape. And suddenly, while his mind was reeling with half-finished thoughts and his body screaming for rest, he blundered into a market square. It was crowded, filled with old men and women standing behind shabby wooden stalls or squatting on rugs, haggling noisily with the passers-by. It was a place in which everything was for sale—mostly food, ripe fruit, meat, dried fish, fresh vegetables still covered with earth, and honey made from the colour of the sun. Other stalls sold tobacco or yellow spirits, or tea served from bubbling samovars, but in many corners there were sad-faced women, often with their arms wrapped round young children, who sat on bare cobbles, trying to trade the last of their possessions for a few copecks.

Nowak's mind was starved of oxygen and overwhelmed with fear, and as he walked between the stalls, struggling to regain his breath, on every side faces were turned to him. Eyes stared at him, hands reached out for him, voices were raised, calling to him, until his mind whirled in ever faster confusion. Then, less than ten paces away, he saw the old guard, his belt now buckled, his rifle raised. And once more Nowak was flying in fear.

Yet this time he was almost spent. He had come

337

to the point when there was little left inside. He began stumbling, slipping on the cobbles, sending stalls and people crashing on either side, clutching at the pocket above his heart, trying to summon up the dregs of his strength, to prime the pump one last, despairing time.

It was as he reached the edge of the marketplace that he saw the truck in a narrow side-street. The door was open, giving cover to the driver as he lit a cigarette. Nowak threw himself at it, sending it crashing into the driver and knocking him senseless to the gutter as Nowak hauled himself inside the cab. But his situation was hopeless. Behind him stood a line of parked trucks while before him he saw a wall of faces—innocent faces, some wrinkled, some young, some no more than babies. One of the younger women was holding a child in her arms of about the same age as his own Kasia. The child was staring at him, helpless. His only path of escape lay through that wall, the memory of his daughter, and he knew he couldn't do it.

He didn't even bother to start the engine. Instead, he kicked the gears into neutral and, just before he jumped from the cab, he released the handbrake. Slowly, desperately slowly at first, the truck edged its way forward down the soft incline that led into the square. They could all see it coming. There were cries of alarm as the truck rolled forward. People screamed, then scattered. A donkey started to panic, chickens escaped in a storm of feathers. Stalls that lay in the path of the truck were abandoned, the fruit and other produce left to be crushed beneath its wheels. Chaos took hold of this corner of the marketplace.

338

The truck didn't get far, as Nowak knew it wouldn't. Before it had gone many yards, someone had the wit to clamber into the cab and yank at the handbrake. It was over almost as soon as it had started, but by that time, in the confusion, Nowak had disappeared. He had found a bicycle leaning against an abandoned stall and stolen it.

Once more, Marian Nowak was running for his life.

*   *   *

Roosevelt gave them lunch in his suite while they were waiting for the papers to be retyped, in the room where once the Tsar had played billiards. The conversation was distracted: they were a little like men who had run a marathon and needed to recover their wits. Roosevelt was exhausted, Churchill in pain, and Stalin as ever watchful of his rivals. The food was mediocre, and they were still toying with it when aides brought in the final papers.

'Ah, history has come knocking,' Roosevelt declared, brightening, and pushed aside his plate to make room for it. As he flicked through the pages of the communiqué and came to the spot where they should sign, he gazed once more at the final paragraph: 'Victory in this war and establishment of the proposed international organisation will provide the greatest opportunity in all history to create in the years to come the essential conditions of such a peace.' Strange, he'd read the phrase a dozen times and always liked it, but now the words seemed ponderous, not matching the heights he had intended. But it was

339

too late.

'So, who'll sign first?' he asked.

'You, as chairman, my dear Franklin,' Churchill suggested, but the American shook his head.

'Not I,' added Stalin, laughing. 'They'll only say I pushed you both into it.'

'Winston, you should sign,' Roosevelt announced. 'Your initial comes first in the alphabet. And, if you'll forgive me pointing it out, you are the eldest, so a little respect is due.' He took off his *pince-nez* to look directly at the Englishman, and his voice grew less flippant. 'But you have also been fighting this war longer than any of us, right from the start, right from the opening salvoes of it all, and for that I respect you a thousand times more. You've never flinched, never failed in your duty. I hope you will do us the honour of being the first.'

Even among old friends who had grown apart, there was room for respect.

'We have come a long way together, we three,' Churchill whispered, fighting so much contradiction inside.

'Then let us take another small step, which will prove to be the most significant of them all,' Roosevelt replied.

The Prime Minister's pen hovered over the paper. 'There's a line from Shakespeare—*Julius Caesar*, I think, just as the triumvirs are signing their own agreement.' His brow creased as he recalled the line. '"Let us do so, for we are at the stake and bayed about with many enemies."'

'Not for much longer, Winston,' replied Roosevelt, happy in his ignorance, for he didn't know his bard or the rest of the couplet.

'And some that smile have in their hearts, I fear, millions of mischiefs.'

There was a brief scratching, and it was done.

Then aides placed in front of them the document securing Russia's entry into the war in the Far East.

Stalin sighed, seeming to hesitate.

'Is there a problem, Marshal?'

'This game of diplomacy you force me to play. I must continue to smile at the Japanese, right up to the moment I declare war upon them.'

'Don't let it worry you,' the President came back. 'Those devils were still whispering sweet nothings in my ear even while their bombers were in the air and on their way to Pearl Harbor. Don't lose any sleep about it.'

'I shall try not to.' And he signed.

Tears welled in the President's eyes. 'My dear friends, we have done a good deed here today. I feel . . .' He was beginning to choke on his emotion. 'I feel ecstatic. Filled with exultation. Supremely happy.'

Stalin's translator was struggling to find sufficiently elevated phrases, but the Russian could see from the President's face all that he needed to know. He beamed and banged the table in approval.

'There should be some fine words to grace the occasion, some historic phrase, but I find my heart too full,' Roosevelt apologised. 'How can words embrace what we've achieved here? We shall have to let posterity speak for us.'

And with that he summoned the servants to clear the table, even though the dessert of fruit in syrup remained untouched.

'You will not finish the lunch, Franklin?' Churchill asked.

'My bags are packed and I've got a car with its engine running waiting in the driveway.'

'Of course. Kings to see. But what, pray, of the Protocol? It'll be some time a-typing.'

'That's for the Foreign Secretaries to sign. They don't need us.'

'But . . .'

'Winston, it's only words. We know what we've agreed. That's enough.'

And in less than twenty minutes, the exhausted Roosevelt had gone. The conference in the Crimea was over.

*   *   *

He was flying with the wings of eagles, soaring, his heart lifting with every mile that passed beneath him. For a while the road from Simferopol dropped away towards Yalta and the old bicycle found nothing but warm air to slow its progress. There were potholes, of course, crumbling pavement, sharp bends, at one point even a fallen tree, but wherever the road descended the old bicycle purred with joy.

Inevitably there were sections when the road didn't help, when it began to climb, sometimes sharply, but only in preparation for the next swooping run down. At one point he got a lift on the back of a truck for several uphill miles: he spent it looking for any sign of pursuit, but there was none. Yet on the interminable stretches that were neither uphill nor downhill but simply rough, he pedalled the bike until he thought his heart would burst.

He refused to grow disheartened when the bicycle began to suffer. It was old, and soon it had forgotten how to purr. Instead it started to offer nothing but a constant shriek of complaint, but it was nothing compared to the pain that had grabbed at Nowak. When it became almost too much to bear, he imagined his daughter sitting on the handlebars in front of him, just as he had once dreamed they would, sharing an afternoon in the park, feeding the ducks, listening to the band that in the summer played in the park near their home, while her mother strolled beside them and showed off some new dress. During his years on the run he had tried not to think too long about his wife: he knew what both Germans and Russians did to Polish women, and whenever the image of her face forced its way back through his defences he knew he would be in pain for many days. So instead he had concentrated on his daughter Katarzyna, little Kasia, and wrapped himself in hope.

And now they were together, flying, even though he was climbing the steepest hill, and while his body begged him to stop, her smile urged him onwards. Whenever he came to the point that he felt he couldn't go on, he shouted at himself that the next push on the pedals would be his last. And the next! And the next! And the next! The old bicycle screamed in torment.

Suddenly, as he pushed on, he was hit by a pain that was greater than anything he had ever felt in his life. He cried out in agony, slowed, faltered, then fell to the ground. It seemed as though he had been shot, but it was far, far worse: for after all this time, Marian Nowak had suddenly realised he could no longer imagine what his daughter looked like.

He lay beside the road, sobbing heedlessly, pathetically, pounding the ground, and the bike at last stopped complaining.

*   *   *

Churchill hadn't expected it would all be over so quickly. He didn't grumble, far from it, he was delighted the bloody communiqué was out of the way. A decision made, a deed done, and no more nights spent struggling with its construction. All he'd have to worry about now were its consequences.

Yet, as he drove back from the Livadia having said farewell to both Roosevelt and Stalin, he began to feel increasingly out of sorts. The American's departure had been abrupt, almost disrespectful, and the truth was that he hadn't shown Churchill much respect throughout the conference, except perhaps for allowing his signature to go first. That had been a single gentle touch amid so many little slights, and it had served only to remind Churchill of how things used to be. And now Roosevelt was off to the desert—British desert. Not that the Middle East was a British colony, but it was most definitely a British sphere of influence. The Suez Canal was under British control, Palestine was a British mandate, and there was all that bloody oil. Now Franklin was up to something. Interfering. There was no better way of looking at it. He was stirring up the waters in a region where the Arabs and the Jews stirred things very adequately themselves. Churchill sniffed; he didn't like what he smelt.

He had planned to make an orderly departure the following morning, but now he grew agitated. Stalin was gone, Roosevelt was gone, leaving him behind like a lost boy. Another evening here, and for what purpose? He had come to loathe this place and all its associations; he wished he could leave them far behind. Fact was, he didn't want to stay a moment longer than was necessary.

As the car drew up outside the Vorontsov, he bounded out and leapt up the steps. 'Sawyers, where are you, man? We leave at five o'clock!'

A wail arose from within Churchill's suite. 'But it's already half-past four.'

'Then get on with it! What the dickens are you waiting for?'

It was typical of Churchill to smother indecision with activity and, frankly, he didn't give a bugger whom it upset.

'Come on,' he shouted to all within earshot, 'why do we stay here? Let's go tonight! I see no reason to stay a minute longer—we're off!'

And soon the entire palace was turned into a scene of chaos as trunks appeared and suitcases were packed and people dashed madly about trying to find those little things that insist on going astray. Washing was reclaimed from the laundry, little tins of caviar were tucked away, and mysterious brown-paper parcels were delivered and piled in the hallway by smiling Russians—ah, the diplomatic 'trifle'! Perhaps they hadn't heard that there was nothing to give them in return.

Churchill charged around shouting instructions, losing his temper, changing his mind, then changing it back again. It wasn't until very late that they knew in which direction they were heading: not to the airport and to Egypt to head off Roosevelt, as for a few moments he had suggested, but to Sebastopol, from where they would sail aboard the *RMT Franconia* for Greece to sort out their wretched civil war. Then they could advance upon Egypt!

Those around him knew the warning signs. They also knew better than to argue. It was what he did when he was deeply depressed. He would charge around and fill up the dark hole in his life with activity, and he showed no mercy to anyone who got in the way. It was as though he was a young man again, back on his horse, leading the charge at Omdurman.

The frantic activity was cut through by a wail that emerged from Churchill's room and wound insistently up the staircase. Sarah rushed in to find a scene that resembled the aftermath of an avalanche. Half-packed suitcases were strewn in every corner, clothes partly in, partly out, and in the middle of it all knelt Sawyers. There were tears in his eyes.

'He can't do this to me, miss.'

'I'm rather afraid he already has, Sawyers.'

'But one minute he tells me he's wearin' his army uniform, the next his Royal Yacht Club suit, then changes his mind again and says he's goin' in his Lord Warden's outfit.'

'What? What?' Churchill demanded, emerging from his bedroom in his underwear. 'Where the hell are my trousers?'

'There are some here, some there, and some on the back of the chair,' Sawyers responded stubbornly.

'So what's the bloody mess all about?'

It was the point of no return for Sawyers. He beat his breast, thumping his heart as though he wanted to bring it to a halt. 'It's the laundry. You weren't supposed to be goin' so soon. And it's all sodden and wet. If I go packin' it like that, it'll all be ruined.'

'Then . . . do something, man.'

Sawyers's eyes brimmed with anguish and hurt pride, and he knelt to attention. 'As always, zur, I'm open to suggestions.'

It was Churchill's turn to show petulance. 'Look, I'm the Prime Minister, not some bloody laundrymaid. Sort it out yourself. The sodding laundry stays, the sodding laundry goes, I don't much care which. But hear this.' He stamped his foot like a child. 'I am off!'

He didn't make it at five, not quite. It was thirty minutes past the hour before he left, the last of the leaders to do so. He made a scrambled and somewhat undignified departure, leaving Yalta all but deserted behind him.

*   *   *

Many things drive a man on: lust, greed, ambition, fear, anger, jealousy, poverty and, particularly, hate. But the greatest motivation of all is love.

There could be no other explanation for how Nowak picked himself up and was able to drive himself onwards, even after a tyre had punctured and filled every yard with rattling confusion and pain. Such things no longer mattered to him. This was his last throw of the dice, his last gamble, and he had come to the point of exhaustion where it

347

scarcely mattered what it cost him. He had one last chance.

By the time he pulled up by the guardhouse at the entrance to the Vorontsov compound, it was growing dark and he was entirely numb. He had lost feeling in his legs, his backside was rubbed raw, his brow was black, his clothes smeared and torn, and he was shaking from the effects of many different types of pain.

'What the fuck's wrong with you?' the guard demanded, spitting a fleck of tobacco from his tongue.

Nowak's streaming eyes looked up. 'I have come to repair Mr Churchill's plumbing,' he gasped. 'It's an emergency.'

'Fucking looks like it, too.'

'Please, comrade. You must let me pass.'

The guard called to his partner. 'Look what we've got here. Some idiot who's come to fix Churchill's bog.'

'Steal the lead piping, more like.'

'Got himself into a right state about it, too.'

'They . . . complained about my work last time. I can't afford to mess up again,' Nowak stuttered.

'Sent for you specially, did they? Is that what you were told? Emergency and all?'

'Yes, comrade.'

And the guards burst into mocking laughter. 'You better go back, you stupid arse. They've played a joke on you.'

'No, comrade. I must go. Please.'

'There's nothing wrong with Churchill's plumbing.'

'But I have orders,' Nowak pleaded.

'Bet Marshal Stalin sent him personally,' the

guards began joking between themselves. 'Get the Order of Lenin for this, he will . . . And all we ever get is a thirty-copeck whore . . .'

'Please, comrades. Let me pass!'

'Persistent swine, ain't he?'

'He's come for the lead piping, for sure.'

'He'll get a labour camp for that.'

'I've been there already,' Nowak said softly, exhausted.

The admission brought a temporary halt to the banter of the guards as the shadow of the camps passed across their souls.

'Well, help yourself, then, if you must,' Nowak was told. 'But take your time. The revolution's been postponed. Put off until tomorrow.'

'That's right,' the other guard added. 'Take all the time in the world.'

'Why? What do you mean? Tell me.'

'You blind fool. We keep telling you. You've been had.'

'How?'

'Churchill left here an hour ago.'

And, as Nowak's legs gave way and he sank slowly to his knees, the guards took up their mocking laughter once more.

The Following Days

CHAPTER TEN

The Americans left Yalta with a huge sense of achievement. Roosevelt told his colleagues that Yalta had paved the way for the kind of world he had been dreaming about. He said he felt he understood Stalin, that Stalin understood him, and that a new era in world peace was at hand. He was profoundly content, and after his detour to the Middle East, Roosevelt sailed back to his homeland and a welcome that compared him to both George Washington and Abraham Lincoln.

But the USS *Quincy* that brought the President home was a ship of sorrows. During the voyage, his old friend Pa Watson collapsed and died, never having made up his quarrel with Hopkins, and Hopkins himself had become so sick that he asked to be put off the ship in Morocco. This displeased Roosevelt, who missed Hopkins's nimble mind. After all, it wasn't as if Hopkins was the only sick man on board.

On the long journey back, Roosevelt spent considerable time with members of the travelling press, relaxing, letting down his guard, and off the record he was withering to them about Churchill. He went out of his way to accuse the Prime Minister of being mid-Victorian and of being too slow or too stubborn to appreciate the inevitable fate that awaited his empire. They were mean thoughts, unworthy of a great man, and understandable only in one racked by illness and exhaustion.

When he had set his wheels once again upon dry

land, he went to the Congress to make his report. He began with an apology. It was the first time he had addressed Congress seated, 'but I know you will realise it makes it a lot easier for me in not having to carry about ten pounds of steel around the bottom of my legs'. Up to that point throughout all the years of his presidency, he had forbidden photographs of him in his wheelchair. Many Americans didn't even know he was paralysed, yet now the secret was out. He was growing too weak to stand, and too weak to pretend any longer, yet his thoughts and ideals shone through as strong as ever.

He told them that the three leaders had spent days in discussing momentous matters such as Poland. He said they had argued, 'frankly and freely across the table. But at the end, on every point, unanimous agreement was reached. And more important even than the agreement of words, I may say we achieved a unity of thought and a way of getting along together.'

They applauded him for that, and it seemed to inspire him. 'Never before have the major Allies been more closely united—not only in their war aims but also in their peace aims. And they are determined to be united with each other—and with all peace-loving nations—so that the ideal of lasting peace will become a reality.'

They were rousing words, yet as he delivered them the President seemed to be growing tired. His wispy hair fell over his face, he digressed from his script, he fumbled with his papers, his speech began to ramble and the words became very slightly slurred.

And at times, when he left the script that he had

354

agreed with his advisers, the right words seemed to elude him. He hesitated, reached for meanings, and couldn't always touch them. He talked disparagingly of what he called 'a great many *prima donnas* in the world' whose tantrums delayed progress, and implied that de Gaulle was one. And, astonishingly, he claimed to have learnt more about the Muslim-Jewish problem in five minutes in conversation with Ibn Saud, the Saudi king, than he had in any number of written exchanges. Yet in private he had mocked the fat king, calling him a great whale. Some of what he told his audience was faltering, a little of it was silly, yet his idealism drew him on.

'The conference in the Crimea was a turning point, I hope, in our history, and therefore in the history of the world. There will soon be presented to the Senate and the American people a great decision that will determine the fate of the United States—and I think therefore of the world—for generations to come. There can be no middle ground here. We shall have to take the responsibility for world collaboration or we shall have to bear the responsibility for another world conflict.' Portentous words, but now he was hurrying, glancing at the clock, misreading one or two words in his script, anxious to finish.

'No one can say exactly how long any plan will last. Peace can endure only so long as humanity really insists upon it, and is willing to work for it, and sacrifice for it. Twenty-five years ago, American fighting men looked to the statesmen of the world to finish the work of peace for which they fought and suffered. We failed them—we failed them then. We cannot fail them again and

355

expect the world to survive.'

Even as he faltered, Franklin Roosevelt kept his eyes fixed on a distant horizon.

Churchill's view, which he expressed to the House of Commons, was far more opaque. When he rose to his feet in a crowded House of Commons on the morning of 27 February, he displayed little of Roosevelt's certainty. The President talked of the world being at an historic turning-point, but Churchill saw a very different world from the one the President gazed upon.

'We are now entering a world of imponderables, and at every stage occasions for self-questioning arise. It is a mistake to look too far ahead. Only one link in the chain of destiny can be handled at one time . . . No one can guarantee the future of the world.'

It was exceedingly cautious stuff, and whereas Roosevelt talked of his hopes for a world of collaboration, Churchill was far more circumspect, particularly when it came to Poland.

'Even more important than the frontiers of Poland is the freedom of Poland,' he told the packed House. 'The home of the Poles is settled. But are they to be masters in their own house? Are they to be free, as we in Britain and the United States or France are free? Are their sovereignty and their independence to be untrammelled, or are they to become a mere projection of the Soviet state, forced against their will by an armed minority to adopt a Communist or totalitarian system? Well, I am putting the case in all its bluntness. It is a touchstone far more sensitive and vital than the drawing of frontier lines. Where does Poland stand?' he asked. 'Where do we all stand

356

on this?'

So many questions. Yet these were not mere rhetorical flourishes. By raising so many questions, Churchill implied that there might be insufficient answers. And by so openly parading these misgivings, he gave legitimacy to others who also raised them. But he couldn't allow himself to be held responsible for knocking down the agreement. He told them that he had 'the impression' that Stalin wished to live in honourable friendship and equality with the Western democracies. He had a 'feeling' that the Russians' word was their bond. 'I decline absolutely to embark here on a discussion about Russian good faith,' he declared. But, once more, by raising the issue, he gave others the right to do so. And there were many who were eager for the chance.

Twenty-five Members of Parliament voted against the Yalta agreement, most of them Conservatives. Others abstained, a minister resigned. There was no jubilation in the streets. Churchill's questions were left hanging in the air.

He had only hours to wait for Stalin's answer. On the very same evening as Churchill told the House of Commons they were moving into 'a world of imponderables', the Russians sent their tanks and troops on to the streets of the Romanian capital of Bucharest and mounted an armed coup. It was in flagrant breach of both the spirit and letter of the promises that had been strewn about at Yalta. Both British and American governments demanded meetings and explanations, but the Russians didn't even bother to lie. They simply ignored their allies, said nothing, and carried on.

It was the beginning of much, much worse to come. The Soviet boot stamped down upon Romania and Bulgaria, the Baltic States, Hungary, Czechoslovakia, the eastern half of Germany, and, of course, Poland. Churchill foresaw it, or much of it. In the month after they had parted at Yalta, Churchill pestered Roosevelt with telegrams urging caution about Russia. His words fell on deaf, and dying, ears.

On 12 April, eight weeks after he had left the Crimea, the President was sitting quietly in his home in Warm Springs, Georgia, when he rubbed his temples and complained of a terrific headache. Then he collapsed. Three hours later, Franklin Roosevelt was dead.

And three months after that Churchill, too, was gone, cast aside by the catastrophic election defeat that Stalin had assured him could never happen.

*   *   *

Nowak the warrior was also dead. During the weeks after the Russian occupation of Piorun, many of the missing men of the town began to make their way home—from gulags and concentration camps, from prisons, from labour details, and from the places that had kept them hidden throughout the years of war. There were many others, of course, who would never make it home and who would lie in unmarked graves, but for those who did they found a town that was still at war. The Home Army was treated as an enemy by the occupying force: its leaders were arrested as traitors, there were executions and mass transportations, so the men of the Home Army fled once more to the forests to continue their resistance.

But there was a new ambivalence among the Poles. Their 'provisional' government was, nominally at least, Polish, and for some that was enough excuse to bring the years of bloodshed to a close. So one night in May, Nowak and his men in the forest were betrayed by a fellow countryman. They woke up the following day to discover, as the mists melted away, that a ring of steel had been thrown round them, and out of the morning sun from the east came bombers who rained death upon their hiding-places. For Nowak and his friends, there was to be no escape. They had no hope of beating off the Russian tanks, and when they tried to flee from the forest they were picked off, one by one, like low-flying pheasants. Nowak was hit in the leg. He knew he would die, but was determined to make it back to Piorun first. They caught up with him in a potato field on the outskirts, within sight of the rooftops, and they did not take prisoners.

Yet at least Nowak the warrior had the privilege of dying on Polish soil. Not everyone was accorded as much.

In March, General Leopold Okulicki, the head of the Home Army, and fifteen other of the most influential non-Communist Polish leaders, including ministers from the government in exile in London, were invited by the Russians to discuss the formation of the new 'broadly based' administration promised by the agreement at Yalta. They had been given personal letters of safe conduct from the commander of the Red Army in Poland, in which he offered his 'word of honour that from the moment of your arrival among us I shall be responsible for everything that happens to you and that your personal safety is completely assured'.

They agreed to meet the Russians in a suburb of Warsaw. Not a single one of the Poles returned from the meeting.

They had been promised that a plane would be provided to take them back to London after their meeting, but instead of flying west it landed in a snowy field outside Moscow, from where they were taken to the NKVD prison at Lubyanka. Two months later they were put on trial in Moscow, accused of subversion, terrorism and spying. Most were convicted, and Okulicki was sentenced to ten years. He died in a Russian prison.

Nowak. Okulicki. And tens of thousands of others. Systematically, the Russians were finishing off the task begun by the Nazis, and wiping out all traces of Polish resistance.

The Mediterranean
June 1963

EPILOGUE

'Nearly twenty years. A long time ago,' Churchill began, leaning forward, trying to adjust his eyes to the glare from the surrounding sea. 'There were so many people, so many different places . . .'

'Yalta.'

'I still don't recognise—'

'I had two good legs then.'

Churchill stared still harder. A Pole? At Yalta? It couldn't be. He'd only met the one and this man was so very much older. The scalp was threadbare, his brow a forest of furrows, his knuckles gnarled like an ancient oak. No, this wasn't the man: this was an impostor, intent on some cruel mischief, no one aged that quickly, not unless . . . Then, as the Pole raised his glass, Churchill saw the gash on his hand where two fingers should have been.

'Is it . . . *you*?' The words came in a sigh, like air escaping from an opened coffin.

'Yes, Mr Churchill. Although it's Sir Winston now, isn't it? So many honours. A man of honour, that's what I think you once told me, or something like that. But I'll call you plain Mr Churchill.'

'How . . . ?'

'How did I escape?' He laughed drily, leaning on the *Christina*'s rail, shifting the weight from his leg without taking his eyes off the old man. 'With luck. With help. Because some angel was watching over me. An angel named Frank Sawyers.'

Churchill shook his head, trying to fend off the confusion that had settled upon him like a fly.

'I know, difficult to believe, isn't it?' the Pole

continued. 'An Englishman whose word could be trusted.'

'Sawyers? What the hell did he have to do with it?'

'Everything. You left him behind, at Yalta.'

'Collecting the laundry. Packing. Some such nonsense.'

'That's when I arrived. You, Mr Churchill, had offered to help. You had promised to take me with you, and I had trusted you, trusted your word. Why, I gambled my life on it.'

Churchill tried to settle back in his chair, pretending comfort, but he was breathing heavily, his nostrils flaring, giving an excellent impression of a goaded bull.

'Tell me, Mr Churchill, I've always wondered— did you forget me? Or simply discard me? Sawyers wouldn't say. Too loyal.'

Churchill scowled. 'They were tortuous times.'

'Ah, I see. Then that would explain it.'

The insolence cut deep. The old man had grown accustomed to getting his own way; he wasn't used any longer to fending off insults, hadn't been for many a year. Once upon a time, his sharp tongue would have sliced the man to ribbons but it was a habit lost long ago, the tongue blunted like a knife left out in the rain, so in some confusion he finished off his champagne and held out the glass, not knowing what to do with it. Without being asked, the Pole refilled it, and his own. To anyone watching they seemed like two old friends.

'Your English has improved.'

'Then it is the only part of my life that has.'

'Please, tell me. What happened?'

'After you disappeared from the Vorontsov

364

without me?' The Pole left a little silence to allow the accusation to sink in. 'I arrived, half dead—it had taken everything I had to get there. And before long I would most certainly have been entirely dead, because by that time they were looking for me. When I discovered you had gone, everything became hopeless. I think I went through some sort of collapse, almost passed out, but then Sawyers appeared. A light in the darkness. He ran me a bath—your bath. He shaved me to make me look decent, then dressed me up to make me look English. He was a very special man, your Mr Sawyers.'

'Bugger left me. Resigned,' Churchill mumbled, a distant stare settling on his watery eyes as he tried to pull back the curtain of time. 'Asked me for a reference, then the bloody man packed up and left. A year after you met him. You know, I don't think he was ever the same after Yalta.'

'No one was.'

'I'd lost the election, you see, been hurled out of office, and everyone assumed that I was nothing more than discarded litter on the scrap heap of history. So he went.'

'You accuse him of disloyalty?'

'I think . . .' Churchill paused. When he spoke it was in a series of gentle hesitations, like the sails of a yacht trying to catch the breeze. 'I think it may have been partly my fault. It hurt when they rejected me after the war, hurt like hell. Clemmie says I was pretty foul to everyone, damnably bad company, and Sawyers said—Sawyers told my wife he had seen me at my best, and that was how he wished to remember me. Was that disloyalty?'

'Sounds to me like a very fine degree of respect.'

'I was angry at the time. He was always scrupulously honest, sometimes to a fault, and his leaving me hurt so very much. It implied criticism—of me! You can take that sort of thing from a creature like Goebbels or even the editor of the bloody *Times,* but from a servant . . .'

'He was a very special man,' Nowak repeated slowly. 'And when I was bathed and shaved and dressed, he pushed me into the car along with all the baggage and suitcases and your hairbrushes and your suits, and we drove out, right through the gates, no questions asked. By that time, Stalin had gone, left Yalta, and taken the clouds of suspicion with him. The guards were relaxed. Why, we even had a couple of salutes.' The Pole smiled grimly at the memory of the sentries, the ones who had mocked him on his way in, standing to rigid attention and presenting arms—arms that in other circumstances might have shot him. 'We caught up with you, a few hours later, at Sebastopol, on your ship.'

'They allowed you on the *Franconia*? While I was aboard?' Churchill asked, his surprise edging into indignation.

'No one bothered to question me there either. I was with Sawyers, he was your man, and his word was enough.'

'Are you telling me he played me for a fool?'

And it was Nowak's turn to grow indignant. 'Oh, how dull-witted can you be? Don't you see? He was trying to prevent you from being a fool—and, even worse, a wicked liar. Sawyers was the one thing that stood between you and damnation.'

They were both rattled. Churchill's glass thumped down on the arm of his chair, spilling champagne over his fingers. 'How dare you?' he barked, as he licked his fingers clean.

'Oh, I dare, Mr Churchill. You see, Sawyers took your word of honour—the word of honour you gave me—as sacred. In his eyes it was a sin to break it. So he wouldn't let you. And you dare accuse him of disloyalty?'

'No, not disloyalty. He was headstrong, wilful, stubborn—and I can't criticise him for that. A little like me, I suppose. Even did a passing good impression of me, so my daughters told me. One of the family, practically, and the only one who didn't shout. That was why it hurt so much when the bloody man just upped and left.' For a moment, Churchill lost himself in regret, then raised his chin once more. 'So we saved you after all.' It was a remark that carried more condescension than compassion. Churchill immediately regretted it; Nowak ignored it.

'You and Sawyers flew off to Athens, and the liner followed, but by the time we arrived you'd already left again. Egypt, I think. But the crewmen were beginning to ask questions about the strange man who'd come unexpectedly on board and, of course, I had no answers. So I jumped ship.'

'You could have entrusted them with your secret,' Churchill encouraged.

'I trusted you.'

In the silence that followed, Churchill trawled his mind to find the words to justify himself, but his net came up empty.

'Then I went back home,' Nowak whispered.

'To Poland? How?'

'I walked.'

'But that must have been . . .'

367

'The best part of a thousand miles, as the crow flies. Except I wasn't a crow.'

'And still no one asked questions of you?'

'The world was in chaos, the whole of Europe overflowing with people trying to get back home—prisoners-of-war, civilians, refugees, demobbed soldiers, a million homeless strangers trying to find their place. We were no more than stray dogs, mongrels, worth a kick if we got in the way, but that was all. No one bothered very much with us, we had little worth taking, not even our lives, unless of course you were Russian and sent back for the amusement of Marshal Stalin.'

'I'm . . . I'm feeling a little hot. Too much sun. I should move back into the shade. Would you mind?' Churchill held out his hand, and slowly the Pole raised the old man and moved his chair back beneath the cover of the canvas awning that had been spread above the deck.

'Thank you, Mr . . . Nowak.' Churchill was surprised that the name had stuck after all these years, embedded deep within his conscience like a splinter of remorse. 'So where were we?' he asked, as he settled back into his chair.

'We were sending Russians back home. No, forgive me, *you* were sending Russians back home. Against their will, most of them, even those who had fought alongside the British. A deal you'd done with Stalin. Sent them all back—just as you'd have sent me back. You hear all sorts of rumours about what happened to them. Ugly whispers, about more graves, about how your friend Marshal Stalin picked up where he left off at Katyn.'

'Stalin was never my friend.'

'Then why, in God's name, did you give him

Poland?'

The question came in a voice that remained as calm as the confessional, but a fire had begun to burn in his eyes that denied any crumb of forgiveness.

'I didn't give him Poland!' Churchill snapped defensively, growling, his voice resembling the grinding of old bones. 'How the hell could I? He already had it.'

He tried to turn away, fumbling to relight his cold cigar and wishing he could get rid of this belligerent bloody man, but he couldn't get the flame to take hold in the breeze that was grazing across the sea. Nowak stooped and lit the cigar for him. Still struggling with his emotions, the old man nodded his appreciation. 'I seem to remember that even all those years ago you had your own way of doing things, Mr Nowak. In England, we call it being bloody-minded.'

'A singularly inappropriate phrase in the context, don't you think?'

And always giving him a kicking: Churchill remembered that, too. He never trod softly, this Pole, always came in his boots, as if he wanted to start an argument. Nothing wrong in that. There had been a time when Churchill had loved an argument, thrilled to its call, but no one challenged him any longer: they simply stuck him on top of Mount Olympus and left him there. He found it so lonely.

'Tell me, Mr Nowak, you said you got home. And I seem to recall . . .' his hand scraped across his forehead, massaging his memory '. . . you mentioned you had a family. Did you find them? I do so very much hope you did.'

The Pole remained silent for a while. He was still standing, propped once more against the guardrail, looking deep into his glass, drinking it, needing it. In the silence there was nothing more than the lap of the sea against the hull and the distant mewing of a seagull.

'The Poland I remembered had gone,' Nowak said eventually, softly. 'Six million dead—more than the Germans, more than the Japanese, far more than the Italians. Nearly one in five of everyone who had been alive in Poland when I left had been killed. No nation suffered as much as we did, Mr Churchill. You think Britain suffered—well, I grieve for your sorrow, but it was the prick of a pin compared to what happened in Poland. It took me almost a year to find my way back.' He raised his hand as though wiping sweat from his eyes. 'I remember that everything had a particular smell. I arrived in the spring when the blossom should have been bursting through, but there were no trees, and instead of honeysuckle and primrose there was smoke and dust and something else, something sweet and sickening. You'll remember it from your time in the trenches. The stench of human flesh that had been burnt and rotted. It was everywhere, seeping out from beneath the rubble. And there was still so much rubble. No schools, no hospitals, no Conservatoire, not anything I remembered. Nothing. You know, Mr Churchill, before the war, Warsaw was the finest city in Europe. It could stand up and look Paris in the eye and gaze down on places like Berlin from a grand height. It was the capital of a renewed nation, full of gaiety, of music and laughter and young people falling in love, that's how I remember Warsaw. But it had gone. All I found was broken walls and lonely chimneystacks standing like monuments in the graveyard. In the very centre of the city, I came across two twisted metal towers. Somehow they seemed familiar. Then I saw the sign and I realised where I was. Jerusalem Street. These broken towers were all that was left of the railway station that was—had once been—the most magnificent railway station in Europe.' Nowak smiled ruefully, feigning light-heartedness. 'Oh, I know it seems ridiculous for a man to get sentimental about a railway station, but it was like the heart of Warsaw, always beating, a place where we said our goodbyes as we went off to war, and where we found our loved ones if we came back. It should have been a place of bustle and beauty, of tearful farewells and the most joyful reunions, yet I found nothing but ghosts.'

'The soldier's return. A most compelling moment in any man's life.'

'I've seen films of what happened to Berlin and Hamburg, even Dresden, but that was nothing compared to what was done to Warsaw. And yet we were innocent. We had started no war, we had done our neighbour no wrong. So why us? Why Warsaw?'

An edge was creeping into the Pole's voice as his passion pushed up against his self-control. Churchill searched for some response that might be adequate, knowing he would fail. 'Warsaw died a brave death, and many times over, Mr Nowak.'

'But what good is that to me?'

'Its name stands as a symbol of hope.'

'You delude yourself. It stands as a symbol of betrayal and inhumanity, nothing more.'

They fell silent for a while, watching as another yacht passed innocently by, slumbering on a sea that was studded with turquoise and diamonds. In the distance the shore seemed to be melting in the midday heat. Yet Churchill felt alive, more vital than he had in years. This man, this Pole, had stirred old passions that he had thought were not simply dormant but stone dead, and if their revival brought along with them memories of compromises and inadequacies, even pain, it was but a small price to pay. His life had become crowded with those who tumbled over each other to flatter and fawn, yet the only loyal companions of old age were loneliness and endless time. Nowak made him feel young again—why, seventy years young! And the fact that he represented a challenge, a threat, even, made the moment all the richer.

'Your home, Mr Nowak. Your family. Pray, what of them?'

The Pole stared directly into the honey-gold sun and for a moment closed his eyes, as though hoping its heat would burn away the memories. Then his hand came up to touch the spot over his heart.

'We lived off Aleja Ujazdowskie. It's a long boulevard that runs to the very heart of the city. Many trees, many magnificent buildings, a place where people loved to be seen. It was also the route that the panzers took, and where the fighting during the Uprising was most fierce. My wife ran a casualty station in the cellar of our house, so a neighbour told me, filled with women tending the wounded, nothing more. But the troops that came were SS. What was left by the tanks and the bombers, they finished off with grenades and flame-throwers. They made no distinctions, and gave no quarter. No one in our cellar survived.'

'And . . . your daughter?'

Suddenly Nowak's foot began tapping upon the deck. It was as though something inside him had been switched on, a motor, a source of energy that was too great to be contained and had to find release in the steady, monotonous movement.

'She ran away. They said she was last seen running down our street in her favourite checked dress—that's how the neighbour recognised her—just as a tank shell hit a nearby house and everything disappeared in a blast of flame and smoke. No one has seen her since.'

'Surely there must have been some trace . . .'

'When a city is razed to the ground, Mr Churchill, when the gutters run with fire, when even the sewers are filled with petrol so they will burn, there is so little place for a young child to hide and so many places for her to vanish. I searched, of course I did. I never stopped. And I found so many lost little girls, begging, hobbling on crutches, shivering in their rags, and every time I looked into their eyes I wondered if . . . if she might be little Kasia. But how could I tell?' The drumming on the deck became more insistent. 'I didn't even know what my daughter looked like. There was no photograph, no image, only a neighbour's muddied memory. And I kept wondering, if she had survived that blast, what might have happened to her? What does a little girl of five do when everyone she knows is dead and her home is broken and she has seen more vileness and brutality than anyone deserves in an entire lifetime? Where does she go? What becomes of her?'

Churchill was openly weeping, yet Nowak's eyes were dry, bruise-grey, tortured with the pain of so many unshed tears.

'Every morning my hopes rose, and every nightfall they died a little more. For an entire year I searched, looking in shadows, in orphanages, in homes and graveyards, scratching away in every dark corner, until it drained my soul.'

'I can find no words to express my sorrow,' Churchill whispered. 'I, too, lost a little daughter. Marigold. We called her the Duckadilly. She was so beautiful and full of delights, and only two.' He produced a huge handkerchief from a pocket in his blazer and wiped his eyes, yet Nowak's tone, like the tapping of his foot, remained mechanical.

'I found myself one day in a gutter. Drunk, of course, desperately drunk. I had no idea how long I'd been there—hours, days, weeks, the difference no longer mattered much to me. Then an old woman spat at me. She crossed the road so she could spit on me. I think I recognised her. She told me I had brought shame on my family. That word . . . "Family" . . . but I had none, not a soul, no one. All . . . gone.' For the first time the mask began to slip and the Pole's suffering twisted his face. 'You know, I imagine them looking down on me, my father, mother, my wife, little Kasia . . .'

'I think I can understand how you feel,' the old man replied softly, his lower lip trembling like the wings of a swallow. 'My father's ghost has walked alongside me all my grown life. He always told me I would come to no good. He still does.'

The Pole was startled—Churchill with his

374

father's ghost? He paused for a moment, struggling to see this man as any other, as one who might have self-doubt or be haunted by his past, but he dismissed the idea as preposterous. They shared nothing in common. What could this man know of family? Why, even his own son treated him with contempt.

'I was in the gutter. It was one of those moments when a drowning man has to decide if he's going to cling on a little longer or simply open his fingers and allow himself to be taken. One more drink and it wouldn't have mattered, but as Fate would have it the bottle was empty. So I got up. And I walked to Piorun.'

'To where?'

'To the home of Marian Nowak. I had been him for so many years. I had nowhere else to go. If I'd stayed in Warsaw I would have ended up in a gutter so deep that I'd never be able to crawl out. Anyway, I thought I owed it to his family, to tell them how he had died. My existence as Marian Nowak may have been imaginary all those years, but it was the one part of my life that remained real to me. So—I walked. Through a countryside that looked as if it had been ripped from the Middle Ages. Nothing but peasants scraping fields for food, living in filth and degradation, in fear. Poland as it hadn't been since the Black Death.'

The Pole's foot was still tapping remorselessly upon the deck and it was beginning to irritate Churchill, making it more difficult for him to hear, but it was scarcely the moment to complain. 'And did you find them, the family of Mr Nowak?'

'Piorun was a town like so many others. It had no airs, no pretensions. It had so very little to lose,

375

but what it had was taken from it. And when I arrived, the people of Piorun had little to offer but suspicion. So many strangers had come to Piorun and left behind them nothing but heartache. They demanded to know my business. I pretended I was a distant cousin of the Nowaks. And that was when they told me what had happened. They were gone, almost the entire family. Wiped away as though they'd never existed. Nowak's father had disappeared, along with an aunt. One uncle killed. Another, a priest, arrested. His mother sat herself down in the town square one night in winter, outside the church, and simply froze to death.' Nowak's lips twisted with contempt. 'And when the liberators of Poland heard that I had arrived in Piorun and was a relative of the most troublesome family in the town, they invited me for a little chat. Wanted to know who I was, where I had come from. And when I couldn't answer their questions, they arrested me, too. Ten years in the gulags, Mr Churchill. Sent to wander Siberia until Stalin was cold in his coffin and they no longer had any use for an ageing man with half a hand and a freshly mangled leg.'

Churchill began to mumble an expression of dismay, but Nowak cut across him.

'The one thing that sustained me until the time I met you in Yalta was the love I had for my family. And afterwards, the one thing that kept me alive was my hate. I carried it with me every stumbling step of the way. Hate. For those who were responsible for what had been done to my family and my country. It was the only way to survive in the camps, to get through another winter or another beating. So I swore vengeance on them all.

376

Promised my little Kasia that, if ever I had the chance, I would make them pay for the many ways we were betrayed at Yalta.'

The old man shuddered.

'But they cheated me, Mr Churchill. They died, Stalin and Roosevelt. It's so difficult to hate the dead. And then, out of the blue, you walked into my life once more. You know, I'd almost forgotten about you, a sad old man surrounded by so many fables. The living legend, the man who won the war. But you and I know better, don't we?'

'My heart trembles for you, Mr Nowak. But these calamities—they were not my fault.'

Nowak sprang to his feet, like an angler striking for a pike. 'Then whose fault was it? Who turned the blind eye to Katyn? Who held out their hand in friendship to the Russians even as they sat on the other side of the Vistula, watching Warsaw—and my family—being reduced to ashes? Who applauded as they marched into Poland and made us all slaves?'

'You cannot blame me for those things.'

'Then who should I blame? Who was it who betrayed not only my country at Yalta but me—me? And who better to pay the price?'

'What price would that be, pray?'

The foot had stopped its tapping. Nowak's battered body was still. And suddenly, Churchill was staring down the barrel of a revolver.

*   *   *

'Is the condemned man allowed a final drink?'

'You think this a joke?' Nowak tightened his grip on the handle of the revolver.

377

'Not at all. I have faced gunfire many times. They have invariably been the most exhilarating moments of my life.' Churchill looked directly at the gun, his voice sounding almost wistful. 'Whatever else you have done, Mr Nowak, you have brought a spark back into my soul and, as strange as it may seem in the circumstances, I thank you for it.'

'If you're thinking of playing for time, I shouldn't bother. Your detective has gone in the launch with your son, your valet is fast asleep in his cabin—a little something I gave him in his coffee—and the crew members have been told by Mr Onassis not to disturb you unless they want—I use his words—their balls to be turned into Turkish sweetmeats.'

'Play for time? Why would I do that? At my age, there's precious little point. Altogether too damned much of the stuff.' He held the other man's stare. 'So, shall we take the neck off another bottle, Mr Nowak? What do you think?'

The Pole shrugged. Cautiously, reluctantly, he set about refilling both their glasses. Pol Roger. Churchill's favourite.

'Your splendidly good health,' Churchill offered in thanks. 'Glad you made it after all.'

'Ah, the Englishman's stiff upper lip, laughing in the face of death.'

'I am not mocking, Mr Nowak. We have both walked with Death, many times, you and I, smelt his breath on our shoulders. The difference between us is that I am very old. There comes a point where life is like a gramophone record, stuck in the same groove, going round and round, constantly repeating itself, and no one dances to the tune any longer.'

'You pretend you are not afraid of death?'

'Since I watched my father die, slowly, by fractions, it is the waiting I have feared. I watched my father being stripped of his wit and his reputation, and eventually his identity. In the end, it was Death who rode to his rescue. Just as he did with Franklin.'

'Your friend,' Nowak sneered.

'Yes, he was a friend, and a splendid one.'

'He was a man who threw away everything we had fought for.'

'That is a question I have often asked myself.'

'It wasn't a question.'

'You'll have to allow a dying man a few doubts of his own,' Churchill snapped back. 'Franklin was weak. His sin was to be ageing and infirm. And, above all, idealistic. If they are faults, then in his case they proved most grievous.'

'You can't pile the blame on his shoulders. You were there, together, side by side.'

'I am English, he was American. Standing together, but separated by an ocean of turbulent water and contesting interests.'

'What? You've spent the last twenty years bragging about your Special Relationship.'

'And it was destined to be special. Just as it was destined to fail. At its very start, on the day of the Japanese attack on Pearl Harbor, the President declared it to be a day of infamy, while I quietly and most secretly rejoiced. It was what I had wished for, had fallen to my bended knee and prayed for over so many months. At last, America at war! It was something I had badgered and bullied him about and he had hated me for it. But

379

when it happened, it was worth a private jig or two, I can tell you.'

'You were one and the same. Franklin and Winston. All but brothers.'

'"We few, we happy few, we band of brothers . . ."' Churchill picked up the refrain, only to cast it aside. 'It wasn't like that. Franklin used me as I used him, as it was right for us both to do. We served interests that frequently coincided, but we saluted different flags.'

'But he—'

'For God's sake, listen, man! And learn. Be the first Pole in Christendom to listen before he leaps to conclusions.' Churchill's voice had found a new edge; perhaps it was the heat, and the drink. 'He was an American, and I was not. He was a sick man in a hurry, and I was not—not then, at least. He was a heady idealist, while I have always preferred my arse to sit on solid ground.' Churchill wasn't any longer used to such outbursts, and he panted with the effort, but was determined to continue. 'Yes, he was a friend, as much of a friend as any foreign politician can be, but he was also in a fearsome hurry and sped off in directions where I had no desire to follow. Why, he was so keen to get the Russians into the war against the Japanese that he gave them everything they asked for. Yet in the end it was utterly pointless. After all that grovelling, America dropped their bombs on Hiroshima and Nagasaki and brought the war to an end before the Russians even got round to loading their rifles.'

'Don't wash your hands of that. You agreed to it all!'

Churchill shook his head. 'It was a deal done by

380

Franklin directly with Stalin and without even the courtesy of consulting me. He was in so very much of a hurry.' Churchill swilled the champagne around his glass before taking more. 'Then in his haste he flew to Egypt to meet with Ibn Saud and the other desert princes. Wanted to interfere, to rearrange the palm trees, to put his stamp on the world before . . . before he died. He knew the flame was almost out. His face had a transparency, an air of purification, and often there was a faraway look in his eyes. Yet there are two sides to every man, and later I discovered that while he was there, talking to the Saudis, he tried to filch the oil concessions right from under our noses. Even as he sang to the angels and talked of peace among men, he was trying to pick British pockets.'

'He deceived you?'

'At Yalta we all deceived each other.'

'You admit you led the world in a lie.'

'No!' Churchill shouted, but the passion had tired him. When he resumed, his voice was quieter, his tone more contemplative, the words trickling in a stream instead of a flood. 'We led the world in hope. And was it wrong to have ambition? Franklin wanted so many things—oh, the bloody oil, of course, and much else that was mercenary besides, but he was American to his roots, and if he planted one foot in the muddy world of war then the other was set on a higher journey. What he wanted most of all was a world of peace. It was his abiding passion. That was why he gave everything—and too much—for his United Nations. He thought it would solve everything. He was wretchedly wrong, of course, but should a man be condemned for embracing his dreams?'

'Did he dream of Poland?'

Churchill wiped his eyes; they were tired, seeping. 'It is a fair point. In all candour I must admit that he didn't care much for Poland, nor for much else in Europe. In his eyes, Europe had fostered the two most barbaric systems ever imposed upon humanity, Fascism and Communism, and he saw us as a source of the most deadly infections. In his own lifetime he had watched the flower of American youth being sent not once but twice to its slaughter on the bloodied fields of Europe, and he swore that was enough. So he was determined that he would win the war, then turn his back on it all. Yes, he was an idealist, but there was also an arrogance, a blindness within him, so typical of his people, who thought that war would be done with once the bullets had stopped flying. Oh, Mr Nowak, if only that could be so. He was like—yes, I shall put it this way—a travelling quack who sells his elixirs and potions from the back of his wagon then departs before anyone discovers that sugar-water isn't truly enough. Americans can be the noblest of creatures in times of war, Mr Nowak, but in matters of peace they can also prove most ridiculously dull.'

'You can't separate yourself from him. You fought the war together.'

'And we fought each other, too. I left Yalta very bitter. He had become like a sheet anchor dragging back our ship. And when he died just a few weeks later I felt—what? Shock? No, for he was a dead man even when I saw him. But I was angry, deeply hurt. I refused to attend his funeral, concocted some excuse, a silly pretension that I quickly came to regret. I even felt a measure of relief, not simply that his suffering was at an end but that a rival had gone from the scene.'

'Roosevelt? A rival?'

Churchill sighed wearily. 'I thought so then. For the laurels, you see. I was envious. He had gone at the height of his fame, acclaimed as the victor, while I was left behind to tread the lonely slope of old age.'

'You were jealous of Roosevelt?'

'He had died. I had merely been sentenced to death, waiting for the maggots and the scribblers.' His eyes closed and his head seemed to drop in sorrow. 'And what will posterity have of me? My paintings? Bugger it, even my detective paints better than I do.'

Nowak began to mock this man, who appeared to see the world as his playground and matters of war and peace as little more than footnotes in his personal chronicle, but even as he raised his voice in rebuke, he saw that the old man had fallen fast asleep.

*   *   *

Only the slant of the shadows on the deck told of the passing time. When Churchill opened his eyes he saw the silver scribble of the horizon and felt the brush of scented air on his cheek. For a moment he wondered whether the deed had been done and he had passed through to Paradise. Then, once more, he saw the gun.

'Poland, Mr Churchill. You betrayed me and you betrayed Poland.'

Churchill wriggled in his chair, trying to revive both his circulation and his thoughts. 'We went to war for Poland.'

'You sold my country to Stalin.'

Churchill shook his head. 'You are beginning to be tedious, Mr Nowak. Just shoot me and get it done with.'

'We fought for you! Our pilots gave their lives for you in the skies above England during the battle of Britain, and our soldiers fought and died like heroes alongside you through the mountains of Italy.'

'They were very brave, the Poles.'

'And you lifted not a finger for them.'

'That is not true.'

'You sent many back to Stalin.'

'It wasn't as simple—'

But Nowak rode right through him, his voice and temper beginning to rise, wanting to pound the old man into submission. 'Every time you were put to the test, you failed. You gave us your word, your solemn word, that you would help. Yet you sat behind the Maginot Line while Hitler devoured Poland, then you applauded while Stalin did the same.'

'No, that's not—'

'We were the first in this war, the very first, yet you denied us an invitation to join the United Nations.'

'Franklin thought—'

'Excuses! So what was your excuse for not inviting us to the victory celebrations in London, then? We were good enough to die with you in Monte Cassino but not fit to walk beside you through the streets of London. You chased us away like stray dogs!'

'But by then I had been hurled from office. It

was not my doing. It was that damned man Hitlee or Attler or whatever he was called. Attlee!' Churchill shook fresh air into his head. 'He was a bloody red, a socialist, too worried about upsetting Stalin.'

'You lied! You lied to the men who fought for your liberty. And you betrayed those who died for it!'

'It wasn't meant—'

'And you betrayed me. Deserted me. Left me for dead. Whose fault was that, Mr Churchill?'

At last, silence.

Eventually Churchill raised himself in his chair, struggling to control his bruised emotions. 'That is a charge I should rightly answer, Mr Nowak. It is something I have been waiting to explain ever since we last met, something I should perhaps have explained then. It may take a few moments.'

Nowak poured himself a glass of champagne, but didn't offer Churchill more.

The old man waved a hand in front of his face as though chasing away moths. 'It was so very long ago,' he sighed, 'and all wrapped up with those things we signed at Yalta. Could the agreement have been different? I have often asked myself, searched my conscience, wondering whether I could have done more.'

'You could have objected, walked away, denounced it as a sham.'

Churchill held up his hand to stem the flow. '*If* I had walked away, it would have made not the slightest difference. I was no longer in control. Yalta was a stage set for a piece that allowed for only two great figures. I played but a bit part. That was why I signed their wretched agreement on the

Far East. It was a shoddy deal, but if I had refused to sign, it would still have gone ahead, except that it would have become clear to every native from Calcutta to Hong Kong that the future of the Far East had been settled without British participation. It would have meant the instant collapse of our authority; our empire would have fallen into chaos. That I could not permit. Surely you can understand.'

'What the hell has that got to do with Poland?'

'Yes, yes, I shall get to Poland in a minute. Don't be so bloody impatient. But first, you must see that power has its limits.' He thrust out his empty glass. 'And you must refill my glass. My mouth is dry.'

'You drink too much,' Nowak said, complying with reluctance.

'I used to declare that I had always taken much more out of alcohol than alcohol had ever taken out of me, and it was true,' Churchill said, as he watched the froth in his glass subside. 'But now I don't give a damn.' He drank, a little of the liquid spilling down his chin. He seemed not to notice. 'Now, where was I? Ah, Yalta. So I signed up to everything, not just the Far East but to Franklin's United Nations—a quack's cure if ever there was—and to Europe. Even had a little influence on the outcome on Europe. You see, it's like potatoes all laid out in a row.'

Nowak looked on as if the old man had lost his mind.

'France, Germany, Poland—Russia, too. One after the other. And Stalin might have had the lot. So I persuaded them that France should be allowed to become a great power once more, perhaps greater than she deserved. I have always had a passion for *la belle France,* even when she played the harlot.'

Nowak was about to interrupt once more but Churchill held up a finger to stop him, like a schoolmaster with a wayward pupil.

'France was the first step, you see, the first bulwark against the red tide from the east. Then Germany. They wanted to devour her, Franklin and Marshal Stalin. They had plans to rip her apart into five or six pieces, to level her so that she would never rise again. But a flattened Germany would have been nothing but an opportunity for the Red Army, an invitation to see just how far their tanks could roll before they were stopped. So Germany, too, had to be rebuilt, in time, and be permitted to take her place in the community of nations once more. That was not a popular message, but it was a necessary one. And you see, Mr Nowak, if France and Germany could be persuaded to co-operate, to come together even in some partnership or union, how much stronger would that bulwark against the tide be?'

'You make it sound so simple, as if you had a great plan.'

'Never simple. I groped my way through darkness, but even in the dark a donkey can find its way home.'

'What donkey?' Nowak demanded, but Churchill's mind had drifted away, distracted by a vapour trail that was stretching out across the cloudless sky, reminding him of a time when the skies above his beloved Chartwell had been filled with such trails, a time when the entire world had been balanced on the wings of a handful of Spitfires and Hurricanes.

Suddenly the old man was back. 'Poland! The next potato. What could we do about Poland?'

'You could have fought for her freedom. That was what you had promised.'

'Oh, and I would have fought, most gladly, Mr Nowak. Everyone says I was a warmonger, couldn't resist the chance to take a pot-shot at someone or other. I would have led the charge myself, be in no doubt. But not a soul would have joined me. Not in 1945. By that time there was nothing to be done in Poland except what Marshal Stalin would agree to. And what he agreed to, free elections, a democratic government, independence, an entire package of liberties, had much merit.'

But by this point Nowak's battered face was contorting with frustration. He spat the words out, one by one, like a man picking his way through a minefield: 'How could you trust that monster Stalin?'

'I didn't! No, not once. Not possible. I knew he was a creature of darkness and utter despair, insatiable in his lusts. Oh, I had to be civil, I had to do business with him, to smile and say generous things about him, but they were no more than the deceits of diplomacy. But trust the bugger? Never!'

'You washed your hands of us.'

'I washed my hands most meticulously, after every meeting with Marshal Stalin. But I never forgot Poland, never gave up hope. And I had my own victory.' He was leaning forward in his chair, wagging his finger. 'I got him to agree to all those things.'

'Words! Useless words!'

'Words, indeed, Mr Nowak. And all your fault.' Churchill began to chuckle, an old man's laugh, hoarse and at first feeble but growing in strength.

'You blame me?' Nowak screamed, thrusting the revolver towards the other man.

Churchill laughed until tears streamed down his cheeks, but he wasn't mocking, merely enjoying the moment.

The Pole was all but convinced he was senile.

'You remember, Mr Nowak, that you went on at me about the importance of giving my word? For you it made a vital difference, for when a man gives his solemn word he opens up consequences which'—Churchill waved a paw in the direction of the revolver—'can be most serious. And you set me thinking. If we could get Stalin to give his word, to sign the agreements on Poland, then if there were to come a time when he blatantly disregarded them, it would have the most serious consequences.'

'Sure. He broke his word and was still enjoying the joke when they buried him.'

'And in so unashamedly breaking his word he admitted his guilt to the whole world. I was determined to give him no excuse for blaming others, no opportunity for muddying the waters. So I smiled, I courted, I praised, using words that I had to force through my craw. Had I once expressed doubt about his good intentions or questioned his honour, he would have used that as a pretext for withdrawing from his obligations and I was determined unto the point of death to give him no such chance.' Churchill's blue eyes were staring weepily into the tortured face of the Pole. 'Yes, even unto the point of your death, Mr Nowak.'

The Pole's face now turned from torment to

389

confusion. 'What the hell did I have to do with it?'

'Imagine if we had been discovered, you and I, if Stalin had been able to reveal to the world that even as I professed goodwill and enduring friendship towards him I was busily smuggling some notorious spy and perverted traitor from beyond the reach of Soviet justice—because that is how it would have been depicted. Imagine how the blame for failure would have fallen upon our shoulders. I had to balance the life of one Pole against the future of the whole of Poland. You lost.'

'Then I praise the mother of Christ for the life of Frank Sawyers.'

'Sawyers was his own soul. But I could not take that risk.'

'Where was the risk? The agreement was useless anyway.'

'I remember one of the American delegation, a young diplomat, Bohlen, I think his name was, who was deeply sceptical about his own country's position at Yalta. He told me a story over dinner about a Negro slave who had been given a bottle of whisky by his owner for Christmas. The master demanded to know whether he had liked the whisky, and the slave replied that it was perfect. This puzzled the plantation owner, for it was but a cheap bottle. So he demanded to know what the slave meant. The Negro replied that if the whisky had been any better, the master would not have given it him, and if it had been any worse, he could not have drunk it. So there could be only one response. That the whisky was perfect. You know, Mr Nowak, at Yalta I felt much like that Negro slave.'

The Pole was clumping around the deck in agitation, dragging his bad leg behind him. 'What in the name of the Blessed Virgin has whisky got to do with Poland?'

'To Mr Bohlen, I think, it suggested the need for compromise and the acceptance of the inadequacies in any agreement. But to me it meant something more. I never forgot that, in the end, that slave was to find his freedom. You see, the agreement we reached at Yalta was far from useless. It had Stalin's name upon it. It promised things that he was never going to allow, so when he broke his word, when, without either excuse or provocation, he took the agreement of Yalta and hurled it beneath the tank tracks of his Red Army, the entire world was clear as to what had happened and who was to blame. Stalin's only justification was brute force. Poland was to become a subjugated nation once more, but this time an entire world would weep in sorrow and decry the injustice of it.'

'Much good did it do my country.'

'Not then, not even now. But what were we saying? That war doesn't finish simply when the bullets no longer fly? The struggle for liberty is ceaseless. It goes on, so long as tyranny is afoot and men still suffer. Just because an Iron Curtain has fallen across the soul of Europe, that does not prevent us looking across it, to the east, and declaring our faith in the ultimate victory of civilisation. We have never ceased to proclaim the great principles of freedom which are our inheritance. In the English-speaking world we have enshrined them in the Magna Carta and in the rules of Habeas Corpus, in trial by jury and in election by secret ballot, in the Bill of Rights and that most famous expression of freedom, the Declaration of Independence. Freedom is our unquenchable cause and it does not cease or surrender because tyranny casts its dark shadow across large parts of our planet. Liberty is no harlot to be picked up by any bully and cast aside once her services are no longer required. It is the fundamental right of all men and we shall not cease to proclaim its virtues until the walls have fallen and that Curtain is drawn aside. You see, Mr Nowak, we are fighting not just for Poland but that the entire world might one day be free. And there, I seem to have made a speech. I think it is the last I shall ever make.' His face had grown pink with the strain of his efforts and his breath was coming in short bursts.

'Walls won't be pulled down by words,' the Pole bit back.

The old man raised himself once more, his words coming more slowly. 'So long as free men shout the words of liberty and there are subjugated souls to listen, then tyranny is in peril. I believe this with all my heart. Those walls will crumble, not now, not in my lifetime, certainly, but one day. Imagine, Mr Nowak, if your daughter were here, what price would you pay that in her lifetime she and all other Poles would be free?'

'Any price, of course. I would gladly pay with my life.'

'And it was precisely that price I was willing to pay at Yalta.'

The two men stared defiantly at each other, but Churchill hadn't finished.

'At Yalta, we lit a flame which casts a light across

the whole of Europe and one day will consume all oppression. That is why I left you behind. For those who will come after us.'

'You served your own interests, nothing else!'

'I admit I am, indeed, an imperfect specimen. I have lived a long life—too long. Examine it closely and you will discover all sorts of failures and vanities. It is easy for a young man to find his way to Heaven, but a man of my age must clamber over all sorts of failings and deceits. I fear in my case they may prove insurmountable. I sit here wondering what they will say when they discover my bloodied body upon this deck. Will they proclaim me another Nelson, or simply a vain and useless old man? Even though I am at the end of my life, such things still matter.' He was panting, but still fighting. 'Condemn me, if you like, but on the day that our sons and daughters come together from all parts of Europe to celebrate their freedom, I hope you will allow me a small fragment of the credit for keeping their flame of hope alight all these years. But . . . no! That's wrong.' He waved his fist at Nowak, his cheeks flushed with passion. 'On that occasion I shall deserve not merely a small fragment but a bloody enormous slice of the glory. So, expect no apology from me. I am proud of what I have done for Poland!'

The old man slumped back in his chair. There was sweat on his brow. He raised his hand to his temple, clearly exhausted by his efforts. Champagne trickled from his tilted glass and dripped into a little puddle upon the deck. 'So, get on with it. I'm tired. Tired of you, Mr Nowak, tired of life. But as you pull your trigger, remember one thing. I don't give a damn!'

Suddenly, Churchill felt a sharp pain in his head. It was a sensation that began to take hold inside until it consumed him, and everything went dark.

But it was not the pain of a bullet. It was another stroke. His mind was closing down.

When he opened his eyes once more, he was alone. He felt limp, shatteringly weak. From somewhere near at hand he could hear voices, but they were indistinct and unrecognisable. He was confused. Sounds, sights, all had become jumbled. His mind raced to regain its grip, stumbling along a path it did not recognise.

Who was he? Well, it couldn't be that bad, could it? For he knew who he was. Churchill. Winston Churchill!

But where was he? Not home, for as his eyes opened and he began to focus, there was sea, blue sky, brilliant light. Ah, that was it. He knew now. He was in Yalta. And out there were dolphins who would be chasing all those sardines.

He felt so wretchedly feeble. Exhausted. Done too much. Time for a rest. A long rest.

'Sawyers!' he cried, but his tongue was thick and wouldn't work properly and no one seemed to hear him. 'Sawyers, where the bloody hell are you, man?'

* * *

A little more than eighteen months later, in the early days of 1965, the tide of Winston Churchill's life reached its final ebb. He died at the age of ninety and was given a state funeral, the first commoner to be granted that honour since the

Duke of Wellington more than a century earlier. Monarchs, heads of governments and leaders came from almost every nation on the globe. On that day the chimes of Big Ben were silenced, the cranes of London's docks dipped in salute, and hundreds of thousands of ordinary men and women watched in pride and tearful silence as the coffin passed through the streets of the capital on its way to St Paul's Cathedral. It was said that he was the greatest Englishman of his time—of any time.

It was to be another twenty-four years before Poland once again found her freedom, along with the other oppressed nations of Europe, after the Iron Curtain that divided the continent had been torn down and left to rust. It isn't known whether Marian Nowak lived to see that most historic of days, but many of his generation did.

As much as any single man, Winston Churchill preserved the liberties of the people of Britain. He was the man who guided them—dragged them, at times—through their finest hour. Yet the freedom of the peoples of Europe, finally secured only many years after his death, was a still greater triumph—perhaps his greatest triumph of all.

POSTSCRIPT

Stalin died in 1953. Undeservedly, he died in his own time and in his own house outside Moscow. He was eventually denounced by the new Soviet leadership for his extraordinary record of brutality, but his shadow continued to be cast across Europe for many years to come. Even today, there are those in Russia who wish to rehabilitate him.

Beria was not so fortunate. He was present when Stalin died and moved quickly to grab the reins of power for himself, but he was feared and loathed by his colleagues. They quickly arrested him on trumped-up charges and sentenced him to death. He died in the manner of so many of his own victims, hanging from a hook and with a bullet to his head.

Molotov, however, was a great survivor. His fortunes waxed and waned, but they never entirely ran out on him. He died in 1986 at the extraordinary age of ninety-six, shortly before the total collapse of the Communist empire in Europe that he had worked throughout his life to build. To the last he remained an unrepentant Stalinist.

The elegant and able British Foreign Secretary Anthony Eden persevered long enough to see his ambitions fulfilled. He succeeded Churchill as Prime Minister, but not until 1955, after Churchill had returned for his second period in Downing Street. By this time Eden was well past his prime and physically ailing. He is remembered largely for the disaster of the Suez War in 1956, which ended in humiliation for the British after the United

States refused to support them. Eden resigned a few weeks later.

The Suez War brought Eden into conflict not only with his wartime ally, President Dwight Eisenhower, but also with his old friend Alec Cadogan. By that time, Cadogan had retired from his glittering career at the Foreign Office to become chairman of the BBC. Eden accused the BBC of reporting the war in a biased fashion, a charge rejected by Cadogan. He, like Eden, retired from public life in the following year.

No one seems to know what happened to the delightful Frank Sawyers. His trail runs cold in 1946, after he left Churchill's employ.

Sarah Churchill led a tumultuous life: failed marriages, an unfulfilled acting career, several scandals, but she always remained loyal to her father.

Averell Harriman served his country in many capacities and under a variety of different presidents. He was one of the most extraordinary diplomatic figures of his age. He eventually married Pamela Churchill, his wartime love, and they lived happily until his death just short of his hundredth birthday.

The United Nations lives on. The United States still has only one vote. When the news leaked that Roosevelt was contemplating asking for three votes, it was greeted with so much public ridicule that he was quietly forced to drop the idea. It was one of many, many ways in which the United Nations was to disappoint the ambitions of its prime founder.

ACKNOWLEDGEMENTS

The records passed down by history can be frustrating. The documents and recollections left behind after the conference at Yalta are incomplete, at times inaccurate, and hopelessly contradictory. Churchill himself wrote that 'one of the most misleading factors in history is the practice of historians to build a story exclusively out of the records which have come down to them', and he knew a thing or two about his art. Yet what perhaps matters even more than the detailed chronology is the spirit of the thing, and that is where novels play their part. Novels can try to fill the gaps left behind by the formal records. After all, history is far more than an assembly of statistics and dates, it's the interaction of countless people fuelled by passion, prejudice, aspiration, intellect, and all those other bits that make us go round, with the mixture occasionally doused in a good shower of alcohol, at least in Winston's case. Throw in a measure of ill health or boundless ambition and the results are inevitably provocative and usually unpredictable. Novels dare to tread along paths that scare off formal historians, but these slippery paths may lead nonetheless to understanding as well as enjoyment.

That, at least, is the ambition behind *Churchill's Triumph*. The events reflected in it are, I think, recorded as accurately as in many so-called academic works, but I should throw in one or two words of caution. Marian Nowak is a fictional character and Piorun a fictional town. However, I believe they both offer a strong flavour of the events that took place in Poland at that time. I don't wish to give a complete bibliography, but anyone wanting to read about what happened in Poland in early 1945 should try to find a copy of *Flight in the Winter* by the German author Juergen Thorwald. Its description of Soviet savagery is chilling.

As for the conference at Yalta, while I have tried to remain true to the course of events, I have omitted large chunks of the proceedings and taken dramatic liberties with other parts, yet most of what I have written about at the major events of the conference actually happened. But one thing that did not happen was Beria's attack on Sarah. That is a little part of the fiction. But the point is, it might have happened—Beria was a notorious and most brutal sexual predator who never showed a glimmer of compassion for the feelings of others, and there was much drunkenness at the dinner in question. The purpose of the episode is to illustrate the exceptional personal conflicts that faced Churchill throughout those days in the Crimea. Winston wasn't great because he found things easy but because he faced impossible dilemmas, yet somehow he dealt with them.

I should also point out that there are people alive today, Churchill's family and friends, who were with him on his last cruise aboard the *Christina*. A little about that voyage is in the public record, and I have been anxious not to seek from those who were present any further details of the desperately distressing scenes they witnessed between Winston and his son, Randolph. I believe I have got the spirit of the occasion right, and I have no wish to revive old sorrows among those family and friends by probing more deeply. This is, after all, a novel.

However, those who share my fascination with Winston Churchill and wish to find out more should consider doing three things. They should join the Churchill Centre and Societies *(www.winstonchurchill.org)*, whose website, officers and journal are an unceasing source of information and encouragement. They shouldn't hesitate to visit the Imperial War Museum, where Terry Charman in particular has responded to all my enquiries with an enthusiasm for his topic that is infectious. And they should make a firm date to go to the new Churchill Museum that has been opened within the Cabinet War Rooms in Whitehall. Its director, Phil Reed, and his staff have worked wonders in bringing together what is one of the finest combinations of exhibition and entertainment I have ever seen. It would undoubtedly have appealed to the old man himself, and brought out the schoolboy in him. I can see him now, charging around the extraordinary interactive displays with a roar of joy. The only thing it misses in being thoroughly authentic is that whiff of cigar smoke . . .

I also want to throw a huge hug of thanks round Rachel, my wife, and our collective band of boys. If marriage is a journey of adventure, authorship is a mountain along the way, yet we seem to have climbed the obstacle with a remarkable degree of happiness even while my desk was covered with dirty plates, schoolwork and builders' dust.

I am indebted to my neighbour, John de Mora-Mieszkowski, who has given me excellent advice on both Polish culture and drinking habits.

Finally, I would like to thank, as so often, my dear friend Andrei Vandoros and his wife Lucy. The book is dedicated to Andrei's father, who was a prime inspiration for this book and its story of Marian Nowak. Dr Pan Vandoros was a man who knew hunger, despair, torture and the insides of both Hitler's and Stalin's prison camps all too well, yet throughout all his suffering he retained both his dignity and his abiding belief in humanity.

Michael Dobbs
Wylye, May 2005.
www.michaeldobbs.com